It-Factor Leadership

ISBN 978-0-9893966-0-8

Contents

Foreword

    I landed my first job as a university president at the age of 37, much too young for this particular line of work. At the time, there were no business sections on leadership at the local bookstore. No executive coaches gave pointers on how to handle hijacked meetings, select team members, create thought diversity, or manage difficult conversations. For me, more than 30 years of practice taught me how to be an effective leader, and, admittedly, left a few skinned knees along the way.

    While there is no substitute for experience, there is a critical advantage to developing skills before you need them. Everyone, at some point, wishes for a time machine to go back and offer advice to a younger self. This is the value of the book you hold in your hands, *"It-Factor Leadership: Become a Better Leader in 13 Steps."* Building on two decades of experience, Claudia and Ruben Fernandez have created a roadmap both for leaders beginning their careers and those who are already well into their journeys. "13 Steps" offers valuable wisdom on how to know yourself better, see your blind spots, find the right job, talk about your skills with grace, not arrogance, and build your emotional intelligence.

As you read, you will encounter the myriad stages of leadership, from the easy and low risk challenges to the advanced and wholly vexing decisions, the ones that can make or break careers. Along the way, this book will offer a menu of best practices that you can apply to your daily work, whether you lead an entire organization, a department, a program, or a team.

It is often said that leaders are not born, they are developed. Few people know this so well as Claudia and Ruben. I met Claudia some years ago at the Food Systems Leadership Institute, a program that teaches leadership skills to professionals in higher education, public service, business and industry. I have always admired Claudia's ability to help individuals find their strengths and gain a competitive advantage. Indeed, both Claudia and Ruben have experience unlocking the "It Factor Leader" within.

This is good news because experience can be an unforgiving teacher. Within these pages, you will learn important lessons before you face the crucible. And you will learn from two proven practitioners in Claudia and Ruben. So enjoy the read, take some notes, and discover the "It Factor" leader inside of you. I am certain that you will.

E. Gordon Gee
President Emeritus and Professor of Law
The Ohio State University

Acknowledgements

We have many acknowledgements to make as this book goes to press. With hearts full of gratitude, we thank Dr. Ken Swartzel, of NC State University, who was so completely generous with his time and advice, as always, giving us unbelievably thorough line-by-line feedback on this work. He has been a valued colleague for a decade, and we will miss his insight and advice after he makes the transition to retirement, leaving his post as the Director of the Food Systems Leadership Institute. Similarly, Dr. Laura Sessums, former Chief, Section of General Internal Medicine at the Walter Reed Army Medical Center, deserves a big thank you as well, as her input shines through this book. We also thank Dr. Shane Burgess, Vice Provost and Dean of the College of Agriculture and Life Sciences at the University of Arizona for his suggestions, advice, and review.

Claudia's mentors, Dr. Sam Smith and Dr. Vincent Covello, who are quoted in this book—your support and guidance have been most valuable. Thank you for all you have taught me. Thank you to Dr. Anita Farel, whose early encouragement pushed Claudia into creating an online learning system and that eventually opened the doors to a much larger world.

Our *FastTrack* team, and particularly Dr. David Steffen. His wise counsel and input to the ideas in this book are greatly appreciated. Both he and *FastTrack* faculty Angela Rosenberg are wonderful colleagues to work with and have helped us hone our understanding of leadership as we have worked with them these past many years. And thanks to our colleague Mitch Owen for your insight and encouragement.

Ms. Jan Chapin, Senior Director of Global Women's Health & Special Issues in Women's Health at the American College of Obstetricians & Gynecologists, and Dr. Bert Peterson, Chair of the Department of Maternal and Child Health at the University of North Carolina at Chapel Hill have both been wonderfully supportive of our work with the medical community. What we have learned has partly come about by the doors they have opened for us, and we are most grateful.

We are thankful to our *It-Factor* leaders, Dr. Bobby Moser, Dr. Daniel Schmitz, Ms. Jill Bemis and Ms. Simone James for sharing their inspiring stories with us. We wish our vignettes had done you justice— you each deserve a whole book written about your leadership. It has been a real pleasure to teach with Dr. Moser in the FSLI program, and we will miss him as he also moves into retirement.

Ms. Pamela Jean Kreigh, who never failed to answer our annoying publishing questions that always seemed to come at the most inappropriate times. She has been a steadfast friend for three decades now.

Our acknowledgments section would not be complete without a well-deserved round of applause to our parents, Barbara and Jim Plaisted and Gustavo and Rae Fernandez, and Carol Rosenbloom, for their unfailing encouragement. And of course, Alexander and Ethan, our little boys, who have been incredibly patient with us during the process of writing this book, deserve some very special hugs. We made all the school dances, the lessons, the practices, did the homework, dedicated ourselves through Read-A-Thon, yet we know you got tired of us constantly talking about the book, debating the content, reading sections to you, and making you practice steps like "The Powerful Apology" whenever you really just wanted to say you were sorry and get back to playing.

And lastly, thank you to all the leaders we have worked with over the past decade-and-a-half through Institutes, coaching, teaching, and advising. You have been our greatest teachers, and it is with such pleasure that we now broadly share the lessons we have learned through our work together.

Meet the Authors

Claudia and Ruben Fernandez of FastTrack Leadership
At *FastTrack*, We Train Leaders

Through our executive coaching work, teaching, and running leadership development programs, we have worked with thousands of leaders across the United States and increasingly across the globe. We have decades of experience in developing leaders in a variety of organizations. It has been an incredible journey—and we have been privileged to work with many individuals who have inspired us along the way.

This book came into being through our work primarily with leaders from across sectors dedicated to the greater good. People we met through our leadership programs and institutes asked us to come to their home organizations—and eventually *FastTrack* Leadership, Inc. was born to meet these requests. And they wanted "tune ups" available as needed—so we created the *FastTrack* learning library. And they asked us to write down all that we were teaching them—so we created this book. While it is a wonderful development experience to combine a leadership institute with this book, it is our aim that the teachings in this book stand on their own merit, and will be useful to you even if we never meet you in person. However, it might be useful for you to know a bit more about us and our professional background as you consider the steps to becoming a great *It-Factor* leader that we outline here.

Ruben Fernandez is a licensed attorney who counsels leaders in change strategies and implementation, including the legal and corporate ramifications of their decisions. He does private consulting for closely-held corporations and practices in the Federal and State Court systems. Ruben also coaches leaders about how to manage crisis communications, build organizational culture, engage employees, create thought diversity and understand the psychological assessment data commonly used in leadership development. He is certified in a wide array of these tools, as well as simulation exercises to foster leader and team development.

Ruben earned his law degree from the University of North Carolina at Chapel Hill. In graduate school, he studied Industrial Organizational Psychology at Tulane University and has an extensive psychological counseling background focusing on interpersonal relationships. He received his undergraduate degree from UNC-Greensboro in Social Psychology, with a minor in Dance. He also has an avid interest in technology and serves on the Technology Advisory Committee for the North Carolina Bar Association, and serves on the Board of Directors for local businesses. *You can contact Ruben at Ruben@wetrainleaders.com*

Dr. Claudia Fernandez is a professor at the Gillings School of Global Public Health at the University of North Carolina at Chapel Hill. In addition to teaching several courses on leadership each year, she creates and directs leadership development institutes. Currently she directs three national leadership development programs: the ACOG Robert C. Cefalo National Leadership Institute (for physician leaders, see

ACOGLeadershipInstitute.org), the Food Systems Leadership Institute (for senior leaders in public and land grant universities, industry and government see FSLI.org), and the Maternal and Child Health-Public Health Leadership Institute (for public sector workers focusing on the well-being of children and families in the US, see mchphli.org).

Dr. Fernandez does extensive executive coaching with leaders from many sectors, specializing in mid-to-senior level leader development. Like Ruben, she is certified in a bevy of psychological assessment instruments commonly used in leader and team development, and uses them extensively in her work. Claudia earned a Bachelor of Science degree from Miami University of Ohio and a Master of Science in Clinical Nutrition from Boston University. She pursued further education in psychology and counseling at the Harvard University Extension School and at the University of North Carolina at Chapel Hill. She later earned her doctorate in Public Health Leadership studies through the Health Policy and Management Department and the Public Health Leadership Program at UNC's Gillings School of Global Public Health. She worked in the Harvard teaching hospital system, and then Duke University before joining the faculty at UNC. Claudia is also a Registered and Licensed Dietitian and a trained hypnotherapist. *You can contact Claudia at Claudia_Fernandez@WeTrainLeaders.com*

Claudia and Ruben work with individual leaders and they travel the country providing leadership development programs to teams and organizations. They live in Chapel Hill, North Carolina and have two young sons, Alexander and Ethan, and two miniature dachshunds, Ginger and Dr. Cornelius.

Introduction

A Note From the Authors

Do you have the *It-Factor* when it comes to being a leader? Being a leader can be immensely rewarding, but it is always full of challenges. Our 20-plus years of studying, teaching, and coaching leaders at many levels have yielded 13 basic steps to great leadership—what the *FastTrack* team calls the *"It-Factor."* We work with leaders: leaders from health care, industry, academia, the public sector. Each year we teach leadership to hundreds of people in groups, teams, or as individuals. We coach leaders to help them maximize their performance and avoid the sticky problems of derailment. One thing that we have seen is that nearly everyone in a leadership position would like to become a better leader. They are all searching for that elusive *"It-Factor"* that can take them to the next level.

No one is really *born* a leader. Leaders are developed: the skills, behaviors, and values are ones you can learn. In fact, they are ones you *must* learn if you really want to make a difference—and have followers. The secret to the *"It-Factor"* in leadership is a set of skills that allows you to work effectively with and through others. We go through 13 of the most important steps in detail in this book—steps that will help you build dozens of skills, tools, and strategies to get you and your team to that next level.

One of the truths of great leaders with the *It-Factor*: they fundamentally understand that the *"it"* is not about them. Nor is *it* about power. Nor prestige. *It* is not about building an organization that looks, thinks, talks and acts like them—or necessarily tells them that they are right. We have found that leaders who live in a world where "it's all about them" don't inspire loyalty. They don't lead a creative or innovative team. They usually have a lot of turnover, particularly among their best and their brightest. While those kinds of leaders might drive a group to excel based on their own raw energy or talent, those outcomes are usually short lived. Those kinds of leaders don't build a legacy—they build an extension of their own egos, but nothing that outlasts their own personal stamina.

You'll find a strong theme of this book is how to be the kind of leader for whom *"It"* is about others. Leaders with this *It-Factor* are focused on creating an organizational culture that invites and nurtures different perspectives, styles, and types to be at their organizational table. Our work shows that while their teams and the entire enterprise benefits from this diversity, the leaders profit individually as well. Through creating this broad and open organizational culture they promote their own cultural flexibility, which allows them to listen better, to make better decisions, and to be better leaders. So work through the 13 steps in this book and become the kind of talented leader who lives "it's not about me." Be a leader with the *It-Factor*.

As you read through this book you will find that these 13 steps build upon one another, with earlier steps laying the groundwork for more sophisticated and nuanced steps later on. Gaining any new skill requires practice in order to gain mastery—while you can practice any of the many practical skills taught in this book, it will be easier (and you'll have more eloquence and grace at the later skills) if you invest in yourself to build yourself sequentially through the tools as they are presented.

For example, the last step teaches you how, when the sticky situation arises, to apologize powerfully. While you will be immediately more effective at this reputation-and-relationship-saving strategy after you read Step 13, *the powerful apology* is a very sophisticated skill. In many ways, doing it right is predicated upon your skills in emotional intelligence (Step 6). Emotional intelligence and building a great team (Step 5) are themselves built upon understanding how to really engage who you've got on your team (Step 7), which builds on understanding what motivates the people on your team (Step 4), which comes after knowing how to build the kind of organizational culture that really builds interpersonal and inter-professional relationships (Step 3). Of course you can't build any of these relationships until you either get yourself on the right team or hire the right people to work for you (Step 2). And in the end, every one of the examples we've given here drills back to the basic home of self-awareness. If you can't know yourself—the good (your assets), the bad (your blind spots that could lead you to derail), and where you are fixable (your "developmental areas") then you really can't do anything else in this book. So follow our framework for developing into an *It-Factor* leader and work your way through an ever-ascending spiral of vital leadership skills.

While leadership theory is interesting if you teach it at a university, we find that real world leaders in practice are mostly interested in skills they can turn around and use tomorrow, if not today. That is why this book is focused on a practical approach. In fact, while we may have "chunked" related skills into 13 steps, we've actually broken these down into more than 100 completely practical strategies, skills, and tools to help you really enhance your leadership. Within these pages you will find your own virtual executive coach. This isn't meant to be some academic tome. We have tried to keep the tone conversational, practical, and easy to read. There are places for you to reflect and self-assess. There are places for you to plan. There are places for you to analyze. As for the 100+ skills: you won't need them all at once, but when you are a leader you face some unpredictable problems. You'll be well served to have a variety of skills and tools at your fingertips. Here they are.

You won't be surprised to learn that our coaching and teaching work focuses primarily on those organizations that contribute to the greater good—enterprises that are out to contribute to society and to offer goods or services that are valuable and make life better for everyone. They are usually out to make a profit (or for the non-profits they still wish to maintain a margin of revenue over expenses), but they don't embrace competition or pursue profit at the expense of relationships. They face bigger challenges than the purely profit-driven companies in that they typically have challenging stakeholders and partners, face complex regulations, and have limited incentives to reward employees. They don't have positional authority. They don't have big prizes to award. They usually don't have huge budgets to buy loyalty. What they *do* have is leadership.

In that context, we have had the tremendous privilege to work with and study some truly great *It-Factor* leaders. They tell us that the coaching and teaching we give them is inspiring—but the truth is that we have learned from them too. Again and again they have shown us the many behaviors, skills, beliefs, and values at which exceptional leaders shine. And some have confirmed for us the career-killing errors to avoid. We decided to write this book to share with you what we have learned about great leadership—real *It-Factor leadership*—because after working with thousands of leaders we are convinced that the *It-Factor* resides in each of us.

It-Factor Leadership is based on the 13 most fundamental steps that represent key aspects of great leadership. Work through these steps to develop and hone the most crucial skills for working with and through others to make a difference with your team, your company, or your community. Whether you're just starting out or a seasoned leader, these 13 fundamental steps can help you become a better leader.

Claudia Fernandez
Ruben Fernandez

The First Step: Know Yourself

Know Yourself:
the Good, the Bad, and the Fixable

Great *It-Factor* leaders know themselves—and we mean they *really* know themselves. They don't just glance in the leadership mirror. They seek to understand the assets they have, the strengths they can rely on. They don't want to be brought up short or blind-sided by their faults. They look to their weaknesses as places they can set goals for development or to partner with others who have that skill as a strength. And they work hard to fix or contain the problems that plague them.

In our work teaching leadership and coaching executives, we hear from leaders that their constant concern is success—for their organizations and teams as well as for themselves, and their greatest fear is derailment—again for both their organizations and for themselves. Luckily there has been a lot of research on these topics[1-6] and in this Step to becoming a great *It-Factor* leader, we'll address both. While *success* is probably not a new concept to you, we do find that *derailment* can be a new one. Technically *derailment* includes failing to progress in your career when you really want to and are actively working to advance, which can include just getting stuck career-wise or having a bad outcome[4-6]. However, when most people talk about derailment they are talking about situations akin to a train going off the tracks, which is usually disastrous. So when most people talk about derailment, they typically refer to the big, colossal, career-altering events that one never forgets, although one might wish to. We'll address the problems of derailment at the end of this section, but first let's look at the things *It-Factor* leaders know, or seek to learn, about themselves and their organizations.

Understanding Competitive Advantage

The path to success is knowing yourself, your team, and your enterprise. If you want to have a successful team or enterprise, then one of the first things you need to know about it is what gives you a competitive advantage[7, 8]. This has always been a key asset to leaders. Think about what has made the difference in history: in the agrarian age, it was land and natural resources that conferred a competitive advantage. Then in the industrial age, it was all about capital and natural resources. Then the information age changed everything for mankind—and what conferred competitive advantage changed with it.

Reflect for a moment on what are the top three elements that give your group, company, or enterprise an advantage against all the other people in your marketplace? Now think about *you* as a product in the marketplace—such as when you're looking for a job or seeking a new opportunity. What gives *you* an advantage over the competition? Mull this over and write down your answers in Table 1.1.

Table 1.1: Defining Your Competitive Advantage

List the top 3 elements that give your group, team, or enterprise a competitive advantage over others who compete for the same work or funds as yours does:

1. _____

2. _____

3. _____

List the top 3 elements that give you, personally, a competitive advantage over others who might want the same opportunities as you desire:

1. _____

2. _____

3. _____

If you work in the business world, your list probably has on it something like, *we have a competitive edge when we offer something valuable*, or *when what we offer is rare and no one else can offer it*.

Another common answer is *what we have to offer is hard to imitate*. For those who value "time to market" the answer is often *we can get what we make to the market faster than anyone else*.

While all of these have some truth to them, there is a more complex picture in cutting edge organizations that lead innovation in their fields.

For the past 20 years, research has supported that three premiere and distinctive resources really make the difference in organizations.

Further, it doesn't much matter whether that organization is in healthcare, manufacturing, consulting, academia, government, public health or technology. The BIG 3 advantages revolve around Concepts— the ideas in an organization. Competence—the people who deliver in an organization. As well as Connections—the organization's ability to make effective collaborations with others. These are called the "3 C's"[9] and as a leader, it's where to focus for the future success of your group. Take a look at your list and note which advantages you listed are really about the people with the know-how who can successfully work with others. Success today is not about getting your hands on the latest technology. The good news for you is that as a leader the 3 C's are all about leadership. What you do—or don't do—in leading the team will mean more than computers or capital or the buildings that house you.

Warning Signs on the Path to Derailment

This is where we get to the uncomfortable topic of "derailment." Just like with any journey, having a destination is important. In your leadership journey it's also important to know the warning signs that you might be on the wrong road, so that you can take corrective action quickly. There are some big classic red flags that are indicators of impending doom career-wise. If you've ever had a bad boss or seriously dysfunctional teammates, then surely you've seen these in action. While you might have seen these in others, the most important person to recognize these red flags in—is you. Dr. Leah Devlin is a valued colleague and a very wise *It-Factor* leader. A dentist by training, she broke the glass ceiling of leadership in her home state of North Carolina, where she was the first female County Health Director and then the first woman to serve as State Health Director. Her sage advice to Claudia's students[10]:

The person who is going to give you the most trouble each day is the one who looks back at you from the mirror each morning.

She's right—that's what the research literature shows too: people derail mostly because of their own choices and actions, not because of what happens to them as innocent bystanders. If you see any of these storm clouds on your personal horizon, then there are many strategies in this book that will be helpful to you. You might also consider getting an executive coach to help you. The strategies in this book will be helpful to you if you work with someone who struggles with derailment behaviors as well.

Derailment is painful. Typically a leader derails because they have what is called a blind spot. That is a characteristic, a set of behaviors, or attitudes that *they* may not see, but are all too visible to anyone and everyone around them. One of the best things that can happen to you is to learn about your blind spots before it's too late. If anyone ever sits down with you to have a compassionate discussion about your development and your blind spots, thank them most sincerely. Far too many people don't find out until it's too late and they've lost a leadership opportunity, or worse still, their job.

Table 1.2 gives this list of the top 7 major personal issues that cause career derailment, which were shown in a classic study of North American and European leaders[4] conducted by researchers at the Center for Creative Leadership (often referred to as "CCL"). This study has given rise to much of what is taught about personal leadership today.

Table 1.2: Top 7 Reasons for Career Derailment

- Problems with interpersonal relationships
- The inability to shift from tactical to strategic thinking
- Difficulty molding or building a team
- Being too narrow in one's functional orientation
- Being over-dependent
- Failing to meet business objectives
- Strategic differences with management

Do some items on this list look obvious? Of course, others might not seem to be quite so intuitive to you—yet they lead to the same, career-altering outcomes. In fact, they all bear some in-depth discussion.

The first of these represents an all-too-common blind spot: **lacking effective interpersonal skills**. Being brilliant or hyper-productive used to be a good excuse to keep a nasty employee on the team, but no more. Organizations are realizing that these folks actually cost them money, which is not compensated for by the work they either bring in or produce. Research shows that 80% of employees who quit don't leave the organization or the job—they leave their lousy manager[11-13]. The behaviors that show up in this category include **being insensitive**, with complaints about the individual's abrasive nature or way of interacting with others. Another bad behavior to be wary of is **overambitious**. This is when the person needs to be seen as powerful and they wield their competitiveness like a club, believing in a "fixed pie" and that the winner takes the largest share. Because of ineffective interpersonal skills, this derailing individual is often **isolated**, which shows up as perfectionism or in needing to have everything done their own way. This is, of course, in direct violation of that third "C" of being able to make effective connections with others. While they might be brilliant and have down the "C's" of concepts and competence, if they can't connect with others then their efforts will be useless in today's interdependent and inter-professional world. Finally, the CCL research showed that these folks tend to be **volatile** as well. Certainly, coming apart at the seams when under fire is a sure fire way to limit your future opportunities. As Dr. Devlin likes to remind emerging leaders, "remember that old adage—the two things you can't take back are the spent arrow and the spoken word"[10]. Those who derail because they lack effective interpersonal skills often find that what they have said in a moment of heat comes back to haunt them and limit their opportunities. No one wants to work with someone who cannot maintain their personal composure at work. Leaders know that volatile people, no matter how smart or talented they might be, represent a liability to an organization and its relationships with external stakeholders.

You may have seen some of these facets in others you've known at work. But the real key here is do you see any of these within yourself? If so, make a note of these and start to keep track of the actions you can take to amend your behavior patterns using the 13 steps described in this book, so you can prevent derailment in your own career. Table 1.3 can help you do this admittedly painful self-assessment. If you feel you don't really have the insight to see your potential challenges in this way, then think about what you hear others say about you, the kind of feedback you get on performance reviews or on a 360-degree assessment, or simply ask someone for their candid feedback. A 360-degree feedback assessment asks for input from your colleagues/peers, those who report to you (often called "direct reports"), and your boss/superiors, and compares their scores on multiple questions to how you score your own performance. They can be administered by someone certified in their use, like an executive coach, who then debriefs the feedback to help make it understandable and useful. Many large multi-national corporations use their own proprietary versions, and are administered by their human resources departments.

Leadership success requires making those tactical-to-strategic shifts in focus, perspective, and skills. **Failure to make tactical shifts** is another major reason people stumble and fall in their careers. Maybe you've been lucky enough to have a supervisor or a leader who you've admired greatly or who became a close personal friend. But things change, organizations evolve, and new leaders come into those positions. If you are unable to adapt to the new leadership and those who have a different style, that is a critical factor in yourself to consider closely. Whenever you have a new boss or a new team that you are leading, it takes some time to learn to adapt to their styles, which may be unfamiliar to you. Inability to cope with the fact that your new boss is not the same as your old boss is a clear factor in derailment.

One manifestation of failure to make those tactical-to-strategic shifts is fear of conflict. Someone who is **conflict averse** is headed for some serious trouble career-wise. You cannot completely avoid conflict. In fact, it is far better for you to learn to harness it constructively as a medium for change rather than to be a poor negotiator. Also related to this area is being **mired in detail** since it represents another way one can fail at moving from a tactical to a strategic perspective. Too great a focus on detail can make it nearly impossible to deal with change, given that it often follows a non-linear and somewhat ambiguous process (we will delve deeper into that topic in a few pages). Similarly, being mired in detail prevents you from seeing the bigger picture or the context of situations that are critical to leadership success.

The next set of derailing factors of which to be wary is the **inability to mold and build a team**. Leaders simply must be able to build the kind of organizational culture that helps a team gel, so the 3 C's of competitive advantage take root. You can't simply hire a person for their intelligence—because the whole person will show up for the job, and then you'll be stuck dealing with (and spending your time on) the overflow of their personality flaws. Leaders must work with and through others in order to create productive organizations in today's marketplace. Those who derail all too often "kiss up and kick down," destroying the team culture in the process. When one cannot create a team that gels there are usually some common underlying issues.

One common problem for a derailing leader is that the individual really doesn't know how to manage others, so they **under- or over-manage** them instead. You'll see that they can't collaborate with others and work inter-professionally on complex tasks. They can't delegate to others, and must do it all themselves. Those who over-manage have disengaged and much annoyed teams. Those who undermanage leave their team feeling unconnected to the vision, unaware of the metrics they should use to verify success, or that management simply does not care about them. Similarly, **communicating poorly** leads others to feel as though they need to be mind-readers to work successfully with their colleague. Since mind reading is a pretty rare skill, people are left blind to the goals, needs, or resources that need to be considered in order to bring a project to fruition.

However, one of the worst mistakes a leader can make when building a team is to **staff in his or her own image**. Hiring based on a gut feeling or "when the chemistry is right" can create an organization that has a homogeneity of thought. It might feel pretty nice to have everyone echo your thoughts, but that can cripple an organization when tough challenges arise. Thought diversity is crucial to a healthy organization— but we'll get to working on this aspect of becoming an *It-Factor* leader in our Tenth Step.

Professionals who are derailing, and particularly those who are insecure, **create mediocrity**. What you will hear from others is that they undermine talented subordinates since they don't like others to outshine them. Or you might hear that they hire weak candidates who *won't* outshine them. Great leaders know it isn't about them: it is about building a strong organization with a deep bench. Any leader who operates like a guru, where everything revolves around them, their ideas, their perspective, their limelight, is doing a severe disservice to their organization. The hallmark point to remember about leadership is: it's not about you. If it *is* all about you then you're not leading, you're being a diva.

Another area of common derailment is **having too narrow a functional orientation**. People generally get promoted because they excel at the job they have. Yet the skills required at the next level may be only partially related to those needed for success in the previous position. It is easy to **become trapped in the mindset** of "I'm a physician..." or for that matter, a nurse, a scientist, an engineer, accountant...whatever your specialty happens to be. But that can lead to being stuck in your role and in having too narrow an orientation to really represent—or even understand—the organization as a whole.

Having too narrow a functional orientation also shows up when a leader gives **too much weight to too few concerns**, thus bringing a limited view to the team. A common complaint is that the only thing that matters to them—or that they truly understand—are concerns that fall into their area of origin or their pet project. Another typical derailer falling into this area is **having limited experience** in the organization. Common issues that come up on reviews or 360 feedback reports are that the person has never really proven themselves on complex tasks.

Stretch experiences are vital to leadership development. They allow the individual to "stretch" and understand the concerns and operation of the organization at a level above where they currently sit. To make a stretch experience successful, emerging leaders (often called "high potential employees") would typically have a mentor or supervisor to give feedback or advice and to serve as a sounding board, coaching them through the process and initiating them into organizational knowledge they would not otherwise have. The lack of stretch experiences can be a sign of future derailment.

Being **over-dependent** is another derailment trap to avoid—and this seems to be more acute for women than for men, perhaps because women tend to balance career with other concerns of life. Women are more likely to stay in a work situation that supports their other priorities of life, which can inadvertently set up some of the situations in this category that can cause career problems. Being over-dependent often stems from working a majority of one's career in the same department. Concerns arise about whether the individual can **perform on their own** or with another team. It is important in your career to make a name for yourself and the quality work that you do. However, some people are a bit shy about making their talents known. Whether admirable humility or incapacitating shyness, the effect can be the same: without a wealth of **personal connections** and a **personal reputation**, it can be very difficult to find opportunities for advancement or leadership, even though they may be well-deserved. It is important to learn to talk about your skills, talents, and accomplishments without seeming cocky or being annoying. The skills presented in the Second Step to great *It-Factor* leadership, about how to select the team (and get hired yourself), can help you in this area.

Overdependence can also show up if you **stay with the same mentor** or supervisor until people wonder if you can stand on your own. A worse situation for derailment is when you lose a mentor, supervisor, or team member who had previously covered up or compensated for your weak spot. This overdependence doesn't necessarily mean you are always associated with the same people. Have you ever worked with an over-enthusiastic, energy-in-hyper-drive colleague who really annoyed you? A classic derailment scenario is when someone who over-relies on their raw energy, a narrow skill, or a natural talent moves up in the leadership ladder. Unfortunately, all too often the skills that made them successful at the previous job are not those that make them successful at the next one. While it might be a blessing to have a strong natural talent, such as being very smart, or to have a great deal of personal energy, these are not enough to carry one through to success at the higher rungs of leadership. For example, emotional intelligence (which we will explore in our Sixth Step to becoming a great *It-Factor* leader) really matters— successful leadership is about a balance of skills and an ability to stretch oneself out of one's comfort zone to meet the needs of others and the team—all without exhausting or bankrupting yourself.

The sixth major derailment factor is **failing to meet business objectives.** This shows up as lackluster follow through, as when someone makes a big splash on the front end of the project but then moves on **leaving a trail of loose ends**. Other common complaints include leaving people hanging with **unmet promises**, or moving way too fast on projects and then losing interest. Finally, **lack of attention to detail** is a way this particular derailment factor can surface. One may not be a detail person by nature but that does not excuse cherry picking the job or failing to pay attention to the details of the organization. This particular derailer has left quite a few leaders facing legal troubles as they claimed they simply did not know that wrongdoing was happening in their organization. The "I don't do details" mindset of leaders leaves a wake of unresolved small problems and a great deal of disorganization for others to deal with. Leaders are often held legally responsible for the ethics and conduct of the organization—so they ignore all the details to their own peril. Jeffrey

Skilling, the famously disgraced leader of Enron, went to jail still stating he never knew of the corruption going on, which was revealed in October of 2001[14]. Of course, successful leaders also know they can't do it all, so they need to balance out effective delegating with sufficient detail orientation.

And lastly, **strategic differences with management** shakes out as our final major derailment factor. Certainly if you have big differences in style, vision, or values then you don't have a good fit in that organization, and you're likely to leave—or be invited to leave. One of the larger issues that looms today is **work-life balance**. Here, opting out is quite different from being shown the way out. Organizations may demand more of the employee's personal time than the employee is willing to give. There is research on the workforce group called "Generation Y" or "Millennials" that suggests their values may not be compatible with the 80-hour work week of the Traditionalists or the Boomer generation[15]. Once again, this is an area where you have to know who you are, what you value, and what you need. If you don't, not only will you never be happy but you will never be a leader worth following. You may be the proverbial company guy and willing to give everything to the job, but then again, you may want to have a life outside of work *and* do a great job for the company. We believe you can have it all—a great career, be a great leader, and not sacrifice your personal life or your health to your career advancement. But you probably can't have any one area to excess. You may also not be able to have it all at once— such as be the CEO and a successful marathoner and an engaged parent. Many successful leaders who value these different aspects of life find that they have phases in which different areas predominate, for instance allowing their career to cool down while their children are young or while they face a family emergency. Then, when they have more time to focus on advancing their career, that aspect of life comes into sharper relief. Integrating your work and life is crucial to renewing your passion. It's important to construct a life where each area supports and nourishes the others, rather than undermines the others. Most *It-Factor* leaders we've met say that having a great leadership career at the expense of a rich personal life or health is not much of a trade to make.

Today, research shows that about one-third of senior executives fail[16]. They derail in their jobs. It's all too common. On our tour of the best research on derailment we've just talked about many of the reasons why this happens. The important take away is don't let it happen to you!

You can use table 1.3 as a quick self-assessment to check if you are at risk of derailing in your career. If you check any of the boxes, it is worth thinking about if that area might negatively affect your career. The more checks you have in one category, the more you may want to evaluate your overall behaviors and results that relate to that category, and how they might affect your future career opportunities.

You should know what your weaknesses are, as well as your strengths. Set your goals for development based on how you want to get better. The 13 Steps to Becoming an *It-Factor* Leader can help you improve in any of these common problem areas—and a whole lot more. Because really it's not just about avoiding derailment: it's much more about maximizing your leadership success.

Table 1.3: Personal Assessment of Risk for Career Derailment

I see myself at risk for: √ the box that applies		
Problems with interpersonal relationships	I have been told that I can be too direct or sometimes abrasive	❑
	Being the best or first is really important to me, all else is secondary	❑
	Things work out best when they are done my way—then I can assure they are perfect	❑
	I have shown my temper at work on more than one occasion	❑
Difficultly molding or building a team	People need to be tightly managed/people should manage themselves and not bother me	❑
	Communicating with people really frustrates me	❑
	It's best to hire people who are like me because I understand them	❑
	My job will be in jeopardy if my staff does better work than I do	❑
Failure to make tactical shifts/to think strategically	Adapting to those with a different style is a huge challenge for me	❑
	I hate conflict and try to avoid it	❑
	Details are crucial and what I like to focus on, but I can get "stuck" on the details	❑
	Change equals risk and should be avoided	❑

Too narrow in one's functional orientation	I am stuck in my role	☐
	I have limited experience	☐
	It's hard for me to understand the needs of those from other disciplines or backgrounds	☐
	I really like to focus on just a few things	☐
	I have never had a stretch experience	☐
Being over dependent	My professional connections are limited	☐
	I've always worked here or for one successful super-star	☐
	I have just one niche area of expertise or skill	☐
Failing to meet business objectives	I am a big picture person—others finish the small details, sometimes I have left little things undone	☐
	I am not in control of the outcomes of my projects	☐
	I see the big picture but really struggle with the details	☐
	I am easily bored by projects and am drawn to the next exciting opportunity	☐
Strategic differences with management	Management has different values than I do	☐
	Management has different metrics of success than I do	☐

Maximizing Leadership Success: A Look at the Research

Those who study leaders have been keenly interested in what makes them successful. The Center for Creative Leadership's studies have found that successful leaders shine particularly strongly in ten areas. What might surprise you is that none of these areas is related to having great hard skills in a particular discipline. And none of them actually are about being smart either. As you look at this list think back on what we know about competitive advantage: it's about concepts, competence, and collaborations. Think about how these success factors relate to nurturing an idea-environment with talented people who can work together in inter-professional settings. Take a look at these "10 areas to shine" and see how you compare.

CCL's research shows that the top ten requirements for being successful as a leader include being able to create environments that welcome **participative management**. Here they capture the best of everyone's ideas, creating both buy in and a shared sense of ownership. Successful leaders also **balance their personal life and work**—in short, they don't die on the job. Personal life, personal health, and stress management matter and successful leaders make a commitment to them. They also have this balance so that they do not fall into the trap of believing they *are* the job, confusing the glory or power of the office with themselves. When people lose this balance they can forget who they are and start to abuse the power they have. *It Factor* leaders are **self-aware** and not caught by surprise by their blind spots. This self-awareness likely helps them with all these other assets that require keeping their egos in check. Successful leaders excel at **putting people at ease** while they maintain their **straightforwardness and composure**, even under stress. Note how many of these success factors stand in direct opposition to those pesky derailment factors we just discussed.

Successful leaders understand that it isn't just about **building relationships**—which they are good at. They also realize that they must be able to *mend* those relationships. Let's face it, you will likely come up against competing needs with at least some of your stakeholders. Competing over scarce resources can cause bruises to professional relationships—a key leadership skill is to **mend relationships** when they do get bruised. Successful leaders shine at **confronting problem employees** –and remember that failing to do so factors into derailment. Being conflict averse is a trait of poor leadership. When you allow a problem to go unchecked it causes organizational culture problems and employee disengagement across all those team members who clearly see the problem and also see the leader ignoring it.

Successful leaders shine at **doing whatever it takes**. They are resourceful, motivated, and role model going the extra mile for the team. They are the model of the engaged employee. Successful leaders also know how to **manage change**. They understand how to sell the change message and how to keep people motivated through the process. And finally, the CCL research pointed out that successful leaders are **decisive**, with an ability to keep projects on track by making the critical decisions in a timely fashion.

Think about leaders you've known and how they compare to this list. How do YOU compare to this list? What areas do you particularly excel at? What areas would you like add to your list for personal development? Reflect on yourself for a moment and use Table 1.4 to chart your insights.

Leaders that really shine at building strong organizations don't let it stop with themselves—they push talent development throughout their entire organizations. Great leaders build great teams. And they develop the talent in their enterprise. These are other aspects in our 13-steps to developing your *It-Factor*. These steps are vital because successful leaders make sure their team has the resources they need, and the coaching and mentoring to know how to use those resources wisely. Great leaders share a vision, they motivate others and they don't turn a blind eye to change—they embrace it, they lead it. Great leaders also delegate and let go.

Table 1.4: Self-Assessment of Strength Areas Where I Need to Shine

My assessment of my ability to:	Poor	Fair	Good
Create participative management	❑	❑	❑
Balance my personal life and work	❑	❑	❑
Be self-aware, both of strengths and weaknesses	❑	❑	❑
Put others at ease	❑	❑	❑
Maintain my straightforwardness and composure	❑	❑	❑
Build and mend relationships	❑	❑	❑
Confront problem employees	❑	❑	❑
Manage change successfully	❑	❑	❑
Do whatever it takes	❑	❑	❑
Be Decisive	❑	❑	❑

Bill Gates is a terrific example of doing exactly this. And when he left Microsoft to pursue his interests with the Gates Foundation, there was no appreciable drop in the stock price of the company. He had built such a strong company that everyone knew it would continue to be strong without him. The company wasn't *about* him and he wasn't a guru leader. In contrast, when Steve Jobs left Apple the first two times, the stock price took quite hit. The difference was that people equated Apple's success with Steve Jobs himself—so without him they were sure the company would struggle. Great leaders build organizations that aren't about them—they build great teams, teams who build great products and build great outcomes.

A good place to take stock of your leadership journey is to understand what makes for successful leadership versus what sinks the ship. You've had a chance to do a quick self-assessment and that should begin to give you an idea of how you'd like to develop, the skills that you'd like to work on, what rough spots you'd like to smooth over. Then the next question becomes how to proceed.

If you want to change the culture of your team, group, or organization, you first need to start with *yourself*. Take a good look at yourself. As an example, let's take the sophisticated skill of *Managing the Difficult Conversation*—which is another crucial aspect to that all-important *It-Factor* of being a great leader. We discuss mastering the art of the difficult conversation at length in our Eleventh Step. That skill alone encompasses many of the attributes listed in Table 1.4, including putting people at ease, confronting problem employees, maintaining straightforwardness and composure, self-awareness, and building and mending relationships. If you feel that managing difficult conversations is an area in which you could develop more skills, then follow this process to improve. First think about the most recent difficult conversation you've had or that you will face soon in the future. Pay attention to this experience. After it is over, reflect on where your skills are now. Then envision using your insights in a future conversation—considering what went right and what could have been better. Rehearse in your mind or with another person how you will implement the tools that make up the art of the difficult conversation. Then, finally, put that into practice in the ACT step listed in Figure 1.1. As you have a new experience, reflect on how that was better or more difficult than others and see what you can learn from it. This is the process of self-monitoring, reflection, and growth of your leadership skills. The process is: Experience, Reflect, Envision, and Act.

Figure 1.1

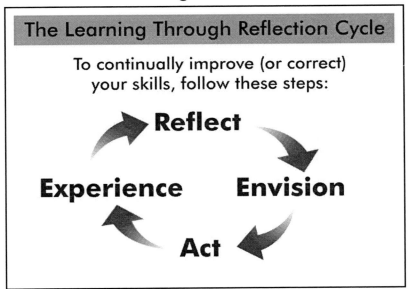

Everyone has a wealth of experiences during their training and their career. The key is to squeeze the meaning out of those experiences so that your capacity as a leader, a manager, and as a teammate is enriched. It is this ability to *get the message*, to extract the meaning out of experiences, both good and bad, that helps define successful folks from those who derail in their careers. Don't make the mistake of merely glancing at your experiences. Study them. Reflect on them. Envision how you'll act in the future—and then act! And then start the process all over again. This is one of the ways you become a life-long learner. And that's another thing we know about great *It-Factor* leaders: they don't stop learning.

Your 1st step to becoming a great *It-Factor* leader is to really, truly know and be aware of yourself.

The Second Step: Get (Or Get On) The Right Team

Get (or get on) the Right Team:
Mastering the Art of the Behavioral Event Interview

Another thing we've learned about great leaders with the *It-Factor* is that they are very picky about the team that sits on their bench. They don't take hiring lightly, they don't slough selection off to the system bureaucracy, and they don't leave onboarding to chance. Similarly, they are also picky about the jobs they take (or choose to stay at). They don't hire out of desperation and don't they take or stay at a job for that reason either. They see the world as full of opportunity—both for finding great teammates and for themselves.

Step 2 to better leadership is about getting the right players on your team or getting on the right team yourself. Individual leadership skills are important, and we'll get to those in later steps, but leadership is also a team sport. You want to make sure that you are choosing the right people for your team—and if you are looking for a position, then you want to make sure you *get* on the right one too. There is a powerful technique to help you do just that, called "Behavioral Event Interviewing"[1]. Truly, this is a technique worth mastering[2]. We teach this skill intensively to about 100 executives and leaders a year. Not only have their careers taken on totally new trajectories, but many of them have revolutionized how they interview and hire too.

In this step of your journey towards becoming a great *It-Factor* leader, we'll talk about interviewing done right and wrong. Think about it: one of the most important things that leaders do is choose the members of their team. Imagine if you could hire the right person for the job the first time, and save yourself those painful corrections after bringing someone on board who just doesn't have the right fit or skill set[3-6]. You want to hire employees who have both sets of skills you want in a position: the hard skills (the technical set of knowledge, skills, and abilities required to actually do the job) and the soft skills (interpersonal skills related to interacting well with people). Yes, you can hire for fit *and* skill.

The "Behavioral Event Interview," or the BEI for short, is a technique based on the premise that the past predicts the future—so when you are considering a candidate for a job, you can make a very educated guess about how they *will* perform for you based on how they *have* performed in the past. And since turnover is one of the crushing cost centers that plagues organizations and drains organizational memory, the BEI technique helps the bottom line. Research shows that when people are well matched to the job, turnover rates are lower[1, 2, 6]. Lower turnover rates save the organization a considerable amount of money.

What kind of performance can you predict? All kinds of performance: on technical tasks, managing interpersonal situations like dealing with conflict, managing upset clients or patients, providing excellent customer service, or managing a work group. You can assess how a prospective employee is likely to implement policies or protocols and how they are likely to innovate and lead change. Using this tool, you can assess if the candidate has the skills to do the job and to get a sense of how well they understand what the job requires. In fact, with any task required by the job you have to offer you can use the BEI technique to assess actual skills, and thus you can gauge how well this individual will function on your team should you decide to hire them.

It-Factor leaders don't get burned by going with their gut—and neither should you. You should also avoid making any of the other "seriously bad" interviewing errors we'll address in this Step. Without a standardized technique like the BEI, it's easy for an interview to feel right but to go very wrong, which can lead you to inadvertently hire the wrong person for the job. There are 5 all-too-common serious interviewing errors that *It-Factor* leaders avoid...and so should you!

Table 2.1: Five Seriously Bad Interviewing Mistakes

1. Talking more than the candidate being interviewed
2. Wasting time on archaic questions
3. Getting a verbal resume from the candidate
4. Asking hypothetical questions
5. Hiring for gut chemistry

The first mistake to make is to talk more than the candidate. You aren't there to sell the job—you are there to find the right person to fill the job. In a job interview the *candidate* should be doing most of the talking. Presumably they are meeting with you because they read the job description and applied for the job. Their application and cover letter should have clarified their interest in the position and basic qualifications. Thus, it should be needless for you to outline the details of the position during your meeting.

The second serious error is to waste time with irrelevant or uninformative questions. One example of such an archaic and useless question is "what are your strengths and weaknesses?" Face it, everyone knows the answer to this question is a well-rehearsed half-truth that has little to do with the requirements for success in the position. People give un-insightful answers like "I'm a perfectionist," which are really designed to make them look like they have no weaknesses. An interview is about assessing competency and skill—so stick to the point. Ask the *relevant* questions.

All too often interviewers look at a resume and use that as a conversational crutch, asking the candidate to repeat the information listed there. Presumably, the candidate will be familiar with the job description before even deciding to apply for the position. Similarly, you should be familiar with their background and experience before deciding to invite them to interview. The best use of the interview time is to assess how relevant their experience and skills are compared to the needs of your organization.

Here's a serious interview error we bet you have heard: The hypothetical question. These are "What *would* you do" questions that present possible situations one might face on the job. The problem is that hypothetical questions invite hypothetical answers which are grounded more in fantasy than they are in fact. What you can get in response to this style of question is not what someone would do, but what they *wish* they would do. If they don't have the experience or skills to do the job, you need to find that out in the interview and not in their first weeks or months on the job.

Of these serious interviewing errors, we've saved the worst for last: hiring for chemistry is the worst mistake you can make when building your team. While at first glance it might *feel right* to hire someone you like, someone who feels comfortable to you and shares your world view, hiring someone based on their personality can do you, them, and your organization a devastating disservice. Now, the interviewee might indeed be a great candidate for the job, but if you don't ask about their skills, you'll be guessing about their competence to perform in the position.

Not hiring for chemistry is a tough issue for many leaders who are building their team. Understandably they want to get along with the people who work for them—and they want everyone else to get along at work too. Hiring someone you like is not a good job criteria, you *aren't* looking for someone to go to lunch with or to serve as a golf partner. You *are* looking for someone with the requisite skills to execute the job duties well–that requires a definite set of abilities and experience. Hiring for chemistry can be toxic to an organization because it can negatively impact the diversity of thought and promote a condition called groupthink. Our Eighth Step addresses how to create thought diversity on your team—and avoid the disaster of groupthink, but first you need to hire right. Since there are great ways to assess skills at getting along that don't depend on your gut level reaction to the person, don't make the mistake of clouding hiring decisions with personal chemistry issues. This is not to suggest that soft skills are not important—they are. They can be critical to job success. And with the BEI you can assess those.

The goal of behavioral event interviewing is to evaluate the candidate's knowledge of specific situations or procedures that they will need for job success in your organization, and to gather data about their interpersonal performance in working with others. The BEI assesses, with a great deal of accuracy, how well a candidate actually executes tasks. Face it, it's easy for a candidate to talk about how they *would* accomplish a given task. A description of how one would act is what researchers call *espoused* theory—but we'll call it *talking the talk*. Those researchers term the behaviors the person actually puts into play as *theory in use*[1], but let's refer to it as *walking the talk*. When you are doing something as important as hiring a new team mate, you want someone who can do more than talk the talk, you want them to walk it as well.

BEI minimizes personal impressions that might cloud hiring decisions and, through predicting future task performance, it helps to make appropriate hiring decisions based on the fit and skill of the candidate.

You may have experienced many job interviews in your life, both as the candidate and as the person doing the hiring. Here are some differences between traditional and behavioral event interviewing:

First and foremost, in a BEI style interview, the candidate is not in control of the process. The interviewer is. They will ask how one DID behave in a given situation. The interviewer will ask for details and won't allow the candidate to theorize or generalize about several events.

Many candidates have polished stories they have prepared that demonstrate their competence and skills—however, they don't usually get to tell these in a behavioral event interview. The only details collected are those relevant to success at the particular job under recruitment.

The person conducting the BEI will ask many questions, and they take copious notes. They probe for depth in answers, asking questions to dig deeper for details to assess the congruency and relevance of the candidate's experience.

It's a highly structured process, not at all a free flowing conversation. The answers are scored on a point system and often multiple interviewers will compare scores after the interviews are completed.

Getting Started With the BEI

So how would you create a behavioral event interview for your next hire? You start with a good job description. First, you list the critical performance areas for the job you need to fill. What are the skills you need the new team member to have? Then you create open ended questions that query a candidate's experience at those tasks. It's also good to have some "probe" questions to help you drill down deeper into the candidate's answers.

Table 2.2: Getting Started With the BEI

Step I: Look at the job description
Step II: List the critical performance areas for the job
Step III: List the skills (both hard and soft) that the new teammate needs
Step IV: Create a list of open-ended questions to ask about those skills
Step V: Create a list of "probe" questions for digging deeper
Step VI: Gather STAR data

In the interview itself, you gather information on 4 areas: the *situation* the candidate faced, the *task* they had to accomplish in that situation, the *actions* they took and the *results* they achieved. That's called a STAR (Situation, Task, Action, Result). Typically you would score each candidate's answers relative to the job tasks and compare your results with those of your colleagues who also interviewed the pool of candidates. The comparison of notes and scores across interviews leads the team to an appropriate hiring decision to bring the right mix of skills and talents on board.

So that you can get a very deep and insightful understanding of the skills this individual has, you use those probing questions to dig down into the details, like peeling off the layers of an onion. Here you want to make sure the job candidate is telling you about just one time, and not generalizing about how they usually handle situations that arise. Table 2.3 lists some helpful "peeling the onion" questions which will allow you to dig deeper into the details so that you can assess if the candidate is telling about one experience or whether they are generalizing about many. With basic questioning, you can find out if they are relating what they *wish* they did or what they actually did.

Table 2.3: Example "Peeling the Onion" Questions

> - *Can you give me an example?*
> - *What did you do?*
> - *What did you say?*
> - *What were you thinking?*
> - *How did you feel?*
> - *What was your role?*
> - *What was the result?*

These will help you to uncover important facts about their performance. Questions such as these can give you insight into the accuracy, congruence and relevance of the candidate's story.

Let's look at an example of how you might ask a question to assess some really sophisticated soft skills in a candidate you are interviewing and considering hiring. First you would take a look at the job description and pull out a few critical skills necessary for success. For the sake of this example let's say that the successful candidate must work with a diverse team while successfully leading change, artfully managing conflict, creating a culturally competent work environment, and nurturing an inter-professional team. Then you would ask a question something like the following:

> *Please tell me about a time when you worked with a group where the players represented a multi-cultural or inter-professional team, and you had to convince them to make a significant change in what you were doing or how you were approaching a project?*

When listening to the answers you would create a chart like the one in Table 2.6, and write down their responses that demonstrate their skills in the appropriate column. Then assign points—perhaps 10 points for each block, but as long as everyone is consistent, it doesn't really matter how many points you assign to each component of the answer. You could give each a single point, or 5, or 10. Then you calculate a total point score to the answer after the interview. Compare your notes with your colleagues who interviewed the candidate. The final scores will tell you a lot about the skill level of the new potential team member.

Table 2.6: STAR Chart

	Lead Change	Manage Conflict	Cultural Competence	Inter-Professional Cooperation
S				
T				
A				
R				
Score:				

Mastering the BEI for Landing the Right Job

Of course, a part of becoming a better leader is finding the right job with the right fit for you, so now let's take a look at the flip side of the interview experience and focus on the BEI technique when *you* are the candidate being interviewed. Since behavioral event interviewing is really growing in popularity you should be ready to handle this type of interview when you are pursuing a new job opportunity. Even if you are not asked traditional BEI questions, by structuring your answers this way you can excel in any interview. Another benefit to preparing for this type of interview is that it will hone your skills at conducting BEI interviews— so you'll be better at using the technique to hire new team members.

Table 2.4 lists the steps to follow when preparing to answer behavioral event style questions: First, visit the job description and note what are the most important skills you would need to excel in that position. Don't forget to analyze it for both hard and soft skills. It's not only the technical part of the job that matters—most work today happens in an "inter-professional" environment, where you have to work with many colleagues from diverse backgrounds. It is in your best interest to clearly demonstrate that you are a team player and can get along well with others.

In order to prepare yourself to answer the questions typical of a BEI interview, you then reflect on situations you have been in that demonstrate leadership, teamwork, initiative, customer service, etc., and relate these to the job opening. These are common themes that arise in

Table 2.4: Preparing to Answer BEI Questions

Step I: Look at the job description
Step II: List the critical performance areas for the job
Step III: List the skills (both hard and soft) that you would need to excel in that job
Step IV: Reflect on your experience that demonstrates your skills in each of these areas
Step V: Create or write out your STAR answers
Step VI: Practice answering questions using the STAR format

higher level positions across all fields. The higher the position level, the more likely you will run into the BEI.

And just a note: you might work in a field where "customer service" is paramount—but if you are in the non-profit sector, such as public health, health care, public service, and academia, customer service is still paramount—you just call it something like community engagement, stakeholder stewardship, or public service.

Your next step will be to prepare short descriptions of each situation that exemplify your skills and experience in the areas relevant to the job you want.

It is important that each example you give comprise a story—not a fairy tale—a true story. It needs to have a distinct beginning, middle and conclusion with you *concisely* relating the situation, your action, and the outcome or result. When you relate the story of your experience, the outcome should reflect positively on you, even if the outcome of the situation you faced wasn't a total success.

Be careful not to embellish or omit parts of the story. And be prepared to give the relevant details when asked—trained interviewers will find out if any part of your story is built on a weak foundation. You also won't be allowed to generalize about several events and make them seem like one experience—you should give a detailed accounting of one event.

We do a *lot* of coaching to help job candidates prepare for very high level and competitive interviews. One thing that we've noticed is a relationship between the level of the position and the number of soft-skill questions asked. Lower level position candidates get asked questions about process or procedure. Interviews for higher level positions are rarely about technical competence. They are about impacting the culture, negotiating, managing others, handling challenges, and leading change. Here are some very typical BEI questions that leaders get asked in these kinds of job interviews.

- *Please tell me about a time when you needed to bring innovation and entrepreneurship to your organization*
- *Please tell me about a time when you managed a difficult interpersonal situation among staff*

- *Please tell me about a time when you had to take steps to change or influence the culture of an organization*
- *Please tell me about a time when you needed to negotiate on behalf of your organization. Who was the other party and what was the nature of the negotiation and the settlement?*
- *Please tell me about a time when you had to communicate across boundaries so that you could connect people, resources and groups despite the obstacles between them?*

When you answer any interview question take a moment to breathe. Listen carefully to what the interviewer is asking. We'll say it again: Breathe and take a moment to formulate your response, think before you speak. Of course, having done your interview preparation homework, you'll in all likelihood have anticipated all the BEI questions since those should be grounded in the job description and company needs.

Example BEI Answers From *It-Factor* Leaders

Here are two example answers to typical questions, one asked at an entry leadership level and one asked at a higher level of leadership responsibility. As we said, we train *a lot* of people in this artful communication technique since it teaches you to speak with eloquence and grace about your experience and keeps you from sounding like you're bragging. So we've heard *a lot* of answers to BEI style questions. The example answers are true stories from real leaders.

Question: Please tell me about a time when a team member wasn't pulling his or her weight. What happened? How did it impact your team? What did you do?

Answer: I have experienced that situation. I had been assigned to a team to work on a particularly complex project. One of our team members wasn't showing up for our preparation sessions or doing her assignments. While frustrations were running high on the team, I thought the real task was to sit down with her and find out what was up. So we met in private, I explained the frustration of the rest of the team, and asked if there was anything I could do to help. She told me she was preoccupied with another work project that was behind deadline and going poorly. We brainstormed on that project and I found someone to help her with the parts that were outside her expertise. She not only was able to spend more time on our project, but was also grateful to me for the help, advice and assistance. The result was that we finished our project on time, and got approval to move onto the next step based on it.

Notice that this answer is quite concise. In general, brevity is better. Long-winded answers tend to lose your audience, confusing them in too many details. You can always invite the interviewer to explore the situation more deeply. And you should be prepared for those "peeling the onion" questions. For an answer like this one, these are typical questions that might follow:

- *How did you feel when you confronted this person?*
- *Exactly what was the nature of the complexity of the project?*
- *What was her responsibility as a team member?*
- *What was your role?*
- *At what point did you take it upon yourself to confront her?*

As you can see, it is key that you refrain from making up or "coloring" information. It should also be obvious why you should have a clear memory of the entire incident.

And here is our second question with a true answer from a real leader as an example. This one asks about a bit more complicated a skill and the resulting answer is a bit longer as well:

> *Question: Please tell me about a time when you needed to bring innovation and entrepreneurship to your organization, even when this was against the tide.*

> *Answer: I really value creativity and innovation so I'm glad you asked about that. Probably the situation that stands out the most is when I was in an enterprise that provided consulting services to clients. When I joined the team, I was brought on board, taught the company way, and quickly became a project leader. But through my networking with colleagues outside of my firm, I began to suspect that what we were offering was not the real cutting edge of what was available. That made me start to investigate our competitors—and I should say, we used to have to hire our competitors as subcontractors to allow us to offer a full range of services. My boss used to call that partnering, but to me it looked like what we were really doing was draining our limited budgets paying our competitors a fortune to do what we could do for a fraction of the cost. To some extent, my Boss had a rather unexplainable attachment to one very expensive subcontractor/competitor in particular. My boss liked the idea of this "partnership" for reasons of self-interest and because they were ranked number one in the field, but the high fees we paid them jeopardized our own staffing lines. To me, clearly what needed to be done was to*

bring the competence level of the internal team up to speed so that we could provide our own full range of services—and better yet, customize them to our client's needs. This was not my Boss' priority, despite some rather distressing customer feedback on the outsourced work. I saw the real task that needed to be done was to have very compelling data to share with my boss to make the case. But in order to do that, I needed to be very innovative. I took some steps that were very "out of the box" for my group. First, I bargained with another division of my company, providing them with services and in exchange they transferred some funds to my group, which I used to pay for the training. After a colleague and I got licensed, I then started offering the services to our clients—and stopped sub-contracting with the competitor on the project that I ran. What happened was that our costs on that project dropped dramatically, which really improved our margins. And I kept careful data on customer feedback—it turned out my clients felt this new approach was really focused on them— and when we compared that to the previous feedback of "it felt canned," and "they (the subcontractor) didn't really understand what we are about," the combination of customer service and financial data presented a very compelling picture indeed. I used the cost savings to pay for my colleagues to go and get the trainings and certifications and the result was that we soon had real capacity in the organization—and a lot more employee engagement. It turned out the staff were hungry for this kind of development. It totally changed the way we did business. I had one client who was a customer to both the old subcontracted-out services and the services my new team offered tell me that the new services clearly out-stripped the old ones, so the tide became too big to fight. It revolutionized what we could offer and created the platform for us to make a national presence a few years down the road, which happily, I got to be a part of.

When using the STAR format, it helps to give what we call, "verbal headlines" in these answers. By that we mean to actually say the words "the SITUATION was….the TASK I had to accomplish was…" etc. That way, you will be able to keep the answer organized, even if the person interviewing you is not. It will also help you to make sure you've covered all the ground you need to in telling a complete story with a definite beginning, middle and outcome.

If we analyze the example answer above, here is how it follows the STAR format:

> Situation: Expensive sub-contractor providing less then optimal services and hired because internal team lacked the appropriate skills
> Task: Build competence of internal team so that services can be customized to clients
> Action: Raise resources to pay for staff training, get trained, implement new services, collect performance data, arrange for staff to get trained
> Result: Client satisfaction improved, significant costs saved on sub-contractor, staff more engaged because of training and development opportunities

Of course, when you are in an interview situation you might answer five to ten questions following the BEI technique, and you don't want to say Situation, Task, Action, Result over and over again—you'd sound like a robot. It wouldn't sound natural and authentic, so we suggest that you use a lot of different ways to say each of the four stages of a STAR answer, as demonstrated in the example above. Some suggestions are in Table 2.5.

In general your answers should be no more than a couple of minutes. Don't worry about getting every single detail in there. The interviewer will ask you questions to "peel that onion" based on the type of skills and interpersonal abilities they are looking for.

In the final analysis, behavioral event interviewing is an important technique and well worth mastering, whether you are looking to add to your team or looking for a new position for yourself. It is powerful in that it helps you to talk about your experience with eloquence, brevity, and organization—all of which help you to give a graceful answer during the stressful experience of an interview.

Table 2.5: Giving Directed BEI Answers Using a Variety of Language Choices

STAR component	Other words to use to describe the same thing
Situation:	The situation was… What was happening was that… The event that I would like to tell you about… I did experience that…
Task:	The task I had to accomplish… What I saw that I needed to achieve was… Clearly what needed to be done was…
Action:	The actions I took were… The steps I took were… There were a few things I did in response to this event…
Result:	And the result was… What happened was… The outcome was…

When you are looking for the best candidates to bring onto your team, using the BEI helps take the bias out of the interviewing process so that you identify the most competent mix of skills and experience to meet your organization's needs. There is evidence that getting the right person with the right skills into the right job the first time reduces turnover and helps control costs as well. With practice you can become quite adept at both administering and answering BEI style questions.

So that's Step 2 towards becoming an *It-Factor* leader: a strong strategy for getting the right people on your bench and playing on your team (or, if needed, getting yourself on the right team!)

Your 2nd step to becoming a great *It-Factor* leader is to hire the right folks the first time.

The Third Step:
Shut Up And Listen

Shut Up and Listen:
Turning Listening Into a Persuasive Art

One of the biggest challenges highly skilled, highly competent leaders face is that they know too much. Having great experience and training can really limit you to seeing only what you know—and leaving you blind to what you don't know. It also can put you into the role of director, savior, and martyr of the organization, and that's not healthy for you or anyone else. We have found that *It-Factor* leaders don't fall into this trap.

One skill great leaders with the *It-Factor* have is listening—really listening. Deeply listening. Listening with the intensity usually reserved for speaking[1].

When leaders talk and tell they fall into a management trap. They give tasks to direct reports, solve their problems, provide all their resources...and stop them from thinking. If you want to have the people you pay to work for you actually think for you, then you can't do their thinking for them.

What *It-Factor* leaders do is they share their vision with the team, and then send their team to solve problems that they themselves, and not the leader, own. When you function as an *It-Factor* leader, then you facilitate a direct report's problem solving, and when people take responsibility for their own problems they generally find their own resources. Leadership is more about having a relationship with a talented, energized, and professional staff. Remember the list of what makes great leaders shine from the First Step to becoming a great *It-Factor* leader? You'll find those types of skills reflected in you when you gain mastery over listening skills.

What kind of staff you have will depend partly on who you hire and partly on the kind of culture you create as the leader. But you have to ask this question of yourself: are you a manager or a leader? How do you function best? What does your organization really need?

Both managers and leaders create culture—the crucial difference lies in what kind of culture you create. You will either create a culture of problem bringers or problem solvers. Managers create problem bringers. Leaders create problem solvers. Now a lot of people hear this and immediately say, "I create problem solvers," but think for a moment about what you actually *do* in your work life. Work can seem all-consuming—and it's very easy to fall into the trap of creating problem bringers. After all, when you create this kind of team they solve the problems *you* identify *your* way.

Why does this management style flourish so? In part because it's time expedient for managers when they don't have to coach or mentor their team through situations they might never have faced before—no learning curve takes less time. And this is pretty subtle but don't underestimate its power: when you do this *you feel valuable.* One of the problems leaders face—particularly emerging leaders—is that once they become leaders they are no longer the highly productive individual contributors they once were. After all, there is a lot of gratification that comes from being the "delivery boy" or the "delivery girl" who completes the mission and produces the end product. If you are having a hard time *facilitating* the work of your team, rather than *doing* the work of your team, you need to do some soul searching: are you struggling with giving up the role of delivery boy? Can you successfully make the move from individual contributor to working with and through others?

After all, that's what *It-Factor* leaders do: they get things done with and through others, with meetings, conversations, and contemplation—and many do say they miss the feeling of accomplishment from getting to mentally mark a task as done. It can be tempting to slip into creating a team of problem bringers without even knowing it.

As a leader, the other thing you should know: people LOVE working *for* a problem solver who cultivates problem bringers. Because if you solve other people's problems, what will they do? Well, they will bring *you* their problems! They will appreciate you as their boss, encourage you, reward you for that—they will want you to stay their problem solver. And you might find that you get so busy solving the problems of other people that you have little time to solve your own.

But if you want to become an *It-Factor leader* and you *create* a group of problem solvers, then you have a very different kind of a team. You'll be building the capacity of the team through empowering *them* to identify and complete the tasks, facilitating *their* ability to both find resources as well as solve problems. Of course, this means you will have to delegate and let go of tasks. In our First Step to becoming a great *It-Factor* leader, we talked about knowing yourself and not letting your ego get the better of you. It is hard to create a team of problem solvers if you are intimidated by the success of your direct reports or colleagues. Leaders who feel threatened by "two bears in the cave" will create mediocrity rather than great outcomes, and *It-Factor* leadership will be elusive to them.

But if you follow the path to *It-Factor* leadership, then you should be aware that creating problem solvers will likely take a bit more time on your part at first, as they will probably need to learn some new skills. While this might feel like the process goes slower at times, in reality it unleashes the power of your team to do more—and often more than you ever imagined[2]. Think about the very real Behavioral Event Interview answer on innovation and entrepreneurship we shared with you in the Second Step to becoming a great *It-Factor* leader. That's a true story. In that case a problem solver understood the challenge, found the resources and despite a culture that didn't want innovation and change, revolutionized her business.

Of course, wanting and having are two different things. If you *want* problem solvers and you *have* a team of problem bringers then you need a good strategy to start moving them in a more independent direction. You can use reflective questions to help them make this transition. But to do reflective questioning, you have to be a good listener. You will need to engage in this reflective questioning with your team, and encourage them to do it with one another as well.

There are some key facets of this kind of team coaching that make this interaction different from other types of discussion or casual conversations. The most important aspect is that you assume that your team member, be it your direct report, colleague, or peer, really knows their situation best. That's where the reflective questions come in. This whole process is about the other person understanding, owning, and solving their own problems, which is why it helps train problem *solvers* rather than problem *bringers*. When you become skilled at reflective questioning, you learn to stop trying to jump in and save the day as a solver of other people's problems. And when you teach it to your team, they learn to facilitate Socratic and critical thinking in others as well.

You've probably run into those folks whose titles say "leaders" but are in reality managers, who think they are "coaching" you. But when they listen to you for five minutes, sure that they understand your world, make their diagnosis about your situation, then provide you a quick prescription—that's not coaching. We call that "curbside consultation." Can one really, in just a few minutes of dialogue truly understand the players, the politics, and the murky waters better than the person who is dealing with the situation day-to-day? Yet often in curbside consultation the well-meaning manager will tell you what you should do, who you should talk to, what books you should read, before they can even know the complexity you face.

When you are tempted to fall into curbside consultation, bear in mind that there may be some sensitive, confidential, or proprietary information that is important but that the other person simply cannot share with you. In those cases, without that particular insight, any strategies you have to offer are likely to be less relevant. And most important, curbside consultation is all about talking and not about listening. Great *It-Factor* leaders really listen.

Here's another reason why you need to learn to listen well. Think back to a time when you were struggling with a complex problem or situation. A time when you were still thinking about what you knew, what you suspected you might know, and what you still didn't know. Probably with this situation, if you think about it, you might not have even finished processing your feelings about what was going on. In those cases, it can be very counterproductive to get advice when what you really need to do is to work through it all. *It-Factor* leaders recognize this and they ask reflective questions. They understand that they can't know it all. They get it that some facts are hidden from view—maybe everyone's view. So they do ask, they don't tell. Great *It-Factor* leaders understand that the curbside consulting approach is based on such little information to go on, it's akin to driving in a heavy downpour at night without headlights: you just can't see the situation well enough to give you good directions about where to go. While the person who is trying to coach might mean well, usually what they *can* offer is just a band-aid solution.

When great leaders listen, they do it with the intensity usually reserved for speaking[1]. When they talk, they ask questions—reflective questions. Not leading ones or judging ones. They never ask questions like "why would you do a dumb thing like that?" They avoid "did you ever think of doing X?" That is *not* a reflective question. That is giving strategy. That is being a manager.

Does this sound intriguing? But are you wondering, *just what is a reflective question?* John Barkai, an attorney and professor at the University of Hawaii, developed a series of questions that fit this category[3] (table 3.1). You should keep these handy and be ready to ask them as you transform problem bringers into problem solvers. This is not an exhaustive list but it certainly can get you started.

You will be amazed at how much more you learn when you really listen. Of course, you don't want to get stuck just going over and over the present situation. Leaders facilitate problem solvers by helping them move forward with strategies and solutions—just not the *leader's* solutions, but rather the team member's solutions instead. When you are asking questions and listening, there are a whole series of phrases you can use to help your team make progress and move towards future action. Some questions that you should keep in mind are listed in table 3.1.

When you cultivate problem bringers you are expected to have the answers. And sometimes you won't. Sometimes you can't. You can't know everything, and you might give some very bad advice when you don't have all the information you need. The good news is that you don't have to, nor should you, provide all the answers. When you use this technique and ask reflective questions, you can help your colleague find their own solution—and a solution they can own.

Table 3.1: Reflective Questions and Statements to Help You Transform Problem Bringers Into Problem Solvers

Discovery Questions	Future-Oriented Questions
• What do you mean by _____? • Can you put that into other words? • Can you be more specific? • Tell me more about that • Explain to me…. • How so? • In what way? • That's helpful, keep going • Hmmm, hmmmm… • How did you (or X) feel in that situation?	• Is what you are talking about now helpful in reaching a solution? • Put yourself in the other person's shoes. How do you think they are feeling right now? • If the other person were to do X, what would you be willing to do? • What can you do to help solve this problem? • What can X do to help you solve this problem? • How do you want things to be between the two of you? • What do you think will happen if you can't negotiate a solution? • Is what you are talking about now helpful in reaching a solution?

Based on the Barkai Chorus, by John Barkai[3]

Move beyond managing your team: really develop them into problem solvers. Develop them into the future and current leaders of your organization. You'll be able to focus on your own problems much more effectively when you have this type of an engaged team to work with, when everyone is working positively and productively.

Listening as the Art of Persuasion

Really great leaders with the *It-Factor* can use honed listening skills to be extremely persuasive. This is a highly sophisticated skill founded upon what is called the Socratic method, based on that good old Greek philosopher, Socrates. When you really listen to what the other party is saying, you can actually use *questions* to be far more persuasive than if you talked a lot about your perspective, knowledge, know-how, or answer. One of the outcomes of this kind of persuasive listening is that when you learn more about the other party and what their concerns are, you build trust.

First, let's talk about why leaders who try to persuade by talking rather than listening run into such strong walls—and all too often meet with failure. Think about a time when you found trying to persuade someone frustrating or an outright catastrophe. Maybe you tried to convince someone that your view of the situation was right, or that the idea you offered should be the one chosen, or that your group was the right one to partner with, or that you were the right person for the job. All too often we think of persuasion like a competitive debate—and so we support our position logically and often provide facts in abundance. We might even think it's wise to overwhelm the opponent with sheer data. Well, even looking at the other party like an opponent with a view to be won is exactly opposite to what research shows will be successful in persuasion. In reality, those techniques more often than not result in the parties locking horns in disagreement. Either that, or one party wins—

leaving the other feeling trampled upon and not likely to partner again where outcomes are so one-sided. Ironically, perfect persuasion is not about you stating your case compellingly or successfully. Let's take a look at what it is about.

Listening Opens Relationships

Great *It-Factor* leaders with acute listening skills understand that their job in perfect persuasion really isn't to convince the other person....it is to open a relationship. As funny as it may seem, what the research shows is that on the important issues you don't persuade people—they persuade themselves! So it's not about convincing them. It's not about data or being logical or being right. It's much more about listening than it is about talking.

There is a basic truth about people that both professional salespersons and trial attorneys know: once we come to a conclusion or make a decision, we don't like to say that we were wrong. Think of someone you've known who sunk a lot of money into a fancy car. Oh how they hate to admit that they made a mistake—and they tell you all the reasons why only true car lovers own this kind of car, that their little baby is just getting a bit of attention in the shop, that they are "an enthusiast." This is known as a "dissonance effect"[4] and it happens on a subconscious level. Subconscious in part because it feels good to make a decision and there is a boost in self-esteem once we have come to a conclusion, and of course, most people feel uncomfortable admitting that they were wrong. People also look at the world very selectively—seeing the data that supports their point of view and conveniently ignoring or dismissing the data that doesn't. The real challenge for you here is that most people have no idea they are making this error of very selectively seeing the world about them. How many people do you know who, when they do see evidence that suggests they were wrong, say "wow, I made a mistake"? When was the last time *you* said that? So you can't get into a battle of logic with most people, because when you are dealing with persuasion, you are not dealing with the logical, rational centers of the brain. You are dealing with the value centers of the brain—and that's a totally different world[5]. If you want to learn more about this you can look at the work of Joel Barker[6] and his writings on paradigms or at Leon Festinger's early research into cognitive dissonance[4].

Researchers have studied gamblers, too. Interestingly, they find that once they make a bet, their confidence in the bet goes up[7]. They start looking for data that justifies their choice. The same "dissonance effect" happens with everything. Especially stories we tell ourselves about each other and conflict. Interestingly, this effect is multiplied the more public the story becomes. If people hear us telling our stories, our need to justify them becomes even stronger.

You might have heard this described as people who are "married to a decision" once they've made it. If you try to be persuasive by dissuading people of their opinion—don't be surprised if they are of the same opinion still. But now they just think you're a jerk.

So, Don't Be a Jerk

If you want to have an effective and potentially persuasive discussion with someone, then the first thing you need to do is to understand where they are coming from. You need to understand who the person is that you're talking with, what they do, what is the situation their company finds itself in. The questions you should ask them are all about fact finding. Are you talking with the right person in the organization? Is this someone you want to persuade to work with your group, partner, or hear your point of view? After all, if you're not talking to the right person, a decision maker or someone who can help you then the conversation might be enjoyable, but it probably won't further the work you are trying to accomplish. Situation questions also help you understand the facts about their enterprise, which might have to do with size, structure, partnerships, or customers. They give you the lay of the land of who they are and why they exist.

Of course, part of this picture you should find out through your own research before you ever sit down with the other person, but you should also inquire about some of this information in your discussion. Ask too few questions about the situation and it feels like you've hired a private investigator to learn about the other person—and spying on someone just feels plain creepy. But don't ask too many of these questions either, or you'll bore the other person and they'll know you haven't done your homework. If they think you're lazy they aren't likely to find you very persuasive. One thing about *It-Factor* leaders: they are prepared.

Once you have an understanding of who the other party is, then you need to understand the challenges they face. What are the issues, problems, and concerns they are up against? If you want to convince them that you are the right group to partner with or that you have a solution that would benefit them, then you need to know their *needs*. Asking about these issues and challenges will help you understand who they are and what they are dealing with. When you can understand their problems, challenges, difficulties, or dissatisfactions then you can start to build a relationship based on really understanding the other party.

A tenacious researcher named Neil Rackham has studied how successful sales agents make the kind of connections that result in large deals[8]. After all, sales is essentially about persuasion. Mr. Rackham is adamant on the point that "if you can't uncover any problems to solve, you don't have a basis for a business relationship." He writes about the sales technique he calls "SPIN selling," but there is much in that strategy that can help leaders listen the right way to help perfect their powers of persuasion.

According to Rackham, the next step is to understand what these challenges, issues, dissatisfactions, or problems *mean* to the other party. All problems have consequences. What's happening to the other party as a result of the challenges they face? The purpose of asking problem questions is so that you can surface those needs. What you will learn about are what Rackham calls "implied needs." These give you valuable guideposts on your way to persuasion, but you can't stop here. When you ask the right kind of problem questions, the other party sees that they have a problem, but despite that acknowledgement they typically won't see the problem as an urgent one. That makes the next step in building this relationship one where you help the other party understand that the problems they see as non-urgent ones might be very significant indeed. So significant that listening to your idea is a valuable use of their time. You are much less likely to be persuasive if you just seem interested in your idea because it is valuable to you.

If you follow this listening-as-persuasion method, then by this point you will have gotten to know them better and to understand the problems they face. Now you should have a good idea if you really do have a worthwhile perspective or opportunity to offer them—in other words if you really do have something to persuade them about. If you still feel this is true, then you need to help them see that as well. Your next step in perfect persuasion is to help illuminate the implications of those problems. You can start to do this by asking about the consequences of the problems they face. You can ask about the effects of those challenges they mentioned. Probe about any dissatisfactions they have about the current situation. These kinds of questions will increase the value they see in what you have to offer them. For one, it shows that you are actually interested in what is going on with them and not just in pushing your idea on them. In fact, if you really want to make a successful persuasive argument, then a large proportion of the questions you ask should be about the implications of those challenges they face.

The best way to persuade someone is to illustrate that you can help them. You do that best by showing that you understand the complexity they face, that you speak their language, as it were. Implication questions build trust because they help both you and the other party to truly grasp the depths of problems they face. Often we can see a problem—but we don't see how all the proverbial dominos fall as a result of those problems. What we're really talking about here is good old systems thinking, first put forth by experts like W. Edwards Demming[9] and later popularized by Peter Senge[10]. By asking implication questions you can help the other party see their problems from a system's level. After all, if problems are only dealt with on a surface level, then they are not likely to be solved. When you help the other party to truly see how they can solve a deep, multi-faceted problem, you will build trust and be much more persuasive.

According to Rackham, questions that surface the implications of the challenges facing the other party are particularly brilliant because they surface a new kind of need: an explicit need. These are needs that you can meet—and *voila*! The combative process of persuasion has just become quite easy as you show how you can solve their deep, systems-level related problem. In essence the questions that you ask by intently listening will lead to them to persuading themselves.

Here's how the culmination of turning listening-into-perfect-persuasion works: you follow up with questions that help you understand how the implications you just discussed, those consequences the other party faces, can be met or solved by what you have to offer, your idea, or your opportunity. When you can get them talking about the need to move to a solution, then you have hit upon explicit needs. According to Rackham's research, explicit needs are directly related to successful persuasion.

When you are successful at asking questions which help the other party understand how their issues must be solved and can be solved, not only are they telling you the benefits of finding a solution, but they will also be increasing the acceptability of your solution—and that translates into persuasion! In effect they sell themselves. You are there to "fill in the blanks" with your solution, which becomes their solution. Suddenly you don't have to argue with them. You don't have to overwhelm them with data. And you don't have to fight cognitive dissonance either. Great *It-Factor* leaders persuade by using this acute listening skill.

So let's look at a real life example of using this strategy in action. To make this as simple as possible, we'll use the example of bringing innovation and creativity we talked about in the Second Step to *It-Factor* leadership, with the Behavioral Event Interview. In this case the leader who brought about a revolution in the way her enterprise did business related the following conversation to us that she had with her #2 manager.

Just as a reminder, she discovered that her enterprise was not, but easily could be, offering cutting-edge services. For reasons of personal self-interest, the #1 boss chose to use a subcontractor who was having less than stellar performance and was outrageously expensive. Our leader felt there was another way to approach the business, but she needed to persuade her #2 boss in order to move forward (we'll call him #2). We'll refer to the expensive subcontractor as "XYX Company." Here is the conversation she relayed to us:

Leader: "Hey #2, many times you've mentioned that we face serious budget problems in this tight economy. Of our three major cost areas, what do you see as the most crucial for our survival?"

#2: "Yes, budget is a huge concern. Well, I guess our 3 major cost centers are salary, our facilities costs, and subcontracting with the XYZ firm."

Leader: "And of these, which are impossible to change, which are possible, and which are easy?"

#2: "Well, we can't really do much about the salary line—we need our staff to stay in business and we don't want to lose any more positions—we're already pretty lean. And we're locked into our space. But we need the subcontract too, since they provide services that we can't."

Leader: "It sounds like the only thing we can give on is staff—but that threatens our survival if we lose any more people. You know, I think we might be paying our competitor good money that we could be saving a bundle on!"

#2: "Why do you call XYZ a competitor? You know the Boss sees them as a partner. They're rated #1 in their field."

Leader: "Yes, that's true. They do have a good reputation. I'll answer your question but first I need to ask you about client satisfaction. Did you see the latest evaluation results and what did you think?"

#2: "Overall the feedback was positive"

Leader: "Yes, overall it was OK, but did you see the comments about XYZ's part? 'I feel this section didn't meet our needs?' and 'this part of the group didn't really seem to understand us. It felt kind of 'canned'."

#2: "Yes, those were disappointing…"

Leader: "You always say our customer service is our life line. Our clients are strapped for funds too—they have to really find value in what we do in order to be willing to pay us for our work. If we get feedback like this, how long will they keep coming to us?"

*#2: "I see what you mean. That is a problem. That's a big problem.
You know, our client load has been drifting down for quite a
few months now. It's a disturbing trend. If that's because
people feel it isn't really worth the money, that could explain a
lot."*

*Leader: "XYZ may be #1 in the field, but they aren't performing like
they are #1...not for us, anyway. I think that to them, we are
very small potatoes. Let me ask you, how sustainable is it to
pay them half the salary of one of our staff—in exchange, they
give us about 2 days-worth of work, and our clients say it feels
'canned? What do you think we could do with that money if
we didn't have to spend it on them?"*

*#2: "In these economic times? A lot, that's for sure. It is a concern that
they aren't performing for us as well as I think they should be.
That raises risks that worry me. If we could save that money—
that would make a big difference to us. We hire XYZ for three
of our projects. If we are getting feedback like that on each of
those projects, that's a huge problem and potentially a huge
waste of money to boot. That could be the difference of
keeping the staff we have."*

*Leader: "You know, the reality is that the only reason we hire them is
because they have this skill set we don't have. What would
happen if we had this capacity in house? We could customize
the services to our clients ..."*

#2: "...We could do it for a lot less..."

Leader: "—neither of which XYZ either can do or wants to do."

*#2: "You make a good point, I think we do need to address this, but
how can we do that? Can you propose some solutions?"*

*Leader: "I have researched how we could get the training to provide
those services. Then we can customize the services to really
meet our client's needs. No one will ever understand our
clients like we do."*

*#2: "Hmm, that costs money too. And it might not work. You know the
Boss loves the prestige XYZ brings. Those are real hurdles."*

Leader: "What would you say to a pilot project—it's pretty low risk. You and I can get the training, I have an idea of how to cover the cost of training—so it won't come from our project funds. That way there's no financial risk. I'll apply the new skills to just my clients and we can see how it works. You'll have gotten the training so you'll know exactly what's going on. If it's successful in their eyes and it saves money, then we can expand it to some of our other team members."

#2: "Well, alright. I'll agree to your pilot project. Make sure you collect really good data about costs and performance. We'll try your mini-experiment."

In the case example above, it was actually the #2 person in the organization who acknowledged some of the problems the outsourcing created. While it is true that implication questions are basically diagnostic ones it is also true that if you just surface problems only, with no solutions, then everyone is going to feel pretty demoralized and defeated. This example moved right on ahead into solving those problems. You already heard the outcome of the story (back in Step 2): the training resulted in significant cost savings, much greater client satisfaction, increased employee engagement, and revolutionized the way the office did business. The pilot project turned out to be a big success.

Table 3.2 lists the steps to Rackham's insightful sales strategy that you should learn if you want to be persuasive.

If persuasion feels more like a battleground than a discussion to you, try this Socratic method to sell your ideas. Build the relationship with the other party. Get to know them. Understand who they are and what they care about. Learn what challenges they face and help them come to understand how those little problems are all too often just symptoms of larger systemic issue that really must be faced. Help them with a viable solution. Remember, perfect persuasion is about building a relationship, and the foundation for that is trust.

Table 3.2: Steps in SPIN Selling

Steps	Symbol	Step	Description
1	S	Situation	Understand the who, what, and how of the other party
2	P	Problem Identification	Inquire about the issues and dissatisfactions (problems) the other party faces
3	I	Implication	Delve into the hidden or unappreciated systems level consequences of the problems
4	N	Need-Payoff	Match the problems with a viable solution that you have to offer

Based on the work of Neil Rackham[8]

One of the best ways you can persuade others, as well as to turn them into problem solvers rather than problem bringers, turns out to be acute listening skills. So be an *It-Factor* leader and learn those reflective questions: hone up on your Socratic method—you can both develop others and persuade stakeholders by listening like an *It-Factor* leader. In short: don't tell, do ask.

Your 3rd step to becoming a great *It-Factor* leader is to shut up and listen. Next we are going to meet an *It-Factor* leader from industry who used the art of perfect persuasion, and really made a difference.

Meet An *It-Factor* Leader: Dan Schmitz

Dan Schmitz is a scientist who exemplifies the idea of turning problem bringers to problem solvers. He works at a major multi-national healthcare company called Abbott. As the Director of Research and Development Operations, he spends his days inventing specialized medical foods to help people who suffer with chronic conditions to live better. He works on problems that are a scourge of modern society, like obesity and diabetes, but also on promoting better nutrition for sick children. If you've had a child who had a really bad GI bug, you've probably purchased one of his products called Pedialyte™. Dan is warm and funny, always ready with a laugh and a smile, and incredibly bright. While it's easy to see Dr. Dan Schmitz as a scientist—you might not see him as a warrior.   But back in 2010 he became one. He led a major battle in the fight against severe childhood malnutrition in one of the most vulnerable places on the planet: Haiti. And he didn't just fight. He won.

Haiti wasn't in great shape before that fateful Tuesday in January 2010 when it was shaken nearly apart by a magnitude 7.0 earthquake. But afterward, it became the poster child for vulnerable. Infrastructure was so fragile that electricity was a come-and-go reality of life. Clean water? Good luck. Educated workforce? Not exactly. Peace and security? Not here, not now. And the lack of food was leading small children to die a slow and torturous death of starvation. This was particularly true if they had other medical issues like HIV or tuberculosis, which couldn't be effectively treated in the presence of starvation. Looking at his Western world where obesity and diabetes were the targets, the starving of small children really bothered a man like Dr. Dan Schmitz. He spends a lot of his time in places like India and China. While these countries have their own challenges to good nutrition, they are nothing like Haiti.

So how could he solve this problem? How can you win a battle so big that tens of thousands of people have fought it around the world with only marginal success? What Dan found is that when it comes to tackling a problem bigger than you: don't do it alone. To fight starvation, get a lot of cooks in the kitchen.

So Scientist Schmitz became a networker of people; a facilitator of ideas; a negotiator of viable solutions. Here's his journey: he started off in Haiti, where he studied the problem. He examined the country. He looked at the assets they had (few) and the challenges they faced (many). One of the building blocks he did find was *Partners In Health* or PIH. This is a non-governmental organization. "NGO"s are businesses that have no profit motive. They exist to run, (usually) sustainably, and solve a human need, often related to promoting health or treating disease. PIH made a type of a fortified "super-peanut butter" that can be used to treat starvation in children. But they did it out of an outdoor kitchen with poor product resources, mitigated success, and an inability to meet the demand. They were there, but children were still dying. However, it was a start.

Dan made a list of the challenges. Then he searched out the people who would bring the best insights and skills to address each of them. He partnered with NGOs, studying them in both Haiti and Africa.

He worked with universities and agricultural extension groups. He found peanut growers and processing companies who were game to contribute to the solution. He rounded up engineers and scientists. He identified nutrition experts and energy specialists and brought them on board. By the end, he had at least 25 cooks in his virtual kitchen, all working on this problem. Since they were scattered around the world while he was situated solidly in the mid-west at a large company with a lot of resources, at first he was the central point of communication, visiting them and talking frequently by phone.

"Well, *that* wasn't working" he said. "This is the kind of project that people get very passionate about...and they have a lot of expertise. They tend to see the solution they know from the angle they know, and I found it was hard, no, *impossible* to try to be the negotiator and broker of their ideas to one another." Dan was trying to be a problem solver, and, as odd as this may seem, in a very real way it *was* his problem to solve—his company, Abbott Nutritionals, had identified this issue as one of their philanthropic activities and assigned it to him: solve child starvation and death in Haiti. And file a report on this by the end of the year. "Big companies have big goals," he shrugged. He worked diligently on the issue, spending more hours on it than on his regular duties, but all he got was frustration.

"The specialists lobbied a lot for their niche, but getting them to see the big picture was a struggle. There was a lot of fighting over details. I heard a lot of *that's impossible*."

The litany of the impossible was endless. The product needed to be very cheap—it was going to be given away. That was the purpose of the NGO. That was their business. With no dairies in Haiti, milk powder was imported from Europe, and it was very expensive. Vegetable oils and the nutrient supplements had to be brought in from outside the country. The base of the product was local peanuts, but they weren't brought in on truckloads by the tons—they were brought in by local farmers by the *pounds*. On top of that, it was typical that 50% of the crop was rotted or contaminated with deadly aflatoxins and had to be destroyed. How do you test for contamination under such circumstances? How can you change the agricultural practices? The site for the new manufacturing facility had no electricity or water. The new plant had to be sustainable. It had to run on its own. If the equipment was modern and sophisticated and broke down, then what? There were no parts suppliers. There were no service technicians to come and fix it. Everything would stop. Everything, that is, except for the dying. Without a solution the dying would just continue on, business as usual.

Dan got tired of being a problem solver of the impossible. So one day he decided that he would be a much more effective leader if he brought all these passionate experts together and *let them solve the problem.* He found that transforming this group of problem see-ers and problem bringers into collaborative problem solvers took excellent facilitation and strong moderation—real *It-Factor* leadership skills.

"I had to be in the middle and also get out of the way. It was tough. Experience is the best teacher but it can be painful at times. You come away a stronger leader with a stronger base of skills for having had the experience—and you use those skills in everything else you do. It changes you."

Through an intense 3-day meeting, he was able to harness their heated discussions as brilliant ideas collided into one another, birthing new innovations and new possibilities. What had been impossible was suddenly worth talking about, then became do-able, then became a blueprint. That blueprint guided 90% of their future efforts. In the end they built a manufacturing plant filled with equipment invented for the Haiti facility that was designed to be rugged enough to withstand the rigors and unpredictability of life there. They worked with the farmers to teach them better agricultural and food safety practices to improve their crops. Abbott leveraged its power to make ingredients available closer to home and cheaper, negotiating on behalf of the small NGO. The outdoor kitchen operation that produced the fortified super peanut butter that could treat thousands of children has been replaced by a sustainable business that can safely produce enough product to treat *tens of thousands of* children. Starvation was put on notice that its days are numbered in Haiti.

Just goes to show the impact a real *It-Factor* Leader can have.

The Fourth Step: Focus On Mortar, Not Bricks

It's About Mortar, Not About Bricks:
Understanding What Motivates People

Great leaders with that *It-Factor* understand the difference between bricks and mortar. Consider a brick building. Bricks are essential; sure, they make up the most of what you see about the building or structure. Being durable and tough, they seem to weather the elements. While bricks are important, don't let them mislead you that they are the whole story. When it comes to your enterprise those bricks are like the people in your organization. But every *It-Factor* leader knows it's not the talent, degrees, or specialized skills—it's not *the bricks* that hold the whole building together: it's the mortar. It's the *mortar* that keeps the bricks together through rain and wind.

The mortar is that gooey stuff that goes on wet and sloppy—after all, clean bricklayers aren't the norm. There isn't an exact technique for perfect mortar placement, it's more like an art form (and in that regard, quite a bit like leadership). But once that mortar sets, *that's* what keeps the bricks in place and the whole building from disintegrating into a jumbled pile of rubble. In organizations, the mortar is the *positive personal regard* that keeps the people (all that talent) there, talking, sharing information, and working together to achieve common goals[1]. A good part of the positive personal regard grows from understanding what people need, from an interpersonal perspective, to feel motivated on the job.

Great *It-Factor* leaders want to understand what makes people tick and they work hard to ensure that the relationships between people are strong. They do this because they realize that it's the relationships between people that make an organization work. In essence, at the core, what we are talking about here is human motivation. The more the organization provides services or works with clients, the more important this facet of motivation will be to your competitive advantage. People work together and produce, innovate, and create because of the relationships they build. Weak relationships (weak mortar) build weak products (weak buildings)—strong relationships build better products. So if your enterprise brings diverse talent together in an inter-professional environment or you count a wide body of the population as your client, then this facet of interpersonal relationships and positive personal regard will be even more important to you. But it still matters even if you bring together a team of experts who share technical backgrounds and serve narrowly targeted markets.

When it comes to human motivation, great leaders get it that what motivates people isn't money. Are you surprised by that? It's really the other elements about work that make people tick, and *It-Factor* leaders know how to understand the players they have on their teams. They use the art of leadership.

Understanding Human Motivation

In the 1970s a psychologist by the name of Bernard Weiner did some of the early research on human motivation, which he called "the attribution theory of motivation"[2]. He gave us a lot of insights into how people learn to feel empowered and smart, or learn to feel helpless. At the workplace that learned helplessness looks like folks who have very low (or no) motivation. Business psychologists have taken that forward to lay prime responsibility at the feet of managers and leaders to create a workplace environment that motivates people who don't bring it with them when they arrive each morning. Now, creating the work environment is important, and we've devoted a whole section to it (the Seventh Step, which addresses engaging the team you've got). But we'd be wrong to say that's the whole story. Even great leaders with the *It-Factor* can't work magic. Not everyone *is* motivated. And not everyone is motivated by the same things.

Inspired by Dr. Weiner's work, and combined with what we've found in working with executives who lead and manage large groups of employees, we propose that people fall into three categories: the highly motivated, the unmotivated, and those in the middle. It's surprising how much the good old Pareto Principle (that's the 80/20 rule) can tell us about people and the work world. According to that theory[3], 80% of the productivity comes from 20% of the people (and 80% of the problems come from a different 20%). Applied to workplace motivation, about 20% of the working population represent these hard working and highly motivated folks who sit on your bench. We find that there might be another 20% at the bottom of the spectrum as well, who have a much harder time bringing their motivation with them. Then there's 60% in the middle. These figures are pretty close to what has been borne out by research in employee engagement—but we'll save that for when we get to the Seventh Step.

First, let's talk about that bottom twenty. The unmotivated are a difficult group for a leader to have. What you do won't make much of a difference to them. Their motivation isn't spent at work. This may be because they have learned to feel helpless, and those folks will usually be poor performers—which is why selection is so critical (remember the Second Step). But it may also be because they have other parts of their lives that are more important to them at present than is their work. Some people who seem unmotivated may actually be quite competent and in reality are struggling to keep their heads above water because of what is going on at home (those huge tidal waves of life like dealing with disability of a parent or a child, the disintegration of a marriage, a personal health issue, financial struggles, or the like). If these folks can get through to the light at the end of their personal tunnel, they are likely to re-join the motivated-looking crew. Others in that not-so-motivated category may have the job because it provides benefits, a regular paycheck, or something to do in life, but they have no aspirations to move up to positions of higher responsibility. It doesn't mean they can't do good work. If you find you have these folks on your bench, then you need to make their work tasks clear, give them quick and meaningful feedback (good as well as corrective), and really think about what is important to them in their lives. It probably isn't what is important to you. Think about what they need, but these aren't the employees in which you are likely to heavily invest.

At the other end of the spectrum about 20% of folks are *motivated.* With these employees, your job as a leader is to get out of their way, because if you block their way they will simply go and be motivated for someone else. These people solve their own problems— and they are likely to let you know when they see the world differently than you do. They generate solutions, and they can feel comfortable bending the rules to achieve their goals. They often create their own rewards. These people typically rise up into the ranks of leadership and then many of them struggle to understand the other 80% of people who aren't like them. The people these highly motivated leaders need to understand are the 60% of the folks who are in the middle of the spectrum and have "latent motivation." Those super-motivated managers need to understand this middle-group in particular because what leaders and managers do will either move their "latent motivation" employees up the continuum toward being highly motivated—or push them downward, towards unmotivated.

The art of leadership includes understanding who you need to forget focusing on (and in some cases let go of), who you need to simply get out of their way and let them achieve, and who you need to nurture a bit. You want to focus on your high potentials—but you may have "high potentials in waiting" gracing your team as well. You'd be sad to miss the contributions they can make, if only given the nurturing they need to really shine.

Tools for Enhancing Motivation

We have noticed these differences between people too, through our work at *FastTrack* Leadership and at the University with groups on developing leadership skills, through our teaching, giving talks, and doing one-on-one executive coaching with senior leaders from many walks of life. We have noticed that the "tool sets" available to leaders (and followers) differ vastly. For example, some leaders are interested in authority. We see this value the most often in the corporate world and the government sector, where job titles confer power: positional power.

In the corporate sector or government world, you do what the Director says because she's the Director, what the Vice President says because you follow the order of a VP. When the Captain says, "make it so" it's often simply because they are the Captain that it happens. People who value and believe in positional power often think in very tangible terms about motivating—or even punishing—employees.

In the corporate sector in particular leaders have many powerful tools to reward their teams in their attempts to motivate them. Options for companies that enjoy healthy profits include benefits like salary increases, stock options, and bonuses. Promotions often come with pay raises as well as enhanced responsibility and visibility. But there are other non-monetary rewards dangled by both the corporate and government sectors including office or lab space, leading a team of direct reports, being assigned support personnel, or having greater visibility with the leadership team. Of course, the corporate corner is rather famous for tangible prizes like company cars or approval for business class travel. Those are some mighty attractive "carrots." We have observed that leaders who like hierarchical structure really like to have carrots to offer their teams. Of course, some of them also like to have the "stick" to apply as a motivational tool as well. These include nasties like demotions, salary cuts, removal of privileges, loss of bonuses, and even dismissal. Titles aside, carrots and sticks motivate performance from people a little bit for a short period of time. But they don't motivate people. You won't change their motivational category with toys like these.

In general, leaders in other sectors (academia, non-profits, public sector like public health, health care) have rarely benefitted from having a basketful of carrots and sticks to mete out when rewarding, motivating, or punishing performance. Interestingly, the great *It-Factor* leaders we've worked with in these sectors often have titles that fall far short of symbolizing any "power of their office." Many of their titles fail to convey what they really do all day, since they are in entrepreneurial or combined roles. But there is an up-side to these often funding-based limitations: they aren't deluded by the false idea that money and toys motivate people. In these sectors it's a very different playing field. The *It-Factor* leaders we've worked with use leadership as an art coupled with a keen insight into what makes people tick.

So what does a real *It-Factor* leader do with pockets empty of such tangible tools? This is our favorite part of leadership coaching because here lives the true *art of leadership*. Great *It-Factor* leaders know their most valuable resources are the people on their team and they spend a good bit of their time focusing on this art of understanding, leading, and motivating people. Great leaders from any sector know that the most important leadership tool she or he must use in order to be an effective leader isn't positional power: *it's personal power*. Personal power comes from understanding human nature and building good relationships. Leadership is about relationships, all else is derivative.

This personal power is a crucial leadership asset. Especially when you don't come from a private sector corporate base, because then being an effective leader means working on a different canvas. A canvas without carrots, without sticks. You have just you and your understanding of what makes people tick. Great *It-Factor* leaders from any world can use those "what makes people tick" insights to truly motivate people and promote the best performance and innovation possible.

However, it doesn't matter whether you're in a business that is for-profit or non-profit: a toxic boss will be akin to weak mortar holding the bricks together, even despite those impressive "carrot" style incentives. It won't take long for a gale-force wind of bad leadership to knock over a brick wall held together with crumbling mortar. And don't overlook the fact that the better the bricks, the sooner they will be seeking opportunities elsewhere. Only the weakest of the bricks will stay in such an environment—which does not bode well for the strength and survival of the organization. If the mortar is weak, so is the organization. The best and the brightest people just won't stay if the positive personal regard isn't there to hold them together and keep them focused on the mission.

What is *positive personal regard*? It is a combination of personal interactions that signal respect and tolerance up, down, and across the lines of the enterprise. For example, how team members speak to and treat one another, their subordinates, their support personnel, and their leaders is an excellent litmus test of a strong culture. Remember those derailing behaviors to be wary of from our First Step to becoming a great *It-Factor* leader? You'll note an absence of them in the enterprise that has strong positive personal regard. Teams with this quality respect each other's role in the organization and appreciate the contributions made by their colleagues. In organizations with healthy positive personal regard, members listen to colleagues with intent and meaning. Members also work to make sure their own personal behaviors are worthy of respect as well[1]. In the workplace, the mortar that is positive personal regard shows up in an honest respect for colleagues and a belief in their genuineness, even if team members might disagree about the best course of action to take[1]. And it turns out that all of these things have more to do with motivation than money, toys, or titles.

When we conduct leadership workshops we typically inquire whether those in our group have worked in a bureaucracy before. The snickers in response are quite telling, as are the knowing nods. Bureaucracies thrive on that red tape called "standard operating procedures." The participants generally agree that no matter how carefully or thoughtfully a position has been designed, that any employee has at least a 10% leeway in how efficiently the procedures are followed.

It's the difference between your request going to the top or the bottom of the in box; the difference between requiring sufficient information to process your request—or exhaustive information before any progress can be made. Sometimes that can make the difference between getting your request processed today or next month.

Of course, the truth is, as the keenly insightful researcher and author Dr. Chris Musselwhite states, that since leadership is not a position but a way of behaving[4], making a person a manager does not necessarily make them a leader. But great *It-Factor* leaders do take stock of the positive personal regard holding their organizations together. And you, too, can grow your own skills in this area and nurture it in your organization. In fact, fifty years of research can help you out.

The famous psychologist William Shutz[5] really boosted our understanding of how people are fundamentally oriented to their relationships with others around them. His work provides fantastic clues into what makes people tick[5-9]. Through capitalizing on his findings, you can make your enterprise or team stronger through mortar, not just bricks. As it turns out, three broad areas are vital to people: he called these Inclusion, Control, and Openness (sometimes termed "Appreciation" or "Affection").

You can use your understanding of these three key areas that are part of *what make people tick* to help meet their needs and thereby spur their motivation. Best of all: understanding what people want and meeting their needs along these dimensions won't add to your bottom line.

Before we explain these motivating and money-saving three dimensions, a few words of caution. You need to also be aware of yourself, much like we talked about in our First Step to becoming a great *It-Factor* leader. This is because your behaviors will speak for you even when your words are silenced. You must understand that there are many behaviors shouting what you—or anyone—is thinking or feeling toward others (or not feeling, in some cases) despite the absence of words. This is one key fact that every leader or manager must realize: for all these domains your behaviors will speak for you, particularly if your words do not. Don't be fooled: there is no silence. You ignore these basic human needs at your own peril as a leader or manager. People will "read" your behaviors in organizations and come to conclusions about you. If you don't follow the basic human expectations of this "brick and mortar behavior" then people will read your behavior as *weird*. Sorry to put it so bluntly, but that is the truth of it. If they think you are weird, they are not likely to follow your leadership. So let's talk about these basic human needs.

Inclusion as a Basic Motivator

The psychological need of inclusion is the first of Dr. Shutz's 3 crucial domains. Many of the people who work on your team are motivated by inclusion, which is about feeling like you belong to a greater whole, something larger and more important than yourself. A core of this domain is about being involved—that is participating and knowing your personal contribution makes a concrete difference. Inclusion as a motivator maps to behaviors around recognizing others and liking to be recognized in turn, an enjoyment of feeling distinct (which can show up in the more mundane as how one dresses or in more organizational contexts such as what value you place on a smart-sounding title). At its psychological root, this is about feeling like one is important and has a valid place in the world. Let's face it: everyone wants to know they have a valid place in the world. This is a basic construct of what makes a person—and it's a huge factor in your relationships at work.

As a leader or even as a manager, you can have a great impact on your colleagues through this motivational domain of inclusion. While your words are important, Great *It-Factor* leaders know that their actions can speak louder than words. They send the non-verbal signals that their team members are significant. Just how do they do this? Through some pretty simple behaviors. First, they make eye contact with them. They acknowledge their presence and make note of their successes. *It-Factor* leaders make sure their members are introduced at meetings and find places for them at the table. They create opportunities for individuals or groups to participate and acknowledge their resulting participation. They don't seek credit for making those opportunities happen—in other words, they don't turn the spotlight back on themselves.

If you fail to do these things then you are sending very definite messages to others that say: "you don't matter around here." So if you don't bother to look up from your work when someone comes into your office, when you don't acknowledge their contribution or accomplishments, and when you skip over introducing them at meetings be aware that you have just shouted out your opinion—no matter what props or pats you might have given them behind closed doors. When you don't create chances for people to have a role, you've just told them they are useless. It's about the mortar, not the bricks. And if they are unmotivated then that could be a reason why.

Now this domain of Inclusion is a complex psychological need, based on feeling important. It can manifest itself in different ways in different people—think of it like a tree trunk with branches heading in all sorts of directions. For some, inclusion is about having a sense of prestige regarding their work, or in the respect others give them. Leaders who fundamentally believe their colleagues are significant really listen (we call that "they show up with ears"). We explored skills for how to do that keen-listening in our Third Step to becoming a great *It-Factor* leader.

Leaders who make mortar work for them integrate everyone into the discussion because they know those contributions are important (for more on how to do this see the Eighth Step on building a culture of conversation; and for why it leads to disaster if you don't, see our Tenth Step on groupthink). Inclusion is a powerful motivator to many. When workers feel significant in the office they are far more likely to give that extra 10%, smoothing out the bureaucracy's red tape. They join teams and task forces to tackle new problems. It is those workers who have no doubt of their importance to the mission that don't leave until the job is done and done well.

Are you doubtful? Let us share a story with you. When we worked with a major multi-national health-related company a few years ago, we were brought in because the leading scientists, the whole team of about 25, were all disenchanted, angry, or disengaged. This is a group of highly respected physicians and PhD-level researchers, the brainchildren of the company. How could they feel unimportant? Their new products and inventions saved or improved lives. They brought us in to help turn things around. It turned out the root of the problem was the new Vice President. He had been there for just under 2 years and made it clear that he was more important than they were. He talked often, and very fondly, about his last job at a different huge multi-national company that served a very different market, and he just couldn't seem to get excited about dealing with their core business model. As for his management style, he always said, "I have an open door policy." But what the docs who worked under him said was, "yeah, that door is always open, but watch out for that invisible force field that will break your nose if you try to walk through it!" We heard that from several people. They all warned us to "watch out for the force field" before meeting with the VP. The VP did not show any of these "weird" behaviors to us. He was perfectly normal. But then someone needed to check something with him, knocked on his door while we were in there, and it was clear what his team experienced on a daily basis. Dismissive, passive, and undermining behavior. An unwillingness to take the time to listen. The force field came out in full force. It was example after example of violating Shutz's most basic behaviors around inclusion. His behaviors screamed, "you are not important, get out of my office with this trivial business", even though his tone sounded polite. When we tried to help him see this impact, he couldn't even grasp the concept.

We came back a few months later to help build skills at leading change. The night before the program, the VP was "invited to leave." While we had intended to spend that first program teaching how to create a healthy organizational culture, in reality we mostly dealt with the rage and pain these senior scientists were feeling. But this second program was different— this time the group was full of anticipation and excitement. They were energized and looked forward to a brand new day. The former VP was far from incompetent but he lost his job because he made very basic Inclusion errors with a vast number of key stakeholders in his organization. You were only important to him if you were above him or an outside consultant, not if you created or invented the products the company sold.

Let's look at this domain from a more positive example. A few years ago, one of our colleagues left his team to join a prestigious research-based group. His team asked us for advice on what would be an appropriate memento to recognize their very warm feelings for him and how they would miss him when he left. They wanted to send him and his wife for a weekend getaway in the mountains or out to a really nice dinner. We looked at where his new job was going to be and suggested a plaque. A bit confused, they informed us that we were really no fun at all, but followed our rather specific counsel and ordered a *really nice*, engraved plaque that bore all the insignia of the various organizations he had partnered with through his work on that team. We got to attend his going away party where he opened his gift—with a look of quickly masked surprise on his face. When he got a moment he came over and said, "OK, this has you all over it. You coached me. You know me—you've got to clue me in to the story behind this—a plaque, seriously?"

Smiling we explained that he was heading into an organization that loved hierarchy, embraced smart titles, and valued lots of letters after one's name (indicating lots of schooling or earned degrees). Our colleague is super sharp, but his master's degree would seem invisible at an organization like this one. We explained that this plaque wasn't for him. It was for his new team mates. He should put it where they couldn't help but see it when they walked into his office. We said, "trust us. This will credential you in a way that will open doors." He did what we told him and reported back 3 months later. It turned out to be a powerful tool to respect. People did a double take when they saw it. They stopped and read it. They asked him about it. They were impressed with his experience—they never would have known he had done all that because no one would have asked a lowly master's-level guy *what* he had done. They wouldn't have thought it worth it. Opportunities followed. People asked him questions and for his advice. He got a window to open, allowing his natural talent and gifts to shine through—and it helped him break a glass ceiling.

Here's another example of Inclusion looming as a large factor at the workplace: at a leading tech company a mid-level leader showed us around the headquarters. We noticed cubes stacked up and prominently displayed on desks as we toured. Examining one, it was engraved with the name of a familiar product in the IT marketplace and a date. "Those," he said, "are product launch cubes. You can tell who is going to be here and who will be gone by a glance at these." He gave us the scoop: small stack—few launches, little future; big stack—key player. It was clear that the heart of motivation for this organization was Inclusion—participation, prestige, being a key central player, having your ideas heard, your position. Other organizations indicate power by trophies or plaques on the wall, and still others by grants, contracts, or publications—but in some way members make known how much they have, what they've accomplished, because those markers play strongly in the organizational pecking order when Inclusion drives the motivation.

Control as a Basic Motivator

Being included and feeling significant on the job aren't the only powerful motivators that make people tick. Some individuals are also motivated by having responsibility, exerting influence, holding authority, and yes, for some it's even about wielding power. For others consistency is very important and they strongly value behaviors such as honoring time limits, staying task-focused at meetings, and bringing closure. This rather wide variety of values and behaviors fall into Dr. Shutz's realm of Control. He found that for some people, Control plays a very strong role in their interactions with others—and it plays an important role for everyone in one way or another.

Let's address Control as responsibility. All *It-Factor* leaders must assess whether and how to mete out responsibility and authority as a part of rewards or job growth. Being able to effectively delegate is a strong *It-Factor* leadership skill and very difficult for many leaders to do. You simply can't do it all yourself—you have to develop your team and trust them to be able to own and achieve parts of the mission. If you are motivated by being in charge, knowing how things stand, and never being surprised, then this particular reality of leadership might feel very distressing for you. Be prepared that being a successful leader will pull you out of your comfort zone as you learn to delegate and really let go.

Why does control feel so good to so many? Why do they seek it out and find it hard to relinquish? When most people are in control of a project, process, or team, they know what is going to happen and when, they can anticipate and orchestrate the process, and that experience makes them feel competent. This can be a huge asset to success. An example: our son, Ethan, had open heart surgery when he was just 10 weeks old. His surgeon, (and our hero) Dr. Mark Galantowicz, of Nationwide Children's Hospital in Columbus, Ohio, is a doctor who likes to know what is going to happen, in what order. He likes to know who is on his team, who he is operating on, and he likes to know even the little things, like how the tool trays are laid out. When he's the surgeon, he is in charge. Like any surgeon, he created the conditions for success on that day in late August of 2005, so that when he worked on our tiny little 9-pound baby boy the only surprises he would face would be the ones Mother Nature had in store for him. Ethan was a fairly complicated case with a few surprises to offer in his tiny little and somewhat deformed heart. Mark sees a lot of complicated cases. He doesn't need any additional surprises from an out-of-control environment in the OR. People who like to guarantee success, in this case saving a life, tend to have strong inclinations around control. It's a good trait when you're the one holding the scalpel. Surgeons like to feel competent. It helps them do their best work. Mark Galantowicz is one of the best in the business— and as an *It-Factor* leader he also comes across as one of the nicest regular guys you're going to meet. Because it feels good to feel competent you will find that many people seek to control the process and reduce those things they are uncertain about. Dr. Galantowicz is highly skilled at this, which is why he is so successful at saving young lives.

However, when a leader (or any employee) is clumsy with Control they tend to come off as a dictator, controlling, manipulative, or secretive. This happened at the once-powerful Nortel. Nortel was a multinational telecommunications equipment manufacturer headquartered in Ontario, Canada. Ruben worked at Nortel when it was at the top of its game and remarks how the organizational culture was one of collaboration and sharing among the teams. Everyone knew what the others on their team were doing. In this way, they could all pinch hit on each other's projects, be flexible as they moved around on duties to help the team achieve the goals, and fill in for one another on their days off. This was a strength of the organization, which wanted to have knowledge and skills duplicated all along the lines. The leadership made that known to the employees and worked to uphold those values.

However, there was a programmer that Ruben ran into who was highly motivated by Control, wielding it like a club with his teammates. For him Control was expressed as power. When programmers write code, they fill it with notes (called comments), written in English, which explain what that section of code is supposed to do. That way, when another programmer contributes to or checks the work she or he can make sense of what they are seeing, fix errors, and add new layers. But this programmer on the team didn't want anyone else to be able to understand what he had created. He rarely put comments in the code, and when he did he used his own unintelligible shorthand. He wanted to be the only one who could work on that code—he wanted to "own" it. He also wanted job security and to be irreplaceable, with everyone needing to come to him for information so the project could progress. Wielding a club of Control doesn't always work out the way you want it to, though.

When the team leader learned of this he was furious. For this programmer, as with some other people you will meet, a sense of personal security comes from exerting Control. That is an illusion. Control handled and used like a blunt instrument will make you very insecure by damaging your relationships with others, reducing the trust in the organization, and eventually in jeopardizing your very job itself. The team leader gave the programmer 30 days to put full comments in the code and to make sure his colleagues could read and understand his code thoroughly. Then the team leader fired him. He had no use for someone who was so controlling that he put his own sense of power and need to be the crucial lynchpin in the system ahead of the system itself. He had no use for someone he couldn't trust. It was a violation of organizational values and ethos.

This leader got it: an organization gets the culture it tolerates[10]. He wasn't going to keep any team members who didn't fit the organizational culture. *It-Factor* leaders set the culture, monitor that culture, and nurture that culture. When you join an organization, understand the culture. Don't let your personal needs push you out of a really great place to work. We call this not allowing yourself "to be had" by your own behaviors or blind spots. When control becomes an obsessive need, others feel you are being secretive, as with the former programmer at Nortel. They will feel their ideas aren't welcome, that they are lectured to, and ordered about. If people perceive you this way, then you need to do some soul and behavior searching on yourself. You may need to make peace with that desire to predict and control everything so that you can give others a chance. Remember, most of the time you won't be doing open heart surgery on babies; most of the time you'll be working on an inter-dependent team.

What happens to your team when you hand over some control to them? When you proclaim: "you're in charge—it's your show" your high performers and high potentials will find a potent source of motivation stirring within them precisely because it feels *competent* to be in control. When you really show faith in their ability to be that capable and successful, even if how they achieve is not a carbon copy of how you would have done it, you tap into the burgeoning *It-Factor* leader in them, too.   Feeling competent feels good. When your team builds their confidence in their own competence they are going to be more motivated and empowered to act.

Let's flip this back over. When a leader refuses to allow those high potentials and high performers to own the task, when leaders micromanage or constantly criticize and correct, they all too often annihilate motivation by making their direct reports feel incompetent[6-8], and that feels bad.   Avoid those behaviors. The only motivation people feel from being humiliated is the motivation to leave or retaliate.

You can help bolster competence and Control-based motivation through developing your team, but also through giving people control on relatively smaller tasks, such as being able to call the shot over their flex time arrangements, the color their office is painted, control over their schedule, or having some choice over the team they work on, volunteer for assignments, or other non-mission-impacting examples can go far in helping people to feel in control of their daily destiny at work.

Shutz's domain of Control is multifaceted, offering another side to consider. Above, we've illustrated exerting or expressing Control to others. But there are some on your team who want Control conveyed *to them…by you*. And if you fail to do this they don't see you as an *It-Factor* leader. In fact, they don't see you as a leader at all and are probably wondering how you landed where you are. They expect anyone leading in any capacity to shine at some of the basics, such as keeping meetings focused, honoring deadlines, and being fair. They expect that the leader won't let sessions descend into chaos or become derailed by an enthusiastic but misguided participant or two. To be mindful of these essentials, as well as time limits, conforms to consistency-based motivation, which is a key factor underlying this Control domain. Other actions you can take to support Control-based motivation include offering structure, gently directing actions, and bringing closure. Shutz's research found that many workers respect these attributes and actions, and furthermore need them in order to get their jobs done efficiently. Organization begets organization in the workplace. The chronically late leader or manager, the individual who is unorganized, letting meetings run over time or descend into disarray, as well as those who cannot honor deadlines, undermine the motivation of their subordinates and team mates.

Jacob was a leader we worked with who was highly respected in his field and, not surprisingly, keenly recruited to a new post. Shortly after his arrival to the organization his new Boss left for a month's worth of travel, having the opportunity to meet only briefly before his departure. This meeting was an enthusiastic greeting of Jacob that talked in broad terms of things like "now having critical mass around here" and a grand vision for what the team would achieve now that Jacob was on board. "But he never told me what he wanted me to do," Jacob mused. "And when he came back he was too busy with catching up to have time for me." It seemed that no one else in the organization could fill Jacob in either—all they had heard were grand visions and enthusiasms as well. Plus, Jacob was their new supervisor and the organization didn't have a history of giving direction and information up the chain. Jacob spent his first six weeks on the job trying to get various projects started (with no direction at all), but keep them flexible enough that they could be changed once he understood what goals his Boss wanted him to achieve. In short, he felt like he was doing nothing. He said it was the most frustrating six weeks of his working life. "I actually wondered at one point whether I was hired to really do anything at all, or if it was just for my name. I have to admit, it crossed my mind that this could be a set up for me to fail so that they could fire me, for what reasons I didn't understand. Maybe to justify terminating a salary line? It was simply bizarre."

Eventually Jacob was able to pin his Boss down on goals, mostly by suggesting them himself and getting the Boss's enthusiastic endorsement and occasional vague rejection. "I learned what it was like to work in an organization where the leadership simply set no specific goals or metrics. I experienced first-hand how demoralizing that can be! But what I also learned was what it must be like for my own team when I gave them too little guidance. I was acutely aware of not wanting to thwart their creativity by controlling them or shutting them down, but I had erred on the side of being too loosey-goosey myself!" Jacob became a very different leader after that. He became an *It-Factor* leader.

Openness as a Basic Motivator

The third area of this positive personal regard side of human motivation is what researcher Shutz termed "affection" or in his later work, "openness." Many also describe this as "appreciation." Of course the word *affection* throws a lot of folks in the corporate sector into a clearly uncomfortable corner, However, organizationally *affection* can be thought of as interpersonal connections between colleagues, or between leadership and the team, or between the person and the work. In a very real sense, this is the mortar that holds a lot of those talented bricks together in your enterprise. If you think of it as openness, it means working in a culture where people can be real and honest with one another about who they are and how they feel. Rather than hiding behind rigid corporate hierarchies and stereotypes, colleagues talk to one another, know one another, and openly appreciate one another's contributions. In our work with thousands of leaders, we have found that appreciation is the most powerful motivating factor of the three.

In your office, this *affection* or *openness* is how team members express support, encouragement, or *appreciation* for others. Saying simple comments, such as, *I liked your report*, or *thank you for your contribution to our team's success,* or even simply asking about a colleague's weekend sends a powerful message beyond the context of the job. When you make statements such as these, you are in effect saying that you appreciate them. What you may not realize from looking only at the surface is that behavior sends a very deep message about their worth to you, the team, and to the organization. It speaks to the sense of the "organizational family."

Leaders who truly appreciate their teams also invest their energy to mediate conflicts. They identify resistance levels in the group and help the group to feel supported. Great *It-Factor* leaders make sure they provide clear, consistent, and fairly frequent feedback to their team members who are motivated by Affection and Openness[6-9]. Does that sound like an odd way to appreciate people? Well, consider this: if you avoid conflict like you avoid the plague then you send the message that your team doesn't mean enough to you for you to *work* for their mutual understanding and harmony.

There are many steps organizations take to give a proverbial organizational hug to employees. The *Employee of the Month* is a common award businesses make to recognize individuals, a well-intended step that sometimes backfires and becomes the butt of jokes. But you might think of other rewards that are more meaningful—for instance, a much coveted parking spot awarded occasionally (not monthly) for those who go above and beyond (particularly when their contribution is to help others succeed—like the players who make an assist on a basketball team). Look around your enterprise and you'll probably see quite a few folks who keep a basket of hand written thank you cards given to them, or perhaps they adorn their walls with thank you plaques from the organizations they have served. When they can tell you who gave them those tokens and why, and speak fondly about their work with those people, you can bet they were meaningful. They hit squarely on the motivational domain of affection.

Wanting to hang the plaques on the walls so that others can see them—that goes back to Inclusion as a motivator. Hanging them to remind you of dear colleagues with whom you served on committees or how the work you did impacted the lives of others—that's Affection. We worked with a teacher who was strongly motivated by this domain of openness-affection. She worked for a year pouring herself into training a group of professionals in a certificate based program. At the end of the year, they had a graduation party for the participants, complete with a graduation ceremony and frame-worthy certificates. As the party broke up, the leader's Boss said, "oh my gosh, I forgot" and hastily ran back to the podium. He had ordered a plaque, which he hastily and rather unceremoniously handed over to her, mumbling a few words about her great service. For their part, the program participants did something quite different. Despite the fact that they were all in those kind of low-paying public service jobs that target highly vulnerable, impoverished, or high risk groups, they had banded together to buy a beautiful baby present for their significantly pregnant teacher. The teacher explained how this event impacted her. "I hung that stupid plaque on my wall because that's what you do at my office. But it's kind of in the corner. I don't actually like to see it because it brings up bitter memories of how little my supervisor appreciated all I did with that program. But the baby gift—oh my gosh, I still have it even though my child is now ten! I'll never let that go. I love those people!" Botching the delivery of a well-intended award actually damaged the relationship this high-potential teacher had with her supervisor. She felt unappreciated, disengaged, and disenchanted with him. Getting it wrong with employees is costly. Research shows that 80% of employees who quit their jobs report that their decision to leave was predicated by a lack of appreciation and respect[11-13]. Not understanding how important that aspect of human motivation is turns out to be costly and pushes turnover.

Getting it right with human motivation can be tricky but it pays off. One leader we worked with added a fun twist to the thank you note, after he learned a painful lesson about human motivation. Laura, one of his valued team members, "worked her tail off" and achieved a great goal that benefitted the whole team. She was very shy and since she didn't talk about it, no one really knew. So the leader, Jeff, decided that people should know and she should be duly appreciated. He gathered his team, made the announcement about what Laura had recently contributed and led everyone in a round of applause for her. Well, for her part she turned bright red and scooted out of the room at her first opportunity. When we followed up with him he was baffled. How could Laura have *not* appreciated that? We said, "Jeff—any chance that might be the kind of gesture *you* would enjoy? Maybe it works for you, but does it work for *her*? What do you think might work for *her*?" His epiphany was that in many aspects he was managing others—not just Laura, but everybody— as he wished would be done unto him, following that good old golden rule. But that was not really working. He had to stop thinking about what *he* wanted, stop making it be all about *him*, and instead really think about what his team wanted. "Jeff," we said, "you're on your way to becoming a great *It-Factor* leader!" Jeff realized that *his* center of motivation was Inclusion—but hers *was* Appreciation-Affection. So he tried again. He hand wrote Laura a thank you note, giving careful consideration of what to say. Then he taped it to a giant candy bar and stuck it in her mailbox in the common mail room. Of course, when everyone got their mail, they saw Laura's treat and everyone went to her to ask what was up (presumably to mooch some candy bar). The result was that although she was a very shy person, she got to tell her story one-on-one while sharing the candy, and that was a very comfortable way for her great achievement to be celebrated. She glowed. And since she shared her chocolate with all her visitors, they celebrated her success rather than being jealous of it.

We worked with one agricultural leader who framed certificates of appreciation celebrating 18 and 20 years of service for the commitment two of his line-employees working on a farm site. One day he stopped the work, called all the men on the team over, expressed his appreciation and presented the nicely framed certificates to the two men. There was no monetary award. There was no promotion. There was no cake. There was just a very sincere thank you from the boss in front of the team. He spoke of how what these men had done every day for decades had contributed to the success of the group, to the mission of the organization, to the benefit of the lives of others. The moment was a tad bit awkward, these tough farm-based agriculture workers being at a loss for words and kicking their boots in the dirt as they accepted the award, mostly looking at the ground. But a week later each independently spoke to the boss, telling him how meaningful that was, that no one had ever thanked them before (in two decades!), how their families made such a fuss over the framed certificates, hanging them on the wall. They had tears in their eyes as they told the boss just how much this had meant to them. Don't make the assumption that an organization isn't motivated by openness, affection, or appreciation just because it is made up mostly of men or that the work is rough and tough. In our work with thousands of leaders, men, and women from all kinds of industries, we find that it is this last domain of motivation that is prominent in most people. People appreciate being appreciated. They like to be thanked. They usually enjoy being connected to other people.

You can share accomplishments in a newsletter, complete with photos of the team members. Or if you are in a non-profit that serves the community in any way, then go one step further: contact your local newspaper or televised news program and see if they will run a story on your best and brightest offerings, products, or programs in their "good news" section. That is a wonderful way to highlight your staff—by sharing with the community just who are their shining stars!

As we'll talk about in our Seventh Step, a personal connection to work plays a crucial role in getting great performance from an individual[14]. This is particularly true if you work in the non-profit sector, where people are not usually motivated by the paycheck. They are geared towards doing something they care about because either they care about serving others or the central mission of the organization.

Great leaders are effective at supporting and appreciating the teams that make up their enterprise—by doing so they help build that much coveted team identity. In part they do this by creating incentives to reward the entire team rather than always singling people out for recognition. Appreciation or affection is the most important area because when it is under-addressed, employees feel like a cog in the wheel and that their work is worthless and unappreciated. That is a major factor that drives people to leave. More than money issues, people leave because they have lost their emotional connection to the work they do and who they do it with. Finding ways to creatively and sincerely thank employees—to acknowledge that they are not cogs in the organizational wheel—is a key strength of good leaders. It's more than good manners. It's good management.

If you work in the public sector, health care, or in a public academic institution, then your leadership is not limited to your direct reports or the teams that make up your enterprise. Anyone outside of the corporate world must also manage their community partners as well. Increasingly corporations are realizing that they, too, have a stake in the communities which make up their markets, so they are not exempt from this concern. Community partners are typically groups of stakeholders over whom the leader has absolutely no authority or control. Understanding how people tick—what motivates them, why they do what they do, what they care about—can be a big asset of personal power for a non-profit sector leader who must convene these diverse groups and lead them to consensus or at least partnership. Getting your own team, other organizational silos, the leadership team, even community partners or perhaps customers to the table with ears and eyes open, hearts and minds present, can be a challenge. Often the most important tool in the cache of a great *It-Factor* leader is positive personal regard. It's the mortar for a strong enterprise and for a healthier organization.

Your Fourth Step to becoming a great *It-Factor* leader is to focus on the mortar of human motivation, not just the bricks of human technical talent.

Now we will meet a medical center leader who understands what makes people tick.

Meet An *It-Factor* Leader: Jill Bemis

The Children's Clinics for Rehabilitative Services in Tucson, Arizona, is a lucky place. They are led by a CEO who is a real *It-Factor* leader. Her name is Jill Bemis—and she has led her enterprise to an 80% "excellent" satisfaction rating from their patients. A striking woman in her mid-sixties, she has the kind of experience and seasoning that leads to real wisdom. Humble yet effervescent, Jill faces the challenges of her organization with grace and a sense of serene watchfulness. Early in her career, Jill's mother provided her with sage leadership advice, giving her a framed picture of a mallard duck on the water. She told Jill that to balance her tendency to be, well, perhaps a little excitable, she needed to be like a duck. To this day, the framed picture hangs on the wall of her office and reminds her to *always behave like a duck: stay calm and unruffled on the surface, and paddle like heck underneath!* She notes, "the challenges that leaders face can be considerable and unpredictable. How you comport yourself as a leader is crucially important to how people listen to your ideas and what you want to achieve. That's where I think of that image of the duck that my mother gave me."

She had another mentor too—she credits a much beloved family dog, her Border Collie, who she says taught her a lot about life and good leadership. "Border Collies are natural leaders—but they need to be trained. I find that people are like that too. They may have natural talents, but they need to hone their skills to make them have real finesse and effectiveness. Some people are motivational leaders, some are technical leaders, but I really believe just about anyone can be a leader. How good you become is a matter of skill—and that takes working on it." She explains what her beloved Border Collie taught her: "What I found is that Border Collies know their herds, which of course are sheep. They know what sheep respond to. They guide them gently for the most part, keeping them headed in the same direction. In my life as a CEO, I need to understand my team, all the people who work here. I need to understand what they respond to and it's my job to guide them to stay on track with the mission of the Children's Clinics. But that's not enough—my Border Collie showed me that she wasn't afraid to gently nip the heels of a sheep who was going astray, and perhaps going to get lost and put itself in danger. It struck me that there are times I need to do that too—I need to correct behavior that is not in alignment with our values as an organization. That might be catching a chart left on a desk as I make my rounds though the clinic. That might be correcting someone who is not using good communication skills around a conflict situation and needs to be brought back in line."

Jill muses that, "but most of the time the Border Collie is laying down and watching, just letting them be sheep. And I try to do what my Border Collie taught me: I know my people. I understand them. And for the most part I need to sit back and watch, be ready to help when needed, be aware of what is going on, but let them do their jobs taking care of the children in our community." She finds her Border Collie an important source of inspiration, particularly when the going gets rough. "Border Collies always watch for what is a risk to their herd. They watch for wolves and protect the herd from them. They *never* throw their sheep to the wolves! They stand between the wolf and the sheep—and that is my job too. I need to watch for danger, for someone who might be angry and turning into 'a wolf'. It's then that I need to step in and intervene, protecting my team. And I take responsibility when things do go wrong, protecting my 'herd' of clinicians and managers, and save them from blame, too. Like they say, the buck stops at the top. If I'm going to protect my group, then that's my job."

When we asked Jill what she was most proud of with the Children's Clinics, she knew immediately what to share. She has a lot to brag about at that organization (just remember that satisfaction rate!), but she chose a story that exemplified both her unruffled duck mantra and her border collie mentor—by how her organization chose to treat people during a difficult and painful downsizing. Back in 2008, the Children's Clinics were both a managed care facility and a clinic operation—but due to state contract changes, the business model changed to an all-clinic structure. So goodbye managed care division. Easy on paper but in real life that new structure came with a 30% staff layoff. As a "border collie leader" Jill knew her team, understood what made them tick, and connected with what they cared about. She thought and thought and thought about how to lead her team through this incredibly difficult process with dignity and grace for the affected staff, the patients, and the organization. She came up with a perfect plan, kind and gentle, slowly transitioning to the new structure, and presented it to the board, sure of how impeccably it would work; but to her surprise they had concerns. She was caught totally off guard. Her feathers were indeed ruffled.

"Much to my dismay, they weren't immediately enthusiastic with all elements of my plan!" she said. "Some Board members wanted to follow a more traditional model in which employees are given their layoff notice and immediately relieved of their responsibilities. I knew these employees. They had been loyal, competent, and caring caregivers and managers. We just could not treat them that way. *I* could not treat them that way." Truly, Jill believes you don't throw employees to the wolves, even when that specter shows up as a reorganization and downsizing. What did she do? She thought of that mallard paddling away on her wall. "You keep calm and unruffled on the surface. You don't let them see that you are upset or worried. You stay in the moment, thinking and churning your ideas so that you can make a more compelling case for what you want to pursue."

You see, the Board worried that people who were being laid off might negatively affect the morale of remaining employees and that they might sabotage the organization, ultimately compromising the care they were giving to the children. "I didn't believe that for a minute," she countered. As a CEO she realizes that they have legitimate concerns based on their past experiences. "You can't just tell them they are wrong. What you *can* do is paddle like crazy underneath the surface to give them alternative ways of looking at things and hope that your compelling arguments are very convincing and that you can sway them." She did that, arguing that there was another approach that would benefit everyone more. After all, Children's Clinics was a partner in the community and some day they would be hiring again—they needed the kind of reputation that would draw the best and the brightest to want to work there. Those valuable caregivers needed to know they would be treated fairly and respected. "I felt that if you treated people well while they worked for you, and if you treated them fairly during the layoff as well, and gave them adequate support and financial reimbursement during the letting go process—basically if you treated them fairly all along the line, then you would have no reason to expect sabotage."

In the end, her unruffled, calm demeanor and her compassion won the board over. The reality was that the layoff was imminent in three months—and they could not afford those corporate style buyout packages. Children's Clinics is a non-profit, so the options she had were far more limited. She was going to give people plenty of head's up and support during the process. After all the negotiating with her Board the Clinic gave employees who would be let go a minimum of 6 weeks' notice, often more, and gave them work-time flexibility to go on any job interview during that time. She also brought in resume counselors to help her employees write their resumes and enrolled them in a job outplacement program in Tucson.

She created a bonus severance package, so that if people stayed to the end they received a generous bonus, but if they found a new position before then she encouraged them to go, saying "If you get a good job before the end of our contract, then you should take it, and then you don't need the severance. But if you don't, you'll have the retention bonus to help you bridge that gap." The Clinic also covered the full COBRA premiums for the employee and family for three months after the lay-off.   A sense of camaraderie prevailed and all employees pitched in to help cover for those that were being laid off or left early for another job.

What happened? Enough employees stayed to the end of the managed care phase that there were no disruptions in care or business functions. The company reputation in the community as a good place to work remained solid. She convinced her Board to take this route, despite their experience that pushed them towards a more traditional (and harsher) approach, changing their views in the process. The downsizing and restructuring was peaceful and orderly, with no sabotage. And she got thank you letters and even a couple of presents from those who were let go. Now that's *It-Factor* leadership!

The Fifth Step:
Build A Great Team

Strategies to Build a Great Team:
A Guide to Developing Others

Leaders make a lot of important contributions to their organizations. They set the vision and lead their group to the goal, providing the resources, gathering the team, setting the metrics to evaluate progress and success, all in the pursuit of achieving the organization's goals. While doing this, leaders have other responsibilities to juggle, too. They serve as the "human face of the organization" to the outside world and it is their job to convey its values and mission to external stakeholders. Leaders must set direction and strategy. They ensure that it gets implemented. The common thread that runs through each of these tasks is that none is accomplished alone. If a leader can't work creatively and effectively with and through others, she or he will fail to achieve the organizational mission.

In the end, one of the most important and longest lasting impacts a leader has on their organization is how they build the team. Great *It-*

Factor leaders build great organizations by building a great team. As a leader, developing people should be among your highest priorities.

Face it, you can't always go outside and find the talent you need. It costs a fortune, you lose time in onboarding, new people have no organizational memory, and heavens forbid you hire poorly and then have to make a painful correction. Great *It-Factor* leaders know that some of the most talented, motivated, and dedicated folks they will ever have work for them already—they just need a bit of coaching and nurturing to fulfill their highest potential. That's why *It-Factor* leaders have a solid plan for developing leadership from within the organization.

In this step to building a great team, we'll discuss some of the reasons why leaders need to develop others and we'll go through a list of 11 important strategies that we've seen *It-Factor* leaders use to successfully develop others and build a great team. Now don't get us wrong: we are fully in support of sending team members to a leadership development program. After all, we run many such programs ourselves both through *FastTrack* and at the University. However, we also recognize that these are expensive and can take people away from work for a week or so at a time. The great news is that there are many tools and strategies for you to bring to your own team which are no-to-low cost to you.

The Advantage of People

Leaders need to develop others. Think about it: great leaders care about production—but not at the expense of people. This is because they realize that *people* are crucial to gaining a competitive advantage[1]. It hasn't always been this way. Back in the First Step (Know yourself: the good, the bad, and the fixable) we investigated what gives a leader competitive advantage. As a reminder, it used to be about the stuff you had—tangible stuff, like money, land, or resources. But this is the 21st Century, and now what makes the difference are the ideas you have, the talent you have, and how the talent you have can work together on those great ideas. By-and-large, it's a technology and information economy— and that means that the rules have changed since your father's time. Hey, now the rules change just about every week. The one constant is people. *Inter-Professional* is the environment of the 21st Century—and *It-Factor* leaders make sure they're culturally competent to work with this diverse group of talent that they need. You should make sure you are, too.

"People development" strengthens your organization's future. It's smart to invest in home-grown talent. You *need* to grow their skills so they can move up in the organization and take on new roles and enhanced responsibilities. You can't leave this to chance since the skills that define competency change with changes in organizational level. For example, at the front line delivery of excellent services is critical. Those services could be delivery of care, teaching, producing research results, publishing, working with clients, or even serving on a production line. However, as people grow into new roles they rely less on the skills involved in production and much more on those involved in working with and through others. They also need to rely on their creativity and innovation to handle the complex and often unexpected challenges that arise. Your emerging leaders need to delegate effectively and manage others without either neglecting or micro-managing them. Growing your own leaders is a wise investment for any organization[2].

And there is more when it comes to developing others: in addition to communication or leadership skills, the *technical knowledge* upon which professionals base their expertise changes—and sometimes rapidly. Great *It-Factor* leaders develop their team to create a *learning organization*[3, 4]. In a learning organization the enterprise enables its members to continuously learn and share new knowledge, thereby transforming itself. Learning organizations develop because of the pressures modern organizations face. Continual and shared learning is essential for them to maintain competitiveness in the business environment[3, 4]. When you do this, you will lead a flexible, nimble, responsive group that can maintain the cutting edge rather than getting stuck in the past. One of the best kinds of teams to lead is a team of life-long learners.

For all these reasons, one of the most important roles of leadership is to develop a strong team.

A Mini-Manual for Building the Skills of Others:
11 Low Cost Strategies to Develop Your Team

It pays to make developing others a leadership priority. Now for *how* to do it. Without a step-by-step process, transforming your organization from feeling like a quaint remnant of a bygone era to a leader in learning and innovation can seem like magic indeed. The good news is that it's not as daunting as it seems. In fact, many of the steps to take are rather simple and quite intuitive, and are listed in Table 5.1. All they take is the dedication of the leadership team to make it so. In this step we will explore each of these 11 strategies, explaining them and illustrating how you might adopt them for your team. As you read, consider the people you work with and how such a strategy might help develop their talents and ability in your enterprise.

Table 5.1

11 low cost strategies to develop your team
1. Hire smart—that bench is important
2. Team not superstars
3. Engage, engage, engage
4. Everyone has a plan
5. Give 'em time
6. Accountability is key
7. S-T-R-E-T-C-H experiences
8. Develop your high potentials
9. Nourish ideas (POINT)
10. Coach and mentor to grow skills
11. Share the learning

Strategy 1: Hire Smart—That Bench Is Important

The very first thing you should do is add only the right people to your team—so hire smart, which we covered in our Second Step to becoming a great *It-Factor* leader. We won't revisit that technique in depth here. By hiring right the first time, it's much easier to promote from within later—and when you continue to develop the people you have, wow! What a bevy of choice talent you'll be able to select from.

If you make the mistake of hiring people only for their technical skills, then don't be surprised when the whole person shows up for the job. Yes, you'll get not only their technical-based knowledge and skills, you will also wind up with their social skills, ability to communicate, ability to lead others, stress management skills...we could go on but we think you get the point. While there are many valuable Steps in this book for working on all these issues (hiring smart, communication skills, listening skills, ability to be persuasive, emotional intelligence, etc.), in this fifth Step we'll talk about different concrete actions to take to develop those who work for you.

Strategy 2: Go for Team, Not Superstars

After you recruit the best candidates, the next step is to foster teamwork. Good leaders know that teamwork is essential to creativity, collaboration, and success, particularly on complex ventures. Your team needs to have a team identity. That is, they have to see themselves as one group, a single unit, connected in fundamental ways[5]. They can't function as a team if in reality they are thinking of themselves as a collection of superstars, all vying for the same recognition.

One important step in developing people is to develop a diverse group of individuals—and then to foster teamwork among them. That harkens back to the "3-C's" of competitive edge that we explored in our First Step to becoming an *It-Factor* leader. Claudia has had the very good fortune to work at Duke University for many years in her career, and there she got to meet famed basketball Coach Mike Krzyzewski. She really appreciated his dedication to his teams, whether they were college-aged athletes or the men of the Olympic Dream Teams. He often says, "a basketball team is like the five fingers on your hand. If you can get them all together, you have a fist. That's how I want you to play."[6] Mike Krzyzewksi owns one of Claudia's sculptures of (quite appropriately) a fist—so they see eye-to-eye on this point. Coach K is right and you can learn from his advice. He knows that with a fist—that is, with an integrated team—you can make a real impact. Single stars derail you, not only in sports but also in organizations. Placing too much weight and responsibility on the shoulders of one or two individuals creates burnout with them, jealousy with other team members, and makes your organization too vulnerable if they leave or cannot work for some reason.

So give your team a team identity. The first thing you need to do here is to make sure they know one another, they understand their differences, and they know how to work together. Reinforce and reward the team. Talk in terms of team. Help them understand the fundamental interdependence they have on one another. Remember, *Inter-Professional* is the world of the 21st Century.

Some organizations use team-building experiences like ropes courses or other outdoor adventures. When you choose these wisely, they can be a marvelous investment. But our advice is to think carefully about what you want the team to get out of the experience. For example, we have worked with many teams that tried to get more interpersonally connected with one another—and they did a high-ropes adventure. Well that's fun but high-ropes is about trust, individual leadership, and individuals achieving things they didn't think they could. It's not really about the team (other than the person on the ground not letting go of the rope...)

Now low-ropes courses, when done well, can be huge eye-openers for a team. Since it's not based on technical competence, it's on no-one's "turf." Low-ropes courses are supposed to put the team in situation after situation they can't solve when everyone is acting as an individual leader. It's only through collaborative leadership that they can even approach the goal. It is through the appreciation of different perspectives and working with different talents that they can crack the solution out of the puzzles facing them, and you know what? That's an awful lot like real life.

Strategy 3: Engage, Engage Engage

A crucial aspect to developing others is to make sure they understand the vision and mission, are connected to it and are committed to it. Jim Collins, author of <u>Good to Great</u>[7], calls this "making sure people are on the right bus." If they are not in sync with what the team, the project, or the organization is all about, then they probably don't have the fit needed to be successful in that role. In other words, they are on the wrong bus and you don't want them on your bench.

What you do want is a team of engaged employees. The good news is that engaged employees are highly motivated, they go the extra mile to deliver, and they will very nearly develop themselves, so it pays off to invest in them *and* in their engagement. Our Seventh Step toward becoming an *It-Factor* leader goes into employee engagement in depth.

Research has shown that the way you speak to and develop a relationship with your employees is critical to their engagement in the mission. Other things to consider: to develop an engaged team make sure they have challenging and meaningful work and that they understand the impact their contributions make to the mission as a whole. As we'll talk about in the Seventh Step, the data on employee engagement shows that the #4 reason for employee retention is development of skills. When it comes to engaging those employees, having challenging work showed up at #2 and career advancement opportunities came in at #5. So your efforts to develop them will be worth it, appreciated, and very likely well-rewarded in productivity and loyalty. We know from the research that people are clamoring for this kind of development.

In the Seventh Step you'll also learn that non-profit employees have a leg up on the commercial sector here. Because of their personal connection to their work, 42% of non-profit sector employees fell into the highly engaged category, as compared to just 17% of industry-employed professionals[8]. They *want* to be in those jobs. It's *meaningful* to them. Make sure that the work is meaningful to your team and they have that personal connection to their work and the mission of the enterprise.

Strategy 4: Everyone Has a Plan

A great tool to use in developing others is the *Individual Development Plan*. Have each team member set two to four yearly goals. These can be goals for their individual leadership skills, their personal technical knowledge or skills, their ability to work effectively within the organization, their ability to create impact with external stakeholders— whatever is relevant to their performance and success on the job. You should both meet with them to assess their individual progress and get their peers involved in supporting one another as well. To promote a culture of goal setting and organizational learning, create small groups of 3 to 4 individuals to serve as "peer coaches." These groups will share their development plans with one another, share progress with one another at least quarterly, and support team members' goal achievement. Make sure they have all those reflective questions from our Third Step and teach them to support problem solvers, rather than rushing in and telling each other what to do. Have them read the Third Step of "Shut Up and Listen," and then let them support one another's learning and development. Bear in mind, it's easy to set a goal. It's hard to explain to a peer how you've made absolutely no progress on that goal in the past 12 weeks. By creating peer coaching teams, you'll have a lot more push toward goal achievement. People are much more likely to do something once they've told someone else they are going to do it. That is clear from a wealth of research in a variety of different behavioral based fields, such as weight loss, smoking cessation, and addictive disorders. And it's also true in workforce development and leader development.

When you set goals for yourself, and have your team do likewise, just how do you do that? Table 5.2 shows you an example *Individual Development Plan*. Customize it to fit what you need, but keep the essential elements. Make sure that individual development goals state:

- what areas/skills the person would like to develop
- where they assess themselves to be at present
- what they want to achieve
- steps they will take to reach the goal
- how they will measure their progress
- the time frame they are working within, and
- the sources of support while they work on achieving the goal

Here is an example plan that illustrates all of these components, as might appear for you or someone on your team:

TABLE 5.2: Example of a Completed Individual Development Plan

Individual Development Plan for Jane Doe
Skill I want to develop: I want to be better at managing conflict and handling difficult conversations
My current skill level: on a scale of 1-10, I put myself at a 3. I avoid conflict as much as I can. In conflict situations I am embarrassed by turning red. Feeling anxious, I tend to make statements that are too harsh, and all too often I end up just giving in so that I can get out of there. Then I sometimes resent the outcome and struggle to support it since I have the definite feeling that I lost.
What I want to achieve: I want to turn the current conflicts into opportunities to understand others better and to surface new ideas while

preserving good relationships among the parties involved. I want to learn how to compromise without feeling like I've lost a battle. I want to feel I've been heard when I make my case.

Steps to reach the goal/my action plan:

1. I will read the Eleventh Step to becoming an *It-Factor* leader: "Don't shirk the tough talk"
2. I will pick 3 strategies to practice with a trusted friend
3. I will ask for feedback
4. I will use a reflection journal to carefully think about what is happening now and how these conversations evolve, and how I can improve in my use of the tools.
5. I will use the Reflect, Envision, Act, Experience cycle from the First Step,

How will I measure my progress: the outcomes of the conversations—whether people are defensive or open and sharing — will be a strong indicator

- I will ask for feedback from trusted peers
- I will look at my reflection journal for how often I feel comfortable with the process and outcome vs. how often I find myself struggling
- I will pay attention to how often I find myself turning red versus staying calm
- I will note my comfort and confidence in my use of the skills

Time frame: my goal is to become markedly more skilled at this within three months

Sources of support: Pat is my trusted friend who will help me work on my strategies and skills; Chris is also working on developing these skills, so I will ask if we can support one another

My personal relationships at home have been supporting me so far and will continue to support me in the next few months

If I can't make sufficient progress on my own, I will hire an executive coach to work with me.

The steps the individual will take to reach that goal may include experiences they will have—such as a training program or attending a meeting; reference materials they will use, such as a book or a review of the current knowledge in an area; or activities they will engage in, such as journaling, reflecting on their performance, or measuring their impact. Each goal should also note what sources they will have to support them in working towards those aims as well as what indicates their success—in other words, how will they know when the goal is achieved?

Those metrics are really important, particularly when it comes to developing others. You need to assess performance *regularly*, not just in that once-a-year-formality of the annual review. If giving meaningful feedback is not a routine activity with your team, then you should assess on a *quarterly* basis people's knowledge relevant to their job tasks, their skills, and whether they have the resources they need to do the job. Are they working to obtain those resources or simply looking to you to provide for them? And, quite importantly, you need to assess their attitude and engagement. Sound like too much—you'd rather have to do that drudgery just once a year? Think about what happens if, at the end of the year, you find out that for the past 8 months your team has been working without the skills and tools they needed for success. That's a tremendous amount of wasted time. How will you explain that to your superiors? When you lead a team, you can't cherry pick the job. You have to do the whole job, and that includes taking inventory of the most important resource you have: your team and their skills. Table 5.2 illustrates for you what a completed Individual Development Plan looks like. Everyone in our leadership fellowships must complete these in order to successfully progress in the program. Those who are in extended programs meet regularly with Peers for Peer Coaching and they meet regularly and confidentially one-on-one with their executive coach to help them achieve the goals they set for themselves. Each component of that plan is important: where they are now, how to gain the skills, support along the way, and measuring progress.

Strategy 5: Give 'Em Time

When creating an organizational culture that supports learning and development, it is critical to ensure that people have the time to learn. Whenever one learns a new skill, productivity temporarily diminishes, but these short term costs yield a payoff in better productivity later on. Just like you invest in capital expenses, such as new equipment, computers, or office space, you need to invest in people. Focusing on learning *rather than productivity* will help you foster an environment of innovation and creativity as well.

While investing the time to learn is critical, it is also true that leaders have to balance the need for efficiency against the need for effectiveness. This is because leaders must be good stewards of their most important resource—which is employee time. Efficiency is being able to produce results quickly, using as few resources as possible. Effectiveness is about producing the *right results!*

To gain efficiency you set the goals based on the outcome, setting metrics that measure performance. You reward for things like decisiveness, action, and productivity. However, to balance that out with effectiveness you set metrics that measure process rather than outcome. You reward for reflection, inquiry, and collaboration and know that positive results that cannot be precisely predicted will grow out of the process.

Why would you do this? Because when companies place too much emphasis on producing results, they lose out on the ability to create an organization that can actually learn how to produce the right results the right way. This is called innovation. According to leadership author Amy Edmonson, when leaders focus on results only, they "discourage (the) technologies, skills or practices that make new approaches viable"[1]. Innovation is a key to long term survival and success. So have your team members set goals for development—and make sure they have the time to devote to this learning and development so that they learn deeply and reap the rewards of improved capacity and productivity.

Strategy 6: Accountability is Key

Building your team is all about growth: personal growth, group growth, organizational growth. Another way to say "growth" is "change." Leaders need to lead change in many ways—building the team is just one of them. Great leaders know that accountability is one of the most crucial factors for change. This is true in any facet of changing people's behaviors.

The picture in figure 5.1 shows a group of women's health physicians completing a ropes course exercise called "the spider web." This exercise exemplifies the impact of accountability on both individual and team performance. The goal here is for all team members to get through a single opening in the ropes without touching the rope with any part of their body or clothing. If a rope is touched then the team has to start all over using a different opening in the web. Needless to say, this is a significant challenge.

Most teams tend to get a little sloppy and not wanting to lose, they often wind up seeing—but not calling it—when a team member brushes up against the side of the rope. A minor infraction you say? Well it may be, but think about the implications in organizations: it might be a minor infraction when teammates don't remind or hold colleagues accountable for washing their hands in a health care setting, but the potential for spreading what are called "nosocomial infections" is great. Nosocomial infections are those pesky ones caught in the hospital from

Figure 5.1: Perfecting Accountability on a Low Ropes Course

the hospital itself. The extra souvenir you don't want from a hospitalization. Think about the very scary *e.coli* cases that have plagued both the meat and vegetable industries and kept public health epidemiologists hopping. It might seem a small thing to not record or mis-record information in an outbreak investigation, but the potential for continuation of an epidemic can be devastating. Many can die before the culprit is identified, the rest of the population warned off, and the causative factors addressed. Accountability is critical. Sometimes it's about money, but all too often it's about outcomes way more important than money.

When teams understand the implications of their behavior and learn how to hold one another and themselves accountable appropriately, performance skyrockets—both on the ropes course and in real life[9]. By paying attention to and learning from events and errors, the whole group performs at a much higher level. This transformation happens very quickly. In organizations, upward accountability—where staff and direct reports hold management accountable—is even more powerful than downward accountability, where managers give feedback to staff.

Strategy 7: S-T-R-E-T-C-H Experiences

A potent tool to developing high-potential team members is to give them a stretch assignment. In a stretch experience, the individual takes on a task that is at the limits of or slightly beyond their current level of experience or skills. They get coaching or mentoring, usually from a supervisor or senior colleague who is skilled at the task, to "show them the ropes" on the particular project. This experience allows a high potential employee to "see" the organization from a different level, to take on new and complex challenges, and to learn new skills and develop new abilities relevant to organizational needs. It creates networking among team members at different levels and shares organizational wisdom. When a team member takes on a "stretch goal", assign a sponsor from upper management. The sponsor can function as a coach, resource person, or mentor to your high-potential team member. Linking your team in this way strongly promotes cross-level networking and shared learning. This is a great tool for growing future leaders in your organization.

Stretch assignments make great goals for your team members' Individual Development Plans as well. Since we know that what gets measured gets done[10], employ measures. Have your team set quarterly goals—both as individuals and as teams. At least some of those goals should be stretch ones—ones that will take a good deal of effort, focus, collaboration, and even learning to achieve. There shouldn't be punishment for not achieving stretch goals but success should be rewarded. Make people accountable for their goals—to themselves, you, and to one another— as with the Peer coaching groups noted above. Your team needs to assess their progress, share best practices, share "lessons learned" (and by that we mean mistakes), and create action plans to re-focus on goals not yet achieved. As a developer of others, you may need to help them develop their action plans to address their missed personal goals. Of course, probably the most important thing to do is to celebrate and reward goals achieved — particularly the stretch goals.

Strategy 8: Develop Your High Potentials

Developing your high potential employees is next on the list. While everyone in an organization needs ongoing development and learning, you will also have employees who are clearly in the "high potential" category. These team members stick out either due to their competence, ability, enthusiasm, or interpersonal skills. One way to focus your development efforts most closely on the future leaders of your organization is to create an acceleration pool[2]. An acceleration pool provides a faster pace of development and more challenging assignments to stretch people's skills. Another benefit: team members can opt into the program by applying for acceptance—or temporarily opt out if their life circumstances change, such as while their children are small or when a family member has a health crisis.

An acceleration pool clearly identifies those interested in moving up and allows you to match their development with both their needs as well as the organization's. As a part of the acceleration pool experience, have your high potentials shadow upper management for specific periods of time. To further support this idea, have upper level management create a list of the special projects they would like to see accomplished, but which they just don't have time to do. These make up the focus areas for the stretch assignments we discussed above for those in the acceleration pool. A high-potential individual or team can be matched with a project and the project sponsor who put it on the list. That project sponsor will act as the individual or team mentor and serve as a resource to them—but not dictate how to accomplish the task (this is supposed to be about learning, after all). This will allow the high potentials to "cut their teeth" on a project of the size, focus, or scope that would not normally be a part of their jobs, yet to do so in a way that has support and advice from leaders who understand those issues and peers who are also working on the problem. In achieving the stretch project, individuals and teams often arrive at innovative solutions that the upper level leaders in the organizations might not have thought of, being busy with their own duties. In this way, focusing on your high potentials can have multiple impacts: greater communication between levels of the organization, skill development of future leaders, and promoting innovative thinking across the groups.

Strategy 9: Nourish Ideas

As a leader, you have to develop a climate that *supports* ideas, rather than shuts them down. There are a lot of ways to brainstorm and generate ideas, but one of our personal favorites is called the POINT process. A version of this process, called *Praise First*, was initially introduced in the early 1980s by Diane Foucar-Szocki, Bill Shephard, and Roger Firestien[11]. It was later further refined by Dr. Gerrard Puccio[12].

The whole concept of *Praise First* and POINT is that when ideas are presented, don't let them get shredded or else you'll never have new ideas to work with. If you see your team shredding every new idea put forth, then you should insist that they use the POINT process instead. The POINT process is a great tool to help your teams create the climate that *supports* ideas, rather than shuts them down.

POINT stands for "P-O-I-NT"—basically a step for each letter. First "P": have everyone note the Plusses—that is, the good points about the idea. Then for "O," explore the Opportunities this idea brings—that's the potential benefits if it works.

Then—and only then—can the group discuss the Issues that must be addressed in order to get this idea to work. Exploring the Issues stage is not the time for criticism, so you want to avoid killer statements like, "That idea will never work!" or worse yet, "That's a stupid idea." Don't allow killer statements if you want to nurture ideas. In the Issues stage the group lists the legitimate challenges to be faced in order to make this idea work. The way everyone speaks here is critical—and you will need to use a strategy called "The Power of How." Get your team to phrase every issue with "how to..." or "how might we..." The use of "how to" or "how might we" moves the conversation from one of criticism that *stops* creative thinking to one that encourages conversation.

And lastly, New Thinking: this is where solutions to those challenges are brought to the floor and discussed. P-O-I-NT: Plusses—Opportunities—Issues—New Thinking. The POINT process is a great way to build a learning culture and to nourish ideas. Try this process with your team and watch how they become creative out-of-the-box thinkers.

Strategy 10: Coach and Mentor to Grow Skills

So just how do you transfer the skills from one valuable player to another? One way is through mentoring and coaching. Let's talk about what each of these terms mean and how it might look in an organization.

Mentoring is a highly personal relationship in which the mentor instructs, shares their perspective and experience, and gives advice to the mentee. Typically mentor-menteeships are relationships characterized by a deep level of respect and personal regard. The Mentor has an investment in developing the career of their mentee—and thus they strive to make opportunities happen for them, provide them with introductions, and give them "off the record" advice on complex situations. This relationship is considered private and the items discussed are to be held in confidence. Having a mentor is one of the criteria that many successful leaders list as key in their development and career progression.

While they share some similarities, Coaching is a fundamentally different relationship from a mentoring one. It is generally time-limited and has a definite scope at the start of the experience. It is helpful for there to be strong personal regard between the coach and "coach-ee," but that actually is not required for a successful coaching experience to take place.

A coach may be a professional executive coach or someone internally in the organization. The coach's task is to teach a defined set of skills to the client, or "coach-ee." These may be hard skills, such as teaching a teammate or supervisee how to run a statistical analysis, how to perform a laboratory test, follow accounting procedures, create a particular code, or perform a clinical service. This focus on a set of hard skills is the typical kind of coaching done within an organization where one person is developing a defined set of skills in a colleague. When contained within an organization, it's a bit like a professional working with a protégé.

Professional executive coaches may teach hard skills, but typically a great deal of their expertise falls under the umbrella of "soft skills." These are the tools for working with and through others, communicating effectively, managing conflict, dealing with negativity, changing organizational culture, managing stress, and leading a team. Soft skills bear a strong resemblance to emotional intelligence, which we'll talk about in our Sixth Step to becoming an *It-Factor* leader. Professional executive coaches generally offer a battery of psychological assessment instruments as learning opportunities, and may work with individuals or teams.

When working with a professional executive coach, you should know that the relationship is considered privileged, much as if the coach were a lawyer or a psychologist. It is unethical for a professional coach to share the content of your discussions or the results of any psychological assessment instruments without your approval. This is true even if the person who is asking for the information is paying for the services on your behalf. Table 5.3 lists some of these important differences between mentoring and coaching.

Strategy 11: Share the Learning

A key facet of developing others is facilitating their learning. But one of the most important conditions for successful learning is to make it safe. That is the job of leaders at every level in the organization. If the office is not a place where organizational mistakes can be studied, learned from, and shared without punishment, then people won't admit where things went wrong and won't share their lessons learned. That sets up a situation where instead of everyone learning from a single mistake together, many learn it independently as the error is repeated over and over again in secrecy and silence.

Table 5.3: Differences Between Mentoring and Coaching

Characteristics of Mentoring	Characteristics of Coaching
Usually a highly personal relationship	A professional or contractual relationship
High degree of positive personal regard between the two parties	Positive personal regard is helpful but not critical
No clear end date, often a life-long relationship	Defined start and end dates
Sharing of confidential personal stories and experiences	Confidential psychological or leadership assessment possible
Advice-based information	Instruction-based information
Open-ended nature of discussions is often characteristic	Defined goals set prior to relationship ("prior to engagement")
Creates opportunities, provides introduction to other important connections	Asks questions, makes suggestions, provides advice and training
Personal ethical values prevail	Follows guidelines of professional ethics

You can encourage this sharing by removing or seriously reducing the individual rewards for success and instead rewarding the team. How you reward success also impacts how safe it is to learn. If you reward production to the exclusion of learning and group-based accomplishment, then you create an atmosphere of competition. This violates the fundamental concept that you are, after all, all on the same team. In this environment, people will withhold their constructive ideas, best practices, and innovations. Even when you reward the *entire* team for a sole focus on production, you create incentives to produce, even if the team is producing the wrong thing.

Creating incentives to share learning doesn't have to be expensive either. We worked with a team once where the leader brought her 12 direct reports together monthly to share their progress on their stretch goals. Since there were no punishments for struggles or failure, team members shared both their triumphs and their challenges. Peers supported, suggested, and assisted. Team members learned from one another. And when there was evidence of shared learning that produced outcomes, the team leader would bring those fabulous chocolate and ice cream confections called Dove Bars to the meeting for everyone—even if they weren't involved in the project being celebrated. Everyone was rewarded for the success of any one of the team members. This cost relatively little, less than $15 a meeting, but the intangibles were amazing. Team members were excited about whether the meeting was a "Dove Bar Day." This reward had no real value—but it impacted the team more than money would have done. Money would have set up an expectation of "I think to be paid" and of internal competition ("I have more than/less than you"), which would have backfired. By using something tasty but relatively meaningless, the team had no real reason to compete with one another, and only had benefits to gain by sharing the learning. So you think your group isn't going to go for Dove Bars? Then think of what they would go for, what they would care about. Don't know—then you don't know them well enough. And that will be your first task: to get to know them. As we'll talk about in our Seventh Step to becoming an *It-Factor* leader, the #1 reason for employee engagement is *senior management's interest in my well-being*.

Creating the culture of sharing the learning is critical for building a great team. And if you work in a knowledge-based organization where collaboration and decision making are critical all along the line, you can't be successful without it. This is very common in public health, health care, academia, consulting, and high-technology innovation enterprises.

Be an *It-Factor* Leader and Build a Great Team

Having a great team doesn't come about by luck. It means creating a culture of investing in people. *It-Factor* leaders develop people. They build competency in an organization. They recruit the right talent, they ensure that people know the mission and are connected to it, they delegate appropriately, and either provide the resources people need, or better still, teach them how to get those resources for themselves. In order words: they develop people. Most importantly, they do all this in order to build their bench—they want a deep bench of talented people who are skilled, resilient, innovative, and capable of assuming leadership on projects, with teams, and with external stakeholders.

Your 5th step to becoming a great *It-Factor* leader is to build a great team.

The Sixth Step:
Build Your EQ

Build Your Own EQ:
How to Develop Your Soft Skills

When most people think about intelligence, they think about a very specific type of intelligence. Cognitive intelligence. That's what a lot of people call book smarts. Cognitive intelligence is measured by IQ and generally it relates to the *hard skills* that make up the core technical skills of a discipline. In healthcare this is the ability to evaluate a patient's condition, make a diagnosis, and provide a treatment. In information technology, this is the ability to program or troubleshoot a computer problem. In education this is the material taught and on which students are tested.

All that kind of intelligence is important, but it's not the whole picture of success. Perhaps you've known someone who was really intelligent, with great book smarts, but who just couldn't seem to make things work for them? Perhaps they struggled with being able to understand others, to communicate effectively, or to build relationships, or in creating effective alliances with others? They wouldn't be alone—all too often these are the central issues that cause very smart people to derail in their careers, as we talked about in our First Step to becoming an *It-Factor* leader. People who are the most successful are not necessarily those with the highest IQ. They have something else going for them.

It takes more than IQ to be smart *and* successful in today's work environment. The other half of intelligence is emotional intelligence, what people often describe as *people smarts*. This term is pretty common thanks to authors and researchers like Daniel Goleman[1, 2], Roger Pearman[3], Howard Book, Steven Stein[4, 5] and Ruven Bar-On[6]. "EQ" is about those soft skills that are also crucial for your success. By these we mean your ability to understand what you are feeling and how it impacts your actions, make the same assessment of others, operate in that knowledge, and cope with changing demands and pressures. That's emotional intelligence, often referred to as EI or more often as EQ, particularly when quantified, as with one of the several available psychological assessment tests[5-8].

Don't be fooled into believing that IQ is all important—or all you need. We've already made that all too common (and all too true) old joke that you hire a smart person for their technical skills...and *then* the whole person shows up for the job. Having a high IQ doesn't guarantee success. Skeptical? Well, there's research by Drs. Steven Stein and Howard Book [4] that supports the role of this key leadership skill.

But first, let us tell you a story of how this works out even on a child's level. One day not too long ago, our 8-year old son, Alex, came to us, sad that he wasn't the smartest kid in his class. And given how super-smart and hyper-competitive the kids in his class were, he was pretty sure that particular distinction would never belong to him. He is, however, great with people, sharing, sensitive to their needs, stands up for the little guys, intuitively makes sure all the kids playing have a role, as well as know and value their role. If one of the kids is angry or upset, he doesn't judge. He investigates. We gave him 100 pennies and had him put 45 of them in a pile and 6 of them in a pile. You can see his pile in Figure 6.1. When we asked him to describe the piles, he said, "well there's the super short one I can hardly see and this tall one is so big it keeps falling over!" Indeed, he had quite the time it getting those 45 pennies to stack up, there were so many.

Figure 6.1　Alexander Examining a "Penny-Bar Graph" of the Difference in Success Attributable to Soft and Hard Skills.

We told Alex that in the real, grown-up world it is great to be smart, but that you can't over-rate its importance. To demonstrate the fact that the studies show that only 6% of job success can be credited to IQ alone—we had him identify which pile of pennies he wanted to have.

Of course, being eight, he said "both," but admitted that if he had to choose, he would take the 45 penny-tall stack. We explained that, depending on the field someone's working in, a whopping 27%-45% of success was predicted by EQ and soft skills[4]—representing the big penny pile. That's between 4 times and almost 8 times as important. Famous EQ author and researcher Daniel Goleman thinks this is an underestimate— he credits about 67% of job success with EQ skills[1]. Either way, Book and Stein have a great statement about the role of emotional intelligence: "regardless of how brainy we may be, if we turn others off with abrasive behavior, are unaware of how we are presenting ourselves or cave in under minimal stress, no one will stick around long enough to notice our high IQs[4]."

As a leader you cannot be callous about these problems. Some of your brightest and most talented players, key people in your organization, can be afflicted with issues that strike at the heart of working with and through others, of collaborating, of networking, and of dealing with challenges in constructive ways[7, 8]. While dealing with these problems is not generally pleasant, it is entirely possible to help people improve in each of these dimensions. These are the typical kinds of issues that bring an executive coach into an organization since they specialize in teaching people more effective interpersonal and leadership skills.

We couldn't agree with them more, as Book and Stein note: "Having a high IQ and an underdeveloped EQ can hold an otherwise smart professional back"[4]. The *It-Factor* leaders we've worked with either have great EQ or they work hard to develop it. They don't fall into the IQ only trap. EQ is just too important to ignore.

The Hard and the Soft:
The Soft Skills Aren't Hard to Develop…
and Those That Have Them Aren't Softies Either

Let's talk about these hard and soft skills. Admittedly, hard skills are essential. Generally, they are well covered in professional training programs since they're the budgeting and strategic issues, the assessment, the mathematical, logical, and engineering skills—those issues of fact finding and data recall that represent the technical knowledge, skills, and abilities of any field. People who have good technical abilities are often promoted, and excel in their work…up to a point.

But take a moment to reflect on the five most challenging work situations you have faced. How many represent budget woes or strategic planning issues? And now think about how many revolve around the results of faulty communication, organizational culture problems, the inability of individuals to understand one another, or their inability to grasp the impacts of their own actions or inaction? While we all have faced budget headaches, it is those latter situations that are the stuff of most organizational migraines.

Emotional Intelligence is more than having a thick skin or a sense of empathy for others. It is a genuine ability to feel emotions in response to others, understand what you are feeling, understand how others are feeling, and to move forward constructively with the interests of the larger group at heart. It's a whole group of abilities that help you effectively manage and regulate your own emotional responses[9, 10]. That's a very big part of leadership[1, 4, 6-8].

Emotional intelligence is a standard skill for the 21st Century. It has to do with creating and maintaining relationships—and being able to maintain and restore those relationships when they are damaged. The ability to empathize, be resilient in the face of difficulty, and manage one's impulses and stress all fall into the realm of emotional intelligence. Our emotional intelligence is what helps us navigate the social and interpersonal tasks and challenges we face, as opposed to the technical tasks we often perform.

The 3 Facets of the Whole Person

Cognitive intelligence, emotional intelligence, and personality are all distinct qualities each person possesses and together they determine how one thinks and acts. You could say that together they make up the whole person. IQ and personality (like whether you are an introvert or an extravert, a feeling type or a thinking type, for example) rarely change over the course of one's life—but EQ is something that you can change, grow, and improve if you nurture this skill in yourself.

Our modern day concept of Emotional Intelligence came from a railway construction accident and a man who experienced a miracle. His name was Phineas Gage, and on September 13th back in 1848 he had a bad day. A very bad day. On that cool Vermont morning in early fall he was a well-liked and capable foreman. By the afternoon he had lost a part of his brain when a 3-foot, 7-inch tamping iron accidentally exploded upwards, striking him in the head, destroying most of the front and left side of his brain. For him, this event changed his life. For the rest of us it forever changed the way we understand the human mind.

His miracle was that he lived. Some months after the accident, most incredibly he went back to work at the railway—but "the once capable and efficient foreman, who was looked on as a shrewd and smart business man, was now fitful, irreverent, and reportedly grossly profane, showing little deference for his fellows"[11]. Because his personality had changed so much, he could not continue at his former job. Reports describe him as impatient and obstinate, yet capricious and vacillating, unable to settle on any of the plans he devised for future action. His friends said he was "No longer Gage"[11].

It was amazing that a man could live through such a traumatic event, but what he showed the world about how the brain functions was also amazing. For a long time scientists didn't have a way to study the way the brain works—but now with PET scans and functional MRIs, we can literally see into the brain in our attempts to help us see into the human mind.

And what we've found is that emotional intelligence is not just an idea—it's a function of the brain itself. In fact, all that you experience in the world is first, in effect, filtered by your emotional intelligence, as sensations are processed by the limbic system (basically the middle of your brain), the place where the emotions are experienced, and only then onto the rational centers in the frontal cortex (your forehead). Emotional intelligence requires effective communication between the rational and emotional centers of the brain.

Even more fascinating is how your brain is hard-wired for the importance of soft skills. You have built-in neurons that cause you to smile back when someone smiles at you (called mirror cells). You mirror the emotions you see, and that affects your brain chemistry. When you are pleasant, smile at others, speak with kindness and patience, you *create* the mirror of those feelings in others. You help to create the kind of organizational culture that *It-Factor* leaders want. When you are harsh, judgmental, critical, and impatient, you create an organizational culture of fear and angst. Perhaps productive for short anxiety-fueled bursts, but not innovative or enduring. Because of the function of these specialized cells, emotions are truly "contagious"[2].

You have another built-in specialist in your brain: Spindle cells. These cells quickly connect emotions, beliefs, and judgments and make up what has been called your "social guidance system."[2] When you have to choose the best response from among many choices—and you have to do it fast—it's your spindle cells that run to your rescue. For example, when you decide whether someone is trustworthy or not or whether you should open up to them. And brain cells called oscillator cells help you move in concert with other people, such as playing music or dancing—or figuring out how to appropriately jump into a lively conversation. Our basic brain wiring gears us, as human beings, to be very social, and emotional, animals.

So, your rational and emotional centers of your brain are located on different islands of the mind, as it were. What *It-Factor* leaders do is work hard to have a superhighway connecting those islands so that there is a lot of brain traffic going back and forth. When too little traffic flows in either direction, you spend too much time ignoring your feelings (or those of others) or getting run over by them, and ineffective behavior is the result.

What Emotional Intelligence Looks Like

Understanding emotional intelligence, or EI for short, is very simple. However, building up your EI requires breaking it down into tiny little parts so that you can isolate specific behaviors to work on to improve your skill. It's not that different than in the Olympics—an Olympian swimmer has a coach for his or her kick, and arm stroke, and strength, and nutrition—and more. To become the greatest expert in the world at what they do they break their complex performance down into tiny little parts, and work to perfect those. Now EI is not about being perfect, but it doesn't hurt to approach it like you're an Olympian, too, by breaking down the complex skills into small parts to make it easy to focus on.

Here is our favorite model of Emotional Intelligence, in Figure 6.2[8]. We use this in our coaching work with executives—and we should add that we didn't make this up. We've modified it based on our experience of working with many great leaders, but this model is based heavily on the early work of Ruven Bar-On[6], and the later work of Steven Stein[5]. This model is particularly helpful to us because we can use it to isolate several key skills of EI so that you can focus on specific exercises to build up your emotional intelligence. It's like personal training for the mind. We agree with Daniel Goleman that EI is based in personal competence (discussed below) and you need to have personal competence in order to have social competence. But we also appreciate all the work of EI researchers Stein and Book[4], and before them Bar-On[6]. Their research points to a much more complicated model of Emotional Intelligence, as measured by Emotional Quotient (EQ). In order to make it easy to improve your EI skills we need to break Emotional Intelligence down into small components.

As Figure 6.2 shows, personal competence is made up of self-awareness (remember that from our First Step towards *It-Factor* leadership?) Knowing yourself and understanding yourself is absolutely key to strengthening your skills in emotional intelligence.

Figure 6.2: Model of Emotional Intelligence[8]

Personal Competence:
Self-Perception, Self-Expression,
Stress Management, Decision Making

In this model, personal competence is the basis on which all the other skills are built. Without personal competence—there is no social competence. With no personal competence happiness is also elusive. Personal competence breaks down into four domains, each made up of three skills you can improve, thus enhancing your overall emotional intelligence.

Self-Perception:
Self-Actualization, Emotional Self-Awareness, Self-Regard

When it comes to EI, self-perception is based on **self-awareness**. Self-awareness is not about being perfect. It's about knowing yourself and doing the most with what you have. It is about being aware of what your feelings are and allowing those feelings to inform—not control—but to inform and guide your behavior. Always remember that leadership and emotional intelligence are like sports—you don't have to be sick to get better! And you're never going to be perfect. See yourself for who you are. Accept yourself. Rather than excusing your faults, constantly work to get better.

How do you see yourself? Do you see yourself as you appear to others, or do you see an idealized version of who you wish yourself to be? When you can see yourself as others see you, you've gone a long way to start your EI journey. More than two-thirds of people have difficulty admitting their shortcomings. Things you do not think about are off your radar for a reason: they can sting when they surface. The short term fix is to avoid this pain, turn a blind eye to your faults or weaknesses. However, allowing yourself to experience the discomfort of looking in the mirror accurately is the only way to change. You cannot manage yourself adequately if you ignore what you need to change. That is to have a blind spot—and the problem with a blind spot is that you are the only one ignorant of it. Rest assured that everyone else sees it plainly. Better to see, than to be blind, to your faults.

Want to work on this part of your EI? Here are some exercises you can try. A great way to see yourself and improve your self-perception is by doing a 360-degree assessment, which are available for general leadership behaviors, personality type, and for emotional intelligence as well. In a 360 you get to compare how you, your boss, your direct reports, your peers, and even a group of others, like partners or clients, perceive your behaviors. There are a bevy of other assessment tools an executive coach can use to teach you a bundle about yourself—and how you are the same as, and different from, others. Some of the best are of the classics—the Myers Briggs Type Indicator, the FIRO-B/Element B, the Change Style Indicator, the Foursight tool, and the emotional intelligence assessments that are available on the market, such as the EQi 2.0 and the MSCEIT. What these assessments can do is show you how competent, normal individuals can be very different from one another. Learning about these differences can help stretch your ability to communicate effectively and work with those who might be quite different from you. Any "debrief" (explanation of your scores) should be about way more than yourself—if it's only about understanding yourself then it's probably not worth what you paid for it. After all, most leaders are not the great mystery unto themselves—and you probably aren't either. Remember, there is a huge difference between having a blind spot and being so totally blind that you run repeatedly headlong into solid walls (that's considered derailing in your career). It is unusual for those with massive blind spots to survive long in leadership. So make sure your self-awareness is a stepping stone to helping you understand—and appreciate—what makes others tick and the advantages that they bring to the table in addition to the gifts you bring to the table.

The great *It-Factor* leaders we work with know themselves—but it doesn't stop there with them. They know that great leadership isn't about them. It's *not* about their type, intelligence, or perspective. It *is* about creating the kind of culture where there is space for those of very different views and talents—but more about that in our Tenth Step to becoming an *It-Factor* leader: create thought diversity.

Self-regard is a key component of emotional intelligence. Self-regard is about respecting yourself, feeling sure about yourself, having self-confidence and being reasonably happy with who you are. It can be a challenge to have a healthy emotional intelligence if you lack confidence or are consumed with guilt, shame, or self-recrimination. At times people can feel crushed by tough experiences, but it is important to realize that tough experiences happen to good people. Good people get divorces, lose jobs, or don't get offered their dream job, even after a good interview. All leaders need to have resilience because leadership is often a difficult job to have. It is important to know yourself, understand what assets you have to offer, and know that you can't be perfect or all things to all people.

If you have trouble liking yourself then you should try to understand why. There are two possibilities going on here: first, your perspective might be askew. If you are too hard on yourself you need to understand why that is. If you are too hard on yourself, you might be being too hard on others too. If you find that others see you very differently than you see yourself, you probably need to change the inner image you hold about yourself.

Of course, if you have trouble liking yourself, there is another possibility: that you are onto something and you need to make changes. If you don't like yourself because you don't have the basic skills and talents that you want, then you need to work harder to develop those abilities that will truly give you self-efficacy. Set a clear path of skills building, identifying the skills you desire and how you will learn or hone them. You will be helped here by getting a mentor, teacher, advisor, or coach to guide you on this path. But let's say that you don't have high self-regard because of some actions you have taken which you regret. Then your path to self-regard is to amend the damage you have done to those relationships. Until those injuries to others are sufficiently healed it is unlikely that you will have much recovery in your own self-regard, or much improvement in your own EI.

It's easy to see how **self-actualization** relates to emotional intelligence. Self-actualization is your ability to realize your potential and to lead a rich and meaningful life. In general this stems from feeling like you have something to contribute to your work group or community. People who feel self-motivated and are driven to achieve, striving constantly to improve feel 'self-actualized'. Those who feel this way tend to be happier and more productive at work as well. They also tend to show more emotional intelligence. If this concept of being self-actualized sounds like a mystery to you, then you need to think about how what you are doing in life fits in with your values. When work and personal values are out of sync, people often feel a sense of "being lost" and unconnected to meaning in life. When a person is connected to meaning in life, it is easier for them to find ways to contribute, which supports a sense of self-actualization. If this is an issue for you, identify your top 5 values. Write your list in Table 6. 1. Then think about how you live your life. What are the values that your life gives evidence for? Consider your personal life, your work, your hobbies—all the elements that make up your life. How do your actions speak for you and attest to the values you show to others? For example, if you take off of work to catch your child's soccer game or school awards ceremony that attests to family values or supporting your children as a priority in your life. If you miss those kinds of events because you are at work, that indicates having dedication to work or a 'doing whatever it takes" orientation to workplace success.

Occasionally someone in a leadership program will interpret "family values" or "work values" as being good and the other as bad—but you have to think more broadly than that. We work with a lot of surgeons who might miss a soccer game, but their job is to save lives, which they can't do if they aren't at the hospital. When you create your list, don't judge. Try to be objective.

Table 6.1: Comparing Personal Values With Evidenced Values

My personal top 5 values	The values my work or life provides evidence of
1.	1.
2.	2.
3.	3.
4.	4.
5.	5.

Emotional Self Awareness:
Another step towards mindfulness

Another component of perceiving yourself accurately is your emotional self-awareness. If this feels like peering through a fog to you, here are some EI boosting strategies in this area. First, try keeping a thought or emotion journal. An emotion journal is described in Figure 6.3. It works like this: set a timer, like on a watch or smart phone, to go off once an hour at an odd time. Every time it goes off write down what you are thinking for a thought journal, or for an emotion journal what you are feeling. At the end of a week look at what you wrote and analyze it for trends. That can tell you a lot about what is going on with you. Are you frequently frustrated, angry, or feeling disconnected to your work?

Figure 6.3: Emotion Journal

JOURNAL:
8:25 AM: Frustrated (stuck in traffic, overslept)
9:25 AM: Angry (interrupted by co-worker during meeting)
10:25 AM: Anxious (deadline looming ... project not complete)
11:25 AM: Really anxious about this deadline ... keep getting interrupted with other people's problems!
12:25 AM: I am SO annoyed (co-eps trying to pitch me ideas when I'm trying to trate!)

Are you energized and excited? Or perhaps you are feeling overwhelmed or optimistic about the challenges you're taking on? This is great information to share with your executive coach if you have one, and can give you good insights into what is going on with you.

Self-Expression:
Independence, Assertiveness, Emotional Expression

The next part of the EI model is about self-expression—that's how you communicate to others. Self-expression is also fundamental to personal competence—expressing yourself is going to be key to your success as a person as well as your success as a leader. This encompasses your ability to be assertive (not aggressive), to express your emotions, and to be independent.

Assertiveness is a core component of emotional intelligence in this model. This is the ability to express feelings, beliefs, and thoughts and defend one's rights in a non-destructive manner (even if this is not popular)[4-6]. Since this can be a tricky talent to master, here are some ideas to help boost your skills. First, think about a time when a conversation didn't go as you wished. Maybe you said something out of turn or perhaps you didn't speak at all. Reflect on that and then write down what you could say next time this situation comes up. Work on your statement, editing it, until you are comfortable with how it states your point of view yet does not insult or damage others.

Another idea is to get feedback from another person. Share your perspective with someone whom you trust and who will be truthful with you, not someone who will automatically agree with you. Ask them for what they heard. Remember to be very non-judgmental of what they tell you—they hear what they hear, and that can be very valuable insight for you. When they share what they heard with you, your appropriate response is to say "thank you" and not to defend or justify your actions. Just listen and think it over. If they are hearing what you say in a way that is inconsistent with what you intend, then you can be reasonably assured that others are too and that what you are saying, or how you are saying it is missing the mark.

Stress Management:
Stress Tolerance, Flexibility, Optimism

Stress management, the third of the four core areas, is built from stress tolerance, flexibility, and optimism. Again, there are many steps you can take to promote your EI in any of these areas. **Stress tolerance** has to do with how you handle adversity, stressful situations, and challenges without falling apart. It's how you "muddle through" when adversity cannot be avoided that's important[4-6]. Stress Tolerance has to do with your ability to use coping strategies to weather difficult situations and to avoid being overwhelmed by adversity. Research has shown that stress tolerance has a significant relationship to overall work success— and certainly, getting overwhelmed and falling apart has a negative relationship with productivity at work[4].

Here are two ideas for promoting your stress tolerance. First, you need to know what is contributing to your stress, worry, or other feelings you may be having. You can make an inventory list of these. If your list is a big one, well, that can seem pretty overwhelming at times, so on your list write down 1 to 3 action steps you can take that will either help reduce the cause of your stress or the effect it has on you.

Since stress is unavoidable, make sure you give yourself lots of potent stress busters, like eating a healthy diet, being physically active, and getting regular checkups with both your dentist and your doctor. Health care professionals can help identify problems early that are caused by stress and work with you to intervene early. Of course, they will likely emphasize healthy diet and regular exercise in addition to adequate sleep. Don't underestimate the importance of good quality, regular sleep! Deep sleep is when much of the cellular damage to your body and brain gets repaired, and there is no substitute for it[12]. Caffeine may keep you awake but it doesn't repair your damaged cells. Don't cheat yourself when it comes to sleep.

Another good technique for stress tolerance is to straighten out your thinking. You might be surprised to learn that the events that happen to you don't cause you to have a reaction to them. Now before you disagree, consider this: It's the *story* you tell yourself about the event that causes you to have the reaction. Let's say your fun plans for a getaway weekend with friends get canceled. Depending on what those plans were and the story you tell yourself about the event, you could be really disappointed, totally relieved, or feeling sad and rejected. Your reaction is based on your *interpretation* of the events—and your interpretation is the story you tell yourself. Take a look at the example in figure 6.4.

Make sure you understand your stories. When you understand what you tell yourself about the events of your day, you can decide whether those stories are helpful to you—or potentially destructive. You can always change the story—and subsequently your reaction to the initial event. Similar to the emotion journal we mentioned earlier, you can keep a journal or a diary to help you understand the stories that create your reaction. Once you can see them, you can think about how true they really are—and consider telling yourself a different story when a situation occurs that doesn't go as you'd like. That's where to start, examine your stories so you are aware of what you are telling yourself.

Assume for a moment that the stories you are telling yourself make you sad, angry, or some other bad feeling—that gives us a situation to examine where you might really need to straighten out your thinking.

Figure 6.4: Schematic of how Beliefs and Self-Talk Mediate Feelings About an Event

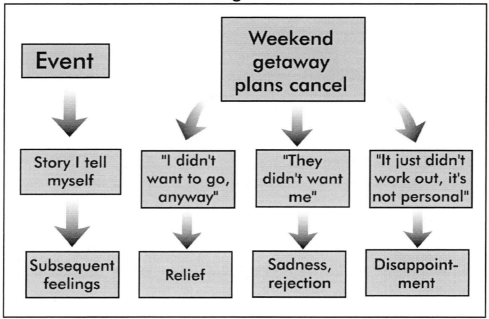

Let's stick with the example of those fun weekend plans cancelling—only this time let's imagine that you have gone down that track of "they didn't want me" and now you're feeling sad and rejected. Of course, other examples that follow this same idea are not getting a job or a promotion, having your project idea turned down, etc. Here is the crucial important insight: when you are telling yourself the equivalent of "they didn't want me," you feel badly about the situation and you label the whole situation with that mood (psychologists refer to mood as "affect"). It's that "negative affect" (bad mood) that really contributes to your stress and will wear you down, making it harder to tap into your emotionally intelligent self, and making it more likely that you will react to your negative affect and make an opportunity-limiting faux pass.

So what can you do? You have basically two options: you can change that story or you can make lemonade out of lemons. Practicing these two exercises will improve your skills in both **flexibility** and **optimism**. Let's first take a look at how you can change that story. You might need to examine a lot of options to find where the truth lies. We'll look at half a dozen in Table 6.2, but there very well could be several different story alternates that you would need to consider.

Table 6.2 Alternative stories that might actually be the truth!

Initial story to challenge: "They don't want me"	
They have a sick child and can't make it.	Money is a factor and now is not a good time for them to commit resources to a fun trip.
An emergency at work has come up and they just don't have the time to go.	Maybe they don't want to be together?
They need some time to deal with some of their own private issues or needs.	The weather is making the trip impossible.

Any of these stories could be entirely plausible and more true than "they don't want me." If any *one* of those other stories turned out to actually be true, how might that change your thinking—and thus your feeling—about the whole situation? You would be thinking "they don't want me" and you find out they have a sick child for instance. The moral of the story here is to dig deeper. You may think you know the "why" behind events, but don't get sucked into believing that you are the omniscient author of your own life. You don't know everything and you'll never see deeper until you take a step back to consider a wider range of possibilities than what immediately pops up for you.

Now consider the "making lemonade" option. For this topic it doesn't matter *what* story is true in table 6.2 (or on your own list). Maybe they *don't* want you along. Time to let that go and now deal with your free weekend. What can you do to build a more positive life for yourself? Catch up with other friends? Indulge yourself in a book you've wanted to read? Dive into an art or home improvement project?

Now consider an even more tense situation where you were not given a promotion you were seeking. You might reasonably be feeling rejected and depressed. You can check out your thoughts, examine all the plausible (not whiney) reasons (stories), and then you're still left with what to do to enrich your life (make lemonade). If you *don't* make lemonade you risk letting your bummed-out feelings (negative affect) pop up when they are most inconvenient—and potentially detrimental to you. In this case, making lemonade might be asking for a stretch assignment (related to a story of "I don't have enough experience"), offering to be helpful to the person who did get the position (related to a story of "I need to be seen as more of a team player"), investing in yourself by getting more training to make yourself more competitive next time (related to the story of "I need more skills"), practicing and improving your interviewing skills (related to the story of "I don't think I interviewed that strongly"), etc. The plausible range of stories you listed will guide you in how to improve (see Table 6.3). When you make your own list of plausible stories remember to separate the whiney ones out. Whiney stories fall into the "they don't like me" ilk and include, "you can't get ahead here as a _____ (insert reason you are marginalized by others)," "I am not the favorite pet of the boss," "they only promote people in their social group," etc. You can't win at those. There is nothing you can really do to change the landscape of these reasons—and if they are true, then it's probably time to leave that organization anyway. Fortunately, the usual reasons are not the whiney "oh poor me" ones, but are grounded in skills, either hard or soft, or experience. Keep your list full of plausible reasons.

Table 6.3 Ways to "make lemonade" when things go wrong

Event: I didn't get the promotion I wanted	
Plausible stories you tell yourself why you didn't get the promotion:	**"Making Lemonade" Strategies:**
"I don't have enough experience for that position"	Ask for a stretch assignment
"I need to be seen as more of a team player"	Offer to be helpful to the person who did get the position
"I need more skills"	Invest in yourself by getting more training to make yourself more competitive next time
"I think I Interviewed poorly"	Practice and improve your interviewing skills

Decision Making:
Problem Solving, Impulse Control, Reality Testing

Research shows that the all-important area of Personal Competence is also based on your skills in decision making, which breaks down into problem solving, impulse control, and reality testing. Here, improving your emotional intelligence is always an option. From our work in coaching mid-to-senior level leaders, we find that **impulse control** is a particularly tough one for leaders in the Western world. While this is one of the most valuable emotional intelligence skills, it can be quite tricky to master. An idea to boost your impulse control skills is to give yourself space between what you are feeling and how you react. Any kind of space can be helpful—people may joke about "counting to 10" or "holding your breath," but strategies like those can actually work because they create a break that allows you to choose your reaction. Creating a break between the event and your overly-quick reaction is the key so that you *decide* what action you want to take. For example, when we work with clearly extraverted leaders who tend to jump in too fast, we counsel them to "breathe before extraverting"—rather than being the first person to speak, wait to be the third or later. They often find this simple advice very helpful in learning to slow down and manage their first-to-participate-impulse. You can also physically remove yourself from the situation, journal about it, or talk to someone else. You can have a statement that you use to ground yourself in your values and goals (some people refer to this as a mantra) that you say to yourself to help you avoid making a knee-jerk impulsive reaction. You can also have a visual reminder, such as a picture or an object to serve as a cue — remember the *It-Factor* leader Jill Bemis.

But what can you do after you've made a self-management error, and you've yelled at someone or done something that you regret?

According to one of our favorite colleagues, business psychologist Roger Hall[13], you can use these experiences to actually change yourself and learn to manage those impulses. While you can say "I'm sorry" this really doesn't quite cut it. According to Roger, what you really need to do is ask for forgiveness. When you do this you give up control—because the other person might not be ready to forgive you. When you ask for forgiveness you give the control to them. It takes humility to do this. Humility is a great way to learn to slow your automatic reactions down so that you can intentionally choose a different outcome.

Another interesting area in emotional intelligence that falls under decision making is **problem solving.** Many competent leaders find solving logical problems easy. The challenge comes when the problems they solve are no longer of the rational world. You are smack dab in the middle of emotionally-mediated problem solving when a) people become involved, b) when decisions create two classes of those affected by it (those who are benefitted and those who are burned), or c) when opportunities or resources are scarce. Most leaders find this much more complex than the simple problem solving in the uncomplicated, straightforward, predictable, logical, and rational world. Unfortunately, they don't get to visit that world very often now that they are leaders. When individuals struggle with EI-based problem solving, they can find that their emotions overwhelm them, interfering with their ability to make a decision or causing them to worry. Worry is merely rehearsed fear. Rehearsing anything makes you more skilled at it—so worrying just makes you more skillful at fear, and practicing fear is not a very productive way to spend your time[13]. Those who have the most struggles in this area feel frustrated, get stuck on examining their options, and eventually give up on solving the problem at all.

So let's explore another skills-boosting idea, this time for emotionally-mediated problem solving. You might have made what is called a fish-bone or tree-and-root diagram to diagnose a problem at work. You can apply the same tool to growing your emotional intelligence as well by linking the outcomes you are experiencing with what else is going on in your life. In our example in Figure 6.5 we'll look at a manager who just couldn't sleep, and then woke up late, and then got stuck in traffic on the morning commute. After getting to work, on edge from his frustrating day thus far—splashes a coffee cup and stains a new shirt. Wow, what a bad start to the morning! While this isn't a fun way to start a day, think about it: none of it has career damaging effects. It's just inconvenient and annoying.

But *then* look what happened—not being resilient and able to deal with these misfortunes resulted in our poor manager snapping at a team mate, rolling his eyes at subordinate's/direct report's idea, interrupting his boss and then missing a deadline.

Figure 6.5 Fishbone diagram of how bad morning events lead to worse afternoon outcomes

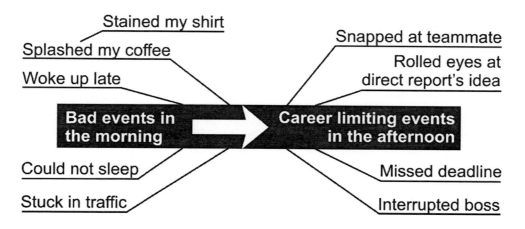

Neither the teammate, boss, nor the direct report caused the frustration and anger but they all bore the brunt of it. And *that* has a career-limiting result for our short-sighted manager. We could write a similar story of those who have a bumpy day at work and then come home to blow up at their children or spouse. It doesn't have to be this way, but it will be until you can see what is going on. Once you understand how you are managing yourself, you can begin to choose new ways to act.

Let's look at an emotionally charged situation, like really damaging a relationship with a partner, who can be another person, group, or company (Figure 6.6). This often happens when the initiating party (on the left hand side of the fishbone chart) makes very self-centered decisions (which is not a very emotionally intelligent thing to do). Examples of such decisions include a) dictating the terms of the partnership to the other party b) so greatly desiring more profit and to

Figure 6.6 Fishbone diagram on
emotionally charged decision making

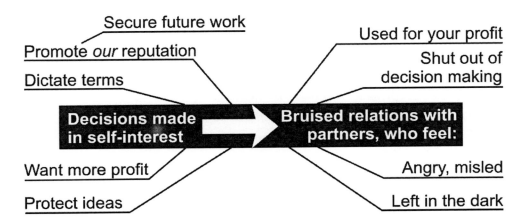

secure future work that one only promotes one's own reputation and welfare in the partnership, c) failing to share ideas with the partner.

This can leave the other party feeling pretty disenchanted, as they perceive they were misled about a partnership that shuts them out of decision making and harvests their ideas while leaving them in the dark. Very quickly they come to the conclusion that this partnership is a one-way deal and they aren't likely to go down that road again—or speak highly of those who they feel used them.

You can use a fishbone diagram to help you diagnose any situation that went awry—or to learn from one that went very well. Use Figure 6.7 to analyze a recent experience you have had.

Figure 6.7 Fishbone diagram

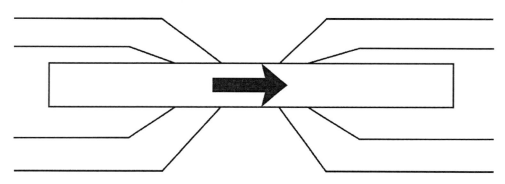

Social Competence:
Social Awareness, Empathy, Interpersonal Relationships, Social Responsibility

Great *It-Factor* leaders have social competence. They are aware of others, and not just themselves. They understand what others are feeling. They work to have good interpersonal relationships and they understand their role in social responsibility.

Social Awareness

Social awareness is the first stage of social competence. Social awareness is about paying attention to others, so that you can identify what another person is feeling and understand how those feelings are influencing that person's behavior. This is important information for you to have since it has significant impacts on teamwork, decision making, and ultimately the outcomes you seek to achieve.

To build your social awareness, try this exercise: after you leave a meeting, write down who attended the meeting, and what you think they were feeling. Then note their behaviors and the things they said that you noticed. Then revisit the feelings you ascribed to each individual and compare your ascribed feeling to each person's actions. This exercise will help you key into what is going on with others around you.

Empathy

One part of social awareness is **empathy**, which is basically the ability to be aware of, to understand and appreciate the feelings of others, being able to articulate your understanding, and behaving in a way that respects others' feelings. Empathy is not the only thing that makes up emotional intelligence, but it is quite important[1, 3, 7, 8].

Recently we worked with a high-potential, very technically competent leader who wanted to build his skills in emotional intelligence—he'd been given some feedback that those kind of skills would help him in the next steps of career success. He relayed an event at work that had annoyed him. His usually excellent support person had been in just a foul mood one morning. After trying to ignore it, he finally decided, "OK, I'll bite" and asked her what was going on since she seemed out of sorts. She replied, "it's my birthday and you didn't notice. You didn't say anything or even remember!" His response? "I don't do birthdays. This is work." We asked, "what motivated her to feel like that?" He indicated that it didn't much matter, since it was inappropriate for the office.

OK, so not the most emotionally intelligent set of responses here (and hence his pursuit of EI skills). Not that he is wrong. Not that he isn't being logical. But when we said, "OK, so did that work for you?" he answered, "no, our relationship was not good after that and her performance wasn't what it had been."

When you are working on empathy skills, you need to think about how the other person feels, what their values are, and what motivates them in the situation. You need to get out of your own perspective, your own shoes, as it were, and into theirs. We offered him the following possible explanation: just perhaps she worked hard to excel at her job not only because of the paycheck she got. That just maybe she didn't identify with the organization she worked for; rather she identified her role in relationship to him, her boss. She worked hard because she felt loyal to *him*. Her excellent performance was because of her relationship with him. And he had just indicated to her that she didn't matter to him. That she was basically gum on the bottom of his shoe. She was a cog in his wheel. No wonder she was out of sorts. He had never thought of it that way. That 'ah-hah' was a game changer for him.

One way to help you build your empathy skills is to practice a basic reflection exercise. When you are having an interaction with someone, you can check in with them by reflecting how you perceive their feelings about the topic, such as, "you seem very happy with this development," or "you seem rather upset about this event, am I understanding you correctly?" They may agree or disagree with you, but it is vital that you remain non-judgmental about their feelings ("I don't do birthdays" would not classify as a non-judgmental response). Learn from them, observe them, and remember that we are all works in progress. Sometimes the other person may not be totally clear on what they are feeling either.

There are strategies for boosting your emotional intelligence when it comes to improving your ability to manage your relationships as well. Two important components of relationship management include interpersonal relationships and social responsibility. These work together as separate skills that contribute to the larger domain of Social Competence[4-6].

Interpersonal Relationships

Interpersonal relationships are all about the ability to establish and maintain mutually satisfying relationships that are characterized by intimacy and the giving and receiving of affection[4-6]. Notice here that the relationship is not about just satisfying your interests. It's not solely about you, nor are you participating in the relationship only in service to the other person.

Here we can explore a couple more EI boosting ideas. First, one of the things that helps make relationships mutually satisfying is sharing what's important to each of you—and that requires active listening (harkens us back to that Third Step towards becoming a great *It-Factor* leader, doesn't it?) So sit down with that other person and take a try at really listening to them. Don't solve their problems, judge them, or advise them. Just listen. You can reflect what you think they are feeling, like we mentioned above. Another idea is to choose someone who has had a major positive impact on your life and write them a letter—tell them how important they have been to you and what impact they had on you. This might be a teacher, a coach, a clergy member, a friend, or a family member.

Another crucial skill of relationship management is managing the difficult conversation, rather than shirking the tough talk—which we'll cover in our Eleventh Step to becoming an *It-Factor* leader. Having a healthy emotional intelligence will help you manage tough conversations well—and not surprisingly, working on your skill in managing those conversations will help you boost your emotional intelligence. This practice will help you accurately perceive the emotions affecting the other person or the group, enhance your ability to interact with others as you respond to difficult challenges, strengthen your ability to be flexible, and hone the group's ability to act effectively across the boundaries of your organization.

Social Responsibility

Social responsibility is working for the interest of the group even though it might not benefit you personally. It is that ability to demonstrate oneself as a cooperative, contributing and constructive member of one's social group, to act responsibly, even though it benefits others[4-7]. There are many ways to become involved in your community and to expand what you care about in life, beyond your everyday experience[8]. In your professional life, you can mentor someone as a way to give back or "pay it forward." In your personal life you can engage in volunteer activities through social organizations, charities, local schools, or your place of worship. You can become a big brother or a big sister. Some individuals find they are most comfortable getting involved by doing what they do best—their profession. We have worked with many individuals who provide pro-bono services or go on trips like medical mission work to contribute to society[8]. By way of example, Ruben provided pro-bono legal services to a non-profit, Spanish language day care in our home town and sat on their board for years as a way to connect with others in our community through something he cared about.

Whatever you choose, it will be an incredible experience when you engage in a world that is bigger than your own life. If your own life seems miserable and lacking in happiness or emotional intelligence, then you probably need to step away from yourself and your concerns a bit and become involved with helping others in some meaningful way.

Strengthening your EI will do more than improve your quality of life: managers with good emotional intelligence make bringing out the best of those around them look easy[4]. They are good at motivating others and, as Executive Coach, Thomas Hayden writes[14], they

> *"… find common ground for solving conflicts, managing stress levels, and providing needed direction for any team effort. Rather than simply managing a business, group, or team, they create an atmosphere of cohesion and creativity. Leaders with EQ possess an uncanny ability to manage up as well."*

We've talked about emotional intelligence as it relates to you, but you should know that each team builds its own micro-culture: in any team or organization, there are unspoken rules about how much or how little emotions can be acknowledged and explored. Being able to accurately perceive the emotions affecting the group is a fundamental part of team emotional intelligence. After all, many team-based work projects are complex—then ice that cake with the fact that humans are emotional creatures at heart. The many challenges, achievements, frustrations, and disappointments all create very real feelings in team members.

But in the end it all goes back to the individual. To you. And to your *Personal Competence*, which lays the foundation for *Social Competence*. Social competence itself starts with *Social Awareness*. This awareness is crucial for the other aspects of relationship management to develop as clear strengths. Relationship management depends upon skills like empathy, interpersonal relationship skills, and social responsibility. We talked about how to hone and promote these skills. You'll also see that happiness is listed in Figure 6.1. We didn't really talk about this component of emotional intelligence, or its close cousin, well-being. It turns out that happiness and well-being are both part of and outcomes of emotional intelligence[5]. Makes sense when you think about it.

Connecting Emotional Intelligence to Workplace Success

A good way to understand and develop your own emotional intelligence is to reflect on what seems to make the difference for others who are successful and focus on those issues for yourself. In a study of more than 16,000 individuals, five subscale categories of an emotional intelligence assessment (the *EQi*) emerged as significantly related to overall work success[4]. These included self-actualization, optimism, stress tolerance, happiness, and assertiveness. Let's take a look at each.

Why does something so personal as *self-actualization* translate to workplace success? The theory is that when someone realizes their potential and they are leading a rich and meaningful life they have a greater sense of fulfillment at work, too. They work harder, finding that fulfillment and joy in life…and not surprisingly they tend to be more productive. With this *joie de vivre*, they tend to be more pleasant to be around, making teamwork easier and more successful. We think that seems to fit.

At second and third places for workplace success are optimism and stress tolerance, which relate to how you handle challenges and problems. When adversity cannot be avoided, these have to do with how you pull it together to make things work out all right in the end for those concerned. That ability to look at the bright side of the situation and find the good in it and in people sums up optimism. People don't think of the hyper-critical or those "Eeyore's" at work as downers for no reason—it is far more comfortable to work with someone who has a good attitude. And the core of good attitude that is optimism and the ability to tolerate ambiguity and stress gives their owners the resilience to not be deterred by the unexpected bumps along the way. It is these individuals who really understand how to make lemonade out of otherwise disappointing events. Certainly, becoming overwhelmed by adversity does not lead to good outcomes at work, or at home.

You might have been surprised to see happiness on the list of EI factors for workplace success[4]. But it turns out that those who can have fun—enjoy both themselves as well as the others on the team—improve the work performance of everyone, including themselves. Goleman's work addresses this as well[2]—remember when we talked about those "mirror" brain cells earlier in this Step to becoming an *It-Factor* leader?

Well, happy people show their enthusiasm at work—and we know that emotions are contagious; happiness is contagious because of how the brain is wired. Happy people tend to infuse their relationships with more of the same, and for that reason they attract others and build relationships with them. Those who are unhappy and dwell on it, sharing it with colleagues, have the opposite effect. Their work and relationships show it.

And rounding out the top five is assertiveness. This is a bit more complex. According to Bar-On, Stein, and Book[4-6] assertiveness is all about standing up for yourself and your personal rights, not allowing others to trample or take advantage of you, even if some criticize (or threaten) you for it. But one of their secrets to real assertiveness is that you never become the bully yourself or let yourself fall into the trap of being abusive or aggressive—that behavior totally crosses the line. Rather, you maintain a non-destructive manner as you take your stance. Assertiveness includes an ability to express your feelings, beliefs, and thoughts openly, even if that means taking some risks to your comfort zone or to the opinions of others. Why does this have such a powerful impact at work? Assertive individuals create constructive compromise and land the highly valued win-win solution. They can defend their deeply held beliefs, walking that fine line of disagreeing with others and yet avoiding that dead end of emotional sabotage or subterfuge. Those who have mastered assertiveness respect the other person's point of view and work to be sensitive to their needs. Sound like a hard path to actually walk? Well, the most successful people—both at work and at life balance—have figured that one out!

EI and the *It-Factor* Leader

Emotional Intelligence is crucially important to successful leadership *precisely because* so much of a leader's job is grounded in soft skills. As leadership authors Kouzes and Posner wrote over a decade ago—and many experts still endorse—leadership is about creating the culture, shared leadership, inspiring a shared vision, modeling the way, encouraging the heart and fostering adaptive change[15]. These are not command-and-control style leadership approaches. Leadership is a much more delicate dance—and requires much more sophisticated skills. It requires soft skills.

It-Factor leaders work hard on their emotional intelligence and soft skills. They use them to make their own lives more enjoyable, to inspire their teams while they maximize everyone's talents. Research shows that qualities like empathy, interpersonal skills, and social responsibility shown by high performers accounts for 90% of the measured difference between them and the medium performers they pass by in their climb up the ladder[3, 16, 17]. If you want to get ahead you will certainly need emotional intelligence on your side—so maybe taking another course in coding, or budgets, or some other set of technical skills isn't what will really give you the edge on success. Just maybe, taking stock of your happiness, managing stress and taking care of yourself, working on your ability to constructively give voice to your views, and to create a fulfilling life for yourself will give you even more impact. So take a look at appreciating silver linings as the home of unanticipated opportunity and give more weight to the bright side of attitude. Learn about your emotional intelligence and work to further your understanding and skills. After all, it's what those successful *It-Factor* leaders are doing. They, and their organizations, are better off for it.

Your 6th step to becoming a great *It-Factor* leader is to hone your EQ skills. Now let's meet a military leader who puts emotional intelligence to work while deployed on duty.

Meet An *It-Factor* Leader: Simone James

It-Factor leaders count people as their most important assets. They work hard to foster good relationships in their organizational culture and to ensure that people feel committed to the company or team. The military excels at creating strong bonds between people, bonds that help soldiers trust one another with their lives.

We'd like you to meet a military leader we'll call Simone James, but that's not her real name. While she believes strongly in what she does as a leader, she is so humble that she does not want attention drawn to herself. We wanted to tell you her story since she an amazing *It-Factor* leader who has emotional intelligence figured out. Simone is passionate about serving her country. She works in state government in Georgia, but has been a member of the National Guard since she was in her early 30s. At 51, she is a fit, commanding, and to be honest, a quite beautiful woman. The military continues to be a huge part of her life. While she and her husband, Randall, have no children, she is very nurturing and calls all the soldiers she works with "my kids." Indeed, most of them are young enough to be her children.

Her latest mid-east deployment to Iraq came on a 1-hour notice. "I remember my cell phone went off when Randall and I were out to dinner," she laughed, sharing her story with us. "I was shocked. I didn't know the call was coming! I didn't even have time to go home and get my uniform, much less a toothbrush. But I figured, heck, they'll outfit me when I get there. So off we went to the airport (and to the mid-east). I said goodbye to my husband. I didn't see Randall again for a year." This incredible and unexpected change-of-course made her more aware of the extreme disruptions to normal life happening for many guardsmen who were under her command—like her, they had been abruptly taken away from family, job, home, friends, responsibilities—often with little time to prepare emotionally or otherwise.

We talked in-depth about leadership and how personal power outweighs positional power. About how good leaders create an organizational culture that welcomes team members who come from diverse backgrounds, embraces their talents, and is tolerant of their differences. We talked about why leaders need to pay attention to others and identify what they are feeling. We agreed that if a leader is going to be successful when leading through high tension or dangerous situations, then she'd better understand how those feelings are influencing the behavior of her followers.

Like us, Simone James thinks of leaders as more than authority figures: the good ones are caring and creative individuals themselves. Simone firmly believes that great leaders know how to apply emotional intelligence to the leadership choices they make, rather than to blindly follow the letter of a policy. A few months after her arrival in the Mid-East, Simone found herself having to make a quick decision that called upon her wisdom in emotional intelligence. And that's what *It-Factor* leaders often find themselves doing as well.

Simone had been in the Mideast a few months, stationed at a deployment camp from which both United States and Coalition Forces landed and then were moved into strategic positions in the active war zones. This was a place where the future was unpredictable and not surprisingly, emotions ran high. "I hadn't had a shower for three weeks. It was a hot, dirty, and exhausting existence," she told us. She knew the end of yet another 18-hour day would be greeted by her hard, sandy cot. On her way to catch some well-deserved rest, she stopped, listened. She heard weeping. She searched and located a young woman huddled in the dark behind a barricade wall. M16 slung across her back, the soldier's head was down and she was sobbing uncontrollably. Simone felt a motherly pang that might not seem too typical in a commanding officer, and yet was typical for Simone when it came to her soldiers. So, despite being exhausted and near tears herself, she went to the crouching figure.

The young soldier's name was Amy. She'd been in the deployment camp about 24 hours. Less than 36-short hours ago she'd been nursing her new baby girl. They'd taken the girl from her arms when it came time to board her transport. Amy was terrified that she would never see her baby or her husband again. In a minute he had become a single father—coupled with mountains of his own anxiety over the safety of his wife and the mother of his child.

Simone listened to the young soldier's story, drying her tears. Quickly she realized this wasn't the homesickness she saw daily in the eyes of the newly arriving soldiers. This was a medical issue. As a healthcare professional, Simone could diagnose that Amy was engorged from suddenly discontinuing nursing. This incredibly painful condition can lead to mastitis, a serious infection which can actually result in death if untreated. This soldier was in no condition to be sent to the front lines.

Simone took Amy to the Medical Clinic, had the physician on duty check her out, and made sure she had the prescriptions she needed to treat her condition and prevent infection. Then she took her to the psychiatrist's tent to make sure that post-partum depression wasn't a part of this picture, too. Post-partum depression is a serious medical condition that can cause a new mother to do unpredictable and sometimes dangerous acts. It is not the condition you want a soldier carrying an M-16 to have. Amy got the prompt treatment and careful medical attention that she needed.

After the hours of medical assessments, Simone's day was not yet done. She spent a long time talking with Amy back in her tent. She learned where Amy was from, and that she had not talked to her husband since that rainy airport in Mississippi, where she called home.

"Ma'am," Amy said respectfully, "once we are 'boots on the ground' we have no phone access."

Simone realized just how true that was. Transient soldiers do not have such privileges—or such access. If pay phone banks are available for calling card use, the lines are long and the conversations are limited. However, Simone was an officer, and as such *she* had access. She had a phone right there on her desk. That phone would connect her anyplace in the world with just the punch of a few buttons.

"Amy, what's your number back home?" she asked.

Amy shook her head, saying, "Ma'am, I am not allowed to call home on a DSN line."

"But you aren't calling. I am. I need to know that things are OK there. I need to know, so that I can assess that you'll be OK, so I can release you back to your regular duties."

A tear stained Amy nodded, and gave her the number.

After three rings a tired voice answered. "Hello," a man's voice said. A baby was fussing in the background, but not crying.

"Is this Jackson Anderson?"

"Yes, may I ask who this is?" came his polite, yet worried reply. A phone call from an obviously military voice when your spouse is on active duty is not always a calming experience.

"My name is Commander Simone James. I am calling from Kuwait. Amy is fine, in fact she is right here. I am calling to see how you are doing?"

She asked about the baby. She inquired about Jackson. Stunned, he gave her the report—the baby was doing fine. Three poopy diapers since her mother had left. Daddy now wished Amy had let him change more diapers while she was home. She'd wanted do to everything before her deployment, but that meant that he had a steep learning curve to figure out how to do everything since that transport took Amy away.

"I have someone here who would very much like to talk with you," Simone smiled. She handed Amy the phone.

"But Ma`am! I'm not allowed...I'm not allowed to call...I'm..." Amy objected while she looked longingly at the receiver.

"You're not calling. I called. I'm the commanding officer and this is the course of action I deem the best and most appropriate to take at this moment."

Simone left the tent so Amy could have a private conversation with her husband for a few minutes, but she could hear when Amy sang her daughter a lullaby. Little Gracie stopped fussing.

We met Simone a couple of years after this incident and she still got teary-eyed as she told the tale. To us, Simone shared an incredible story of leadership—and of having the judgment to bend the rules when necessary to meet the over-riding needs of a soldier. A true example of *emotionally intelligent* leadership.

"Were you in the right to make the call?" Claudia asked Simone.

"Depends on what you mean by *right*" Simone answered calmly. "Was it regulation? No. I suppose I could get busted for that. But was it the *right call* to make? Yes. Undoubtedly. It was a necessary ingredient for this young woman to successfully make that transition from new mom to soldier. It was the right call to make. Amy had to have some closure, to know they were OK so she'd be OK."

Amy was shipped out the very next day and Simone never knew what happened to her after their brief encounter. She never heard from her again, but for 18 months, the length of Amy's deployment, Simone checked that list of soldiers killed in the war. "I never saw her name on 'the list'."

Simone is a real *It-Factor* leader. While a strict interpretation of the policy might have been the easy answer, it would likely not have been the right course of action. Her leadership made tremendous impact in intangible ways. She is a wonderful example of when real leadership means knowing when to apply emotional intelligence to the rules.

To this day we wish that we, too, could talk with Amy. We want to know that she made it through her stint in Iraq and returned safely home to be a wife to Jackson and a mother to Gracie. We can only imagine that "an army of one" had a whole new meaning for Amy after that experience. That the phrase "no one left behind" was more than a phrase to Amy, as it was more than a phrase to Simone. The army wasn't just the cavalry coming in with firearms brandished. Clearly in that long, dusty night in the Mideast the cavalry came in the guise of a 51-year old woman who had the emotional intelligence to know what a young soldier needed in order to keep herself together before, in the defense of our freedom, she put herself in harm's way.

The Seventh Step:
Engage Your Employees

Engage Your Employees:
Turning Retention Into Commitment

Great *It-Factor* leaders know that mission critical turns into mission accomplished when you have an engaged workforce. Most managers and leaders would say that what they really want out of their teams is high productivity. But employee productivity doesn't happen by luck. It is the result of a carefully planned and implemented strategy that great *It-Factor* leaders and managers thoughtfully consider. They understand that productivity is an outcome with many steps leading to it. They create and nurture the right kind of organizational climate. If you want to truly engage your employees, it is important to understand a bit about what causes people to become dedicated to performance at work. Be prepared for some surprises.

Both for profit and non-profit ventures need to accomplish the mission-critical tasks and outcomes—and do so with few-to-no errors, all while managing costs. If where you work involves a production line then getting high productivity out of your workers will have a lot to do with training for efficiency. But what about leaders whose teams consult with stakeholders to help them improve *their* outcomes or *their* client satisfaction? Or leaders of organizations which target those difficult and elusive measures of health improvement, fields like health care or public health? What about those organizations that produce people and not widgets, like educational institutions? What about innovation-based enterprises, where inter-professional teams work together to discover new technologies, new drugs, or new cures? Or what if you advise others, counseling them on technical matters? Then your path to *mission accomplished* is not all about improving efficiency. You have to work with *people*. Their productivity will depend on their engagement.

High productivity is built upon high job engagement and low job turnover. These, in turn, are more likely to be seen where employees have high satisfaction and high morale. High engagement and morale happen in organizations where individuals understand the mission of the organization, they have a personal connection to that mission, and they are committed to it as well. Of course, all of this rests on the employee having the skills and resources required to actually do the job.

When it comes to leading your team, start at the bottom of the pyramid shown in Figure 7.1. Then think: what are three things that you do to help your team understand the mission? What are three things you do to foster their personal connection to the mission? Work your way up through each of the components, identifying what you do as a leader and what aspects of your organization contribute to the ultimate goal of high productivity. Track your list in Table 7.1. After you take a pass at filling in the blanks, note if there are holes across any of the lines: any aspects of that pyramid to employee engagement and high productivity that you simply don't know how to address? If you have many strategies to focus on *understanding the mission*, for example, but you don't have any to reinforce *keeping turnover low*, then you will still have a problem reaching real engagement and productivity.

Figure 7.1 The Pyramid of High Employee Productivity

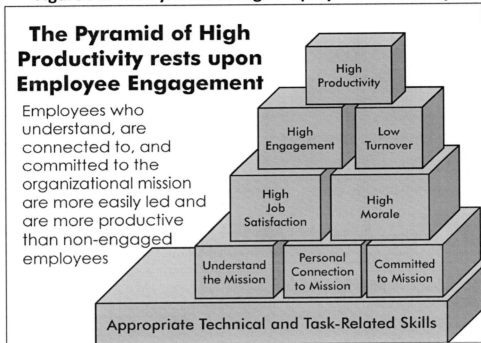

The Pyramid of High Productivity rests upon Employee Engagement

Employees who understand, are connected to, and committed to the organizational mission are more easily led and are more productive than non-engaged employees

High Productivity

High Engagement

Low Turnover

High Job Satisfaction

High Morale

Understand the Mission

Personal Connection to Mission

Committed to Mission

Appropriate Technical and Task-Related Skills

You need to understand what engages the people on your team because the flip side of engagement is employee turnover—if your people aren't engaged, they are more likely to leave your team. That is expensive—in fact losing employees, and then having to find, hire, and train new ones is a financially crushing cost center that plagues many organizations. Turnover slows productivity because new employees have serious learning curves to master all the skills of their new jobs—and they rarely have the organizational memory so crucial for efficiency.

Table 7.1 List strategies you can use to promote high employee productivity all along the pyramid

Target Area	Strategy 1	Strategy 2	Strategy 3
Understand the mission			
Personal connection to the mission			
Commitment to mission			
Promote job satisfaction			
Promote high Employee morale			
Promote high engagement			
Promote low turnover			
Promote high productivity			

Towers Perrin (now Towers Watson), one of the largest management and human resource consulting and administration firms, has recently conducted two major studies of workforce engagement. They showed a strong link between lack of engagement and turnover. In their first major study[1] they found that while only 6% of the highly engaged are out hunting for their dream job, for the moderately engaged that rises to 11%.

What about the disengaged? How many of them are on the hunt? According to Towers Perrin it may be as high as 29%—that's nearly a third and could have a significant impact on your team or enterprise. You might be thinking, "if they are disengaged let them go," but not so fast. Not only are they very costly to replace, they might also be in key positions in your organization! Fortunately for you, you can engage most of your entire team without spending a fortune.

This exploration of workforce engagement was a landmark study and well worth checking out. In all, 40,000 American and Canadian workers took part. The researchers found that they share a very strong work ethic, with 78% of them being personally motivated to help the company succeed by putting in the extra effort to make that happen. More than three-quarters care about the company's future and nearly two-thirds felt it was a good place to work. This study noted a strong sense of "good will" between employees and their companies—this matters because it is the groundwork for future engagement. And of course, engagement is related to productivity. What all this means is that if you value productivity, then you have to value people.

Great *It-Factor* leaders are careful to avoid the trap of confusing employee *satisfaction* with employee *engagement*. They are not the same—and the difference between them shows up in which of your top talent will stay with your team. The Walker Loyalty Report[2] indicated that satisfied employees are not the same as engaged employees. Satisfied employees might talk about company commitment, but even though 80% of them report liking their duties and activities, the Walker Report showed that they would leave your organization tomorrow if someone else offered them better salary or benefits.

The Walker Loyalty Report classifies workers into four categories: loyal—who have a personal attachment to your organization—they identify with the organization and how they are a part of it. Leaders appreciate having these kinds of team members to work with! Accessible—these individuals go the extra mile but intend to leave. This group can contain some of your star performers as well. These two categories are strong contributors to the organizations of today—but they aren't the majority. The Walker Report found that 60%—that's more than *half* of employees—fall into the last two categories: trapped, that is, those who want to move on but feel they can't; and high risk: these individuals are just waiting for the right door to open. This data was collected prior to the great recession that started in 2008. After that time, the US experienced unemployment between 8-11%, with heavy layoffs in many sectors but particularly in housing, manufacturing, and state and federal jobs. Leaders should ponder the engagement level of those team members who remain—are they loyal to the organization, identifying with the mission and vision of the enterprise? Or are they biding their time and keeping their heads down until new opportunities emerge? What if those on your team feel trapped because they feel they have nowhere else to go? Why are they really there? There is a difference in performance between those who are engaged and loyal and those who are scared of losing a job.

Let's think first about those top performers. Leaders need and should want team members who are truly loyal—since loyalty is priceless. Priceless because it leads to extra effort towards achieving their best at work. When the Walker researchers examined the loyal group, they found that 95% said they go "above and beyond the call of duty." But not everyone feels that way. When they looked at those who lacked loyalty, only 62% said they would do likewise. Keeping these loyal employees just that—loyal—is key.

Since you can't rely on employee satisfaction to help keep your high performers, what can you rely on? Employee engagement becomes a critical factor in retaining your key workforce and talent.

According to the Towers Perrin report 17% of employees are "highly engaged," falling at one end of the spectrum, while 19% of their colleagues fell at the far end of the continuum, in the disengaged category. The majority of employees, a full 64%, are moderately engaged. What does this mean? Well, "the fact that nearly one out of five employees may be 'marking time' should concern any manager" or leader[3]. This is not just "too bad." This is expensive! A Gallup study estimated that lower productivity of actively disengaged employees cost the US economy about $382 billion dollars annually[4].

We doubt you'll be surprised to learn that the non-profit sector wins when it comes to employee engagement—a whopping 42% fell into the highly engaged category, far more than their industry-based peers[1]. What does the non-profit sector have that makes it so special? Why do team members in non-profits perform with so much more engagement at work than the rest of the economy? The key seems to be a link between their sense of personal passion and the organizational mission. Remember that people *choose* to work in the non-profit environment, often electing a smaller paycheck than they would receive working in the for-profit sector. Before you dismiss this as the do-gooder economy, there are lessons to learn for *any* workforce. The first take home message: a personal connection to work is fundamental to building employee engagement.

Let's talk about those folks at the low end of the engagement spectrum. How do you work with them and promote their engagement? The challenge here is to identify the disengaged on your team and determine how to re-engage them. You might recall some of what we talked about in our Fourth Step to becoming a great *It-Factor* leader, which addressed understanding human motivation, as you think of employee engagement as well. If you want to re-engage someone then you need to understand how they see their world. Typically, disengaged employees feel their contributions are being overlooked, they concentrate on tasks rather than outcomes, and because of that, quite often you'll find that they want to be told what to do. They don't feel they "own" the job they do. All too often, disengaged employees don't have productive relationships with their managers or with their coworkers. Figure 7.2 illustrates what's often happening in the head of the disengaged employee.

Figure 7.2 Common thoughts of the disengaged employee

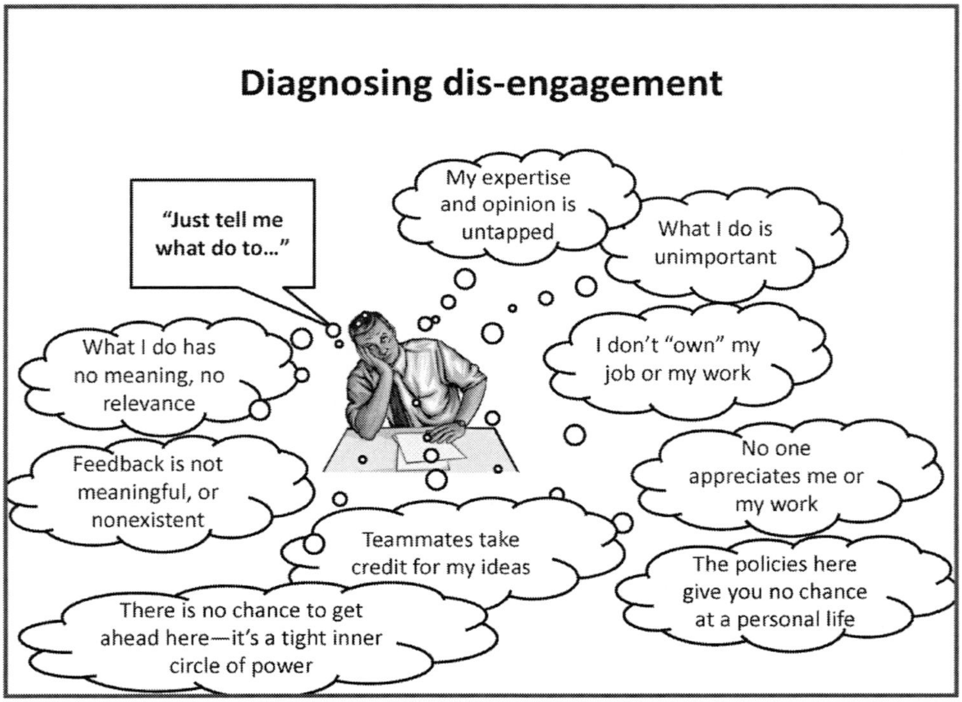

So what do you do when you're the team leader? Should you just give a disengaged employee a list of tasks to do? While in some cases, that might be the right course of action, there is some debate about whether simply providing tasks reinforces those non-engaged behaviors, which is the opposite of the true goal. The real job is to get them on the proverbial bus, to understand the mission, be connected to that mission, and committed to it as well.

In reality, people become disenchanted at work for many reasons, some are personal while others are related to the organizational culture or values. For example, if your organization doesn't have flex time, then don't be surprised if a great deal of your workforce between the ages of 25-50 chafe at those restrictions. There is a growing body of evidence to show that flexible policies, including flex time and job sharing, allow your employees to meet the other demands in their lives from children or aging parents. And what do they give their organizations in return? Greater loyalty, greater productivity, and greater engagement[5].

As the leader it is your job to set and enforce the organizational culture. So if you have disengaged employees then take a look at your enterprise and make an inventory of what the contributing factors might be. Some of them will belong to the individual, but you will be surprised at how many belong to the system itself. W. Edwards Demming taught us that 85% of the problems that crop up lie with the system itself and not with individuals[6]. As the leader you can't control individuals. But the system, well that is your job. Your job is to create the system—that's the policies, the culture, the processes. That is the most important job of leadership.

Let's focus on that critical spot in the middle of the continuum, that whopping 64% who are moderately engaged. How do you move them up into the highly engaged realm and keep them there? If you do nothing, leave them and well enough alone, then you risk having them slide into disengagement, which can impact your organization's performance, bottom line, and turnover. Lucky for you the vast majority of your team is just waiting for an *It-Factor* leader to come along with the right steps to launch them to full engagement. When employees make the shift up to high engagement, they are nearly twice as likely to want to stay with their job and give the extra effort required to get the job done, and done well.

If you are a leader or a manager and you aren't actively nurturing your engaged employees, then you are missing the boat. Engaged team members produce more and contribute to good working environments where people are productive, ethical, and accountable. In the corporate world they make more money for the company and create emotional engagement and loyal customers. They stay with the organization longer and are more committed to quality and growth than are *not-engaged* and *actively disengaged* workers—who tend to leave organizations more frequently.

How do those engaged employees manage to do all this? The secret is that they tend to build strong relationships with others, including their managers, and they work to have clear communications with everyone above and below them, as well as with lateral teammates. Your highly engaged employees are focused on a clear path based on their strengths, and they work with others who have different assets to bring to the table. They can take risks and make that stretch to excellence because these strong relationships serve as a solid foundation for them to work from. Don't leave these excellent employees alone! For best results, spend most of your time with the most productive and talented people because they have the most potential[7].

Building Engagement on your Team

Let's take a look at some of the things you can do to build engagement on your team. Cultivating good relationships with your motivated employees is key to strengthening their foundation of engagement. But just having a relationship is not enough: you still have to communicate your expectations and metrics on a regular basis. Try reframing the language you use, and instead of focusing on tasks, focus on the goals and outcomes that the tasks accomplish. Here are some good questions to ask of your team members:

- *What are the outcomes you are supposed to achieve?*
- *What were you hired to do?*
- *How do you contribute to making this a great place to work?*
- *What are your metrics around goal achievement?*
- *How are you sharing your learning with others?*
- *How has the team celebrated its success at achieving goals?*

Focus your disengaged employees on outcomes as well as the steps it takes to get to that result. Focus them on goal achievement. Using m*easurement* is crucial to an employee's feeling of success, as long as what you are measuring is outcome-oriented. This helps people have a sense of control and investment in their work. Make sure they understand where their part of the puzzle impacts the whole—so they can see the importance of their work.

Building Good Relationships with Employees

We'll focus a bit more on this idea of building good relationships with employees. One of many steps you should take in this area is to sincerely and authentically thank all the members of your team who make achieving the goal possible—and in most organizations, that is pretty much everyone. Occasionally we coach a manager who says, "Why should I thank them? I pay them! They get a paycheck for their work!" This is a very unenlightened and egocentric view. Yes, workers get paid. But talented employees who produce the best results can work for anyone—why should they work for an organization that doesn't appreciate them? Remember our discussion about human motivation? Appreciation rings high with most talented folks in the workforce. When you create a culture of "money equals success" and measure people by dollars, you will easily lose your best and brightest to the highest bidder. Unenlightened leadership does the opposite of employee engagement. You learned about the unenlightened leader in our First Step to becoming an *It-Factor* leader. Be an *It-Factor* leader. Don't let yourself be the unenlightened leader.

Have you ever wondered what brings all those talented team mates to your enterprise? The Walker Loyalty Report[2] looked at why people come to an organization—and why they stay. If your first thought is MONEY, well, you'd be right, but that's only a part of the story. According to the Report, the factors that *attract, retain,* and *engage* employees can be divided into four categories: 1) *Pay,* 2) *Benefits,* 3) *Learning & Development*, and 4) *Work Environment.*

Remember we have four categories to think about when it comes to why people take a job in your organization and why they stay there. Of *Pay, Benefits, Learning & Development,* and the *Work Environment* people actually take a job with an organization based on competitive benefits, pay, and "work-life balance" (Table 7.2). These are the important factors—and that may not surprise you. If you think work-life balance is for sissies, think again—without offering this factor you could be losing both valuable diversity as well as top talent[5].

Now let us move onto the next step: you've got the team, but why do they stay with you? (Your HR manager calls this employee retention). The answer: they want to have someplace to go in their careers, which means that people want to be successful. They want to work with other colleagues whom they respect, and they want an overall work environment that is conducive to working together well. It is the leader's job to create and nurture that work environment. When it comes to retention, way down the list at #6 is salary and benefits. Money is just not the reason your best and brightest will stay with you and it's not the primary reason they will leave you either. They will leave you because they become disengaged.

Table 7.2 Attracting vs. retaining employees[2]

What Brings People to Your Organization	
Attracting Employees	**Employee Retention**
1. Competitive benefits	1. Career advancement opportunities
2. Competitive base pay	2. Retention of high caliber people
3. Work/life balance issues	3. Overall work environment
4. Competitive retirement benefits	4. Development of skills
5. Career advancement opportunities	5. Resources to get the job done
	6. Salary and benefits

And remember that disengagement is *not* usually the fault of the employee—it's usually due to the leader or the system the leader has created. When people leave a job they usually leave a person.[8-10]

Now let's look at the data about what *engages* your employees (Table 7.3). You might be surprised that *Pay* and *Benefits* don't even make the top ten! All the top factors fall into the categories of *Work Environment* and *Learning & Development*. The most important factor for employee engagement is *senior management's interest in the employee's well-being*. Think about that. That means *your* interest in their well-being is the number one factor influencing whether they give their work their all—or their second best. As a leader, if you give your employees *your* second best then you'll get that or worse from them. You also need to think about providing them with *challenging work* and *decision-making authority*, since these rank 2nd and 3rd. Customers matter to the engaged employee, so make sure that the *customer orientation* of your enterprise is clear and communicated. Of course, having *career advancement opportunities* is important, as is *company reputation*. Remember that engaged employees have good relationships with others, so *collaboration with co-workers* ranks high on this list. They are focused on achieving objectives, so having the *resources to get the job done* and *input into decision making* are vital for them. Notice that 10th on this list is *senior management vision*—it's still important, but it won't replace the nine elements that come before it.

Table 7.3 The top 10 for employee engagement[2]

Factors that Engage Your Employees
1. Senior management's interest in the employee's well being
2. Having challenging work
3. Having decision making authority
4. Customer orientation
5. Career advancement opportunities
6. Company reputation
7. Collaboration with co-workers
8. Resources to get the job done
9. Input into decision making
10. Senior management's vision

Along with (and even before) the great recession beginning in 2008, what people were looking for in a work environment started to change. Sadly, the many shocking revelations of corruption and deceit in corporate America, such as the economy-rocking scandals of ENRON and Arthur Anderson in 2001, followed shortly thereafter by the deplorable Wall Street greed that precipitated the mortgage-backed securities debacle later in that decade led the start of a sea change in work-place values. Towers Watson updated that employee engagement survey in 2011—finding that in addition to the big three "engagers" at work (good leadership, learning, empowerment), engagement was now also driven by corporate social responsibility[11, 12]. Yes, it finally happened. No one wanted to work for the bad guys anymore. People really did want that personal connection to work and to know that what they did, and who they did it for, mattered just a little bit more than what could be measured in a paycheck.

An update of the Walker research[13] indicated that what the employee thinks of you, their leader, is crucially important. In the later Walker Loyalty Study researchers found that 91% of those who are truly loyal believe the organization is highly ethical—and 89% feel positive about the leader's integrity. But take a moment to consider what they found out about high risk employees—*they* don't feel the values of their organizations are in the right place and about two-thirds of them feel the ethics and integrity are missing or misplaced. If you or your enterprise fall into that category, then look for those "best and brightest" ethics-embracing teammates to be poached by another enterprise that has the ethical intangibles to offer.

We have a particular interest in health care. Claudia is a registered dietitian and both she and Ruben have worked for many years in public health environments, so we are always looking for what this corporate research means for the healthcare sector. A recent study by Tower's Watson[11, 12] found that leadership matters a lot to the healthcare workforce. They are looking for their leaders to be trustworthy, care about others well-being, be focused on patient satisfaction, encourage development of people's talents, be highly visible, and they want to know they are managing the books, not cooking them. Integrity matters all the down the line. It might not have mattered enough a decade ago, but it matters now. *It-Factor* leaders understand these principles.

This values-centered leadership showed up in another, later research work examining how to land and engage top *leadership*. Interestingly this engagement literature applies not only to those who work *for* you but to those who work *above* you—and to *you* as well. Good leaders want to engage employees throughout the organization—and that applies to your top talent too. In this study, 8000 senior executives and those in the pipeline right behind them were asked about what drove their engagement in their global organizations[5]. Their top six reasons are listed in table 7.4—but we want you to know that women in particular valued the top three—much more so than their male counterparts.

Table 7.4 Drivers of engagement in a global economy[5]

- Having a challenging job
- A supportive work environment
- Good fit between life on and off the job
- Opportunity for high achievement
- Being well compensated
- Working at a company with high values

So, if you want to engage both women and men on your team, and to promote diversity at the top echelons of your enterprise, then there are some zero-cost ways to do so.   Offering flexible schedules and a supportive work environment will go far to lower your bottom line when it comes to the retention of your most valuable women leaders. These actions will appeal to a great number of your male leaders as well. Since turnover is one of the most expensive cost factors to an organization— keeping the best talent engaged and part of the team is a smart strategy for any savvy enterprise.

Leaders with that *It-Factor* focus on engaging employees. While pay and benefits will help you recruit the top talent, so will having an organization where people want to work. Your top talent is much more likely to stay with you if your policies and the relationships at work engage them, even if a competitor tries to woo them away with more money.

So, know your team. Be interested in their well-being. Support their learning and development. Make sure your organization has good supervision and that team leaders provide meaningful and timely feedback. Implement effective performance management strategies. Most importantly, clearly tell your team—and tell them often—how what they do leads to results that really matter!

The data on employee engagement is great news for leaders in the public or non-profit sectors, where great performance cannot be financially rewarded as it is in the private sector. While people may take a job for the money—it's not why they stay and it's not why they give their absolute best to the team regardless of whether they are in the private, public, or non-profit world. As a leader there is much you can do to create a team of highly engaged employees who boost the productivity of your enterprise.

Your 7th step to becoming a great *It-Factor* leader is to engage your team.

The Eighth Step:
Build A Culture Of
Conversation

Build a Culture of Conversation:
Multiplying Options Through Effective Communication

One thing we've learned about leaders with that *It-Factor* is that they get people talking. They get ideas on the table—all the ideas, not just their own ideas or only those from the most talkative folks.

Ever run a meeting where some members dominated the entire conversation? And some members didn't participate at all? When the meeting is dismissed, did you wonder if all the ideas were really put on the table? You may not want to admit that it happens to you, but know that you are not alone. Interestingly, when we coach and teach on this topic, all too many leaders snub this crucial leadership skill, as though it were a freshman error. The more senior the leaders are, the more likely they are to overlook the fundamental importance of creating a culture of conversation. We give leaders a "pop quiz" and in teams have them come up with as many of these strategies as they can to create this kind of team environment. How many strategies do you think they can muster? Typical is five. The record we've seen is an entire room of 30 leaders (6 teams) coming up with 14-15 different strategies—with the participants nodding and furiously taking notes as they hear their colleagues' new ways to fully harvest ideas from the great minds they work with back at home. Getting people to share their ideas, perspective, information, and thoughts is vital—and *It-Factor* leaders know how to do it.

How can you get the most out of the great minds on your team? Creating a culture of communication where dialogue fosters ideas, promotes the sharing of information, and supports creativity can be a significant challenge. All too often, individual members can either dominate or avoid the dialogue. This unbalanced contribution to the discussion narrows the field of ideas and options being generated, limiting thought diversity, and stifling creativity and innovation[1]. These are high prices for you to pay for a simple lack of a communication-supporting climate in an organization. However, there are positive steps you can take to foster an organizational culture that supports more varied and efficient discussions. Our Eighth Step to becoming a great *It-Factor* leader gives you 21 strategies you can use to get the players in your meetings well down that road of sharing ideas. These tools will help you create a culture of conversation on your team. You may not need to use all of them, but some of them will certainly be helpful.

When some members dominate the discussion and some seemingly avoid it, here's what's going on that you need to know. To understand, we need to go back almost a century ago, to a psychologist named Carl Jung. He came up with the idea that people have a set of behaviors that they pretty much stick with for the most of their lives—he called his theory Psychological Type,[2] which is the foundation for the popular Myers Briggs Type Indicator, often simply referred to as the MBTI,[3, 4] and is widely available today. Psychological Type Theory gives an explanation for those marked differences in how we interact with others—attributed to innate preferences for either Extraversion or Introversion, with individuals commonly referred to as "extraverts" and "introverts." In Jung's view, "extraverts" become engaged when they have others with whom to share ideas. They tend to be expressive, demonstrative, share personal information about themselves, and often engage in an activity called *external processing*, wherein they come to understand how they think or feel by hearing themselves talk about it. Typically extraverts enjoy groups and they tend to join committees, gatherings, or social events easily and with comfort. They generally like to come to an understanding of meaning through dialogue. In discussion and conversation they tend to cover a breadth of ideas. In team meetings this exuberance can translate into dominating the conversation, perhaps unwittingly, via frequent contributions or jumping on or finishing the thoughts of team members[3-5]. In the US population, recent data indicate that 45-53% of the population identify as extraverts. When broken down by gender, 45-55% of women and 45-50% of men fall into this category[6].

Introverts, on the other hand, function quite oppositely of their extraverted counterparts. Rather than engage in that external processing mentioned above, they tend to enjoy quiet reflection on ideas, coming to greater understanding through contemplating their thoughts. Sharing the ideas can be distracting until they have had sufficient time to consider and refine those ideas. Introverts are more likely to be seen as calm individuals who like to connect with others in small, intimate groups in settings conducive to focused discussion. They lean towards covering ideas in depth. They tend to have a higher threshold of privacy than do their extraverted counterparts and might be described as harder to know or a private kind of person. In team meetings this reflective stance can seem like disengagement or lack of dominance[3-5]. In the US population, recent data indicate that 47-55% of the population identify as introverts.

When broken down by gender, 45-55% of women and 50-55% of men fall into this category[6].

Since we are both certified in the MBTI and use it ourselves, we are, perhaps understandably, whole-heartedly in support of you finding out your Myers Briggs Type by taking the 15-minute assessment and meeting with a certified counselor (or better yet through experiencing a group-based debrief, whereby you will get to see many types in action). However, we realize this may be the first time you've ever given serious consideration to the problems your organization is facing because the leadership doesn't know how to create that vital culture of conversation. Until now, you might not have thought about how a group of introverts and extraverts can mix poorly, effectively creating a culture of abdicators" and "dominators" if the leadership isn't there to do its job. After all, heralded expert Edward Schein notes the leadership and organizational culture are two sides of the same coin. Leaders set culture. That's a huge part of their job[7].

To help you get a clearer grasp on this concept of how personality factors can really influence both you and the culture of your team or organization, Table 8.1 provides an "at a glance" type of assessment to help you figure out which side of the introvert/extravert poles you stand on—and how far out (or close to the middle) you might be. In no way is this a replacement for a true MBTI, which is well worth the money and the time for the assessment, but it might help you make sense of what you are seeing in your team meetings and it might help you get some sense of yourself.

To use table 8.1, simply circle the statement that you feel fits you best on each row. Add up the number of circled statements in each column in the area at the bottom of each column. The larger the difference between the two totals, the more of a preference for Introversion or Extraversion you probably have.

Table 8.1: Quick Introversion-Extraversion Assessment

For each line in the chart, circle the statement that you feel fits you best:

	OPTION A		OPTION B
1	If I'm working on a project but then hear others talking about something relevant to me, I'm likely to join them to see what's up	OR	If I'm working on a project but then hear others talking about something relevant to me, I'm likely to shut my door so I can focus
2	Interacting with others energizes me and gives me ideas	OR	I am energized by working on ideas by myself in a focused way
3	I am undaunted interacting with a lot of people at a time	OR	I find I need to take a deep breath before interacting with a lot of people at a time
4	I tend to act quickly...maybe at times too quickly	OR	I tend to reflect a lot before I act...sometimes delaying acting more than I'd like or should
5	I am easy to get to know	OR	I am a private person
6	I can sometimes say too much about myself or the situation	OR	I can sometimes say too little about myself or the situation
7	I really appreciate interacting with others—it makes ideas better	OR	I really appreciate quiet reflection—it makes ideas better
8	I don't mean to interrupt people but sometimes I jump in with ideas	OR	I am careful to wait until others finish what they have to say
9	I feel I get my point made in meetings and discussions	OR	I feel it's hard to break into a conversation or meeting to make my point
10	When I share my thoughts, I find that I correct or refine what I'm saying as I'm saying it	OR	I prefer to share my thoughts only when they are fully formulated
	NUMBER CIRCLED IN THIS COLUMN:		**NUMBER CIRCLED IN THIS COLUMN:**

Where do you have the most checks? Is there a side you fall further out towards? Or maybe very far out on? It is good for you to understand yourself—and also how you are the same as, and different from, other people. Once you understand if you have a strong preference (or not) for introversion or extraversion, you can be aware of your behavior that may be a result of those preferences. Once you are aware of your behavior, you can change it when it is advantageous to do so.

Now let's work on some strategies that you can use to get people talking—and listening—no matter if they are clearly introverts or extraverts or somewhere in between.

Strategies for Creating a Culture of Conversation:

1. Send an Agenda in Advance

Have you ever had to go to a meeting where you had no idea what the topic was until you got there? You had no way to prepare in case you were asked to share your ideas, data, or your perspective? Many people are unnerved by this bad habit of the leadership team, feeling that going into a meeting blind is tantamount to walking into an ambush. There are some folks who are not at all bothered by the surprise agenda, and they are more likely to fall into that extraverted category. Even if the surprise agenda doesn't bother you, don't make this mistake. Your #1 take away is to not be an ambush leader. Instead provide an agenda in advance. Letting everyone know what to expect in advance of the meeting is particularly important to introverted types, who typically do *not* appreciate being surprised with an agenda upon entering the room. Introverts typically like to think about the topics ahead of time and are more likely to contribute ideas if they have had the opportunity to reflect on their ideas in advance. So do what an *It-Factor* leader does and let everyone know in good time what to expect from your upcoming session. Send an agenda in advance of the meeting.

2. Open the Agenda

Another way to get greater participation in the sharing of perspectives, ideas, data, and information is to open your agenda. Send it around ahead of time and allow team members to add items to it. You may not know everything that is important to talk about, so this strategy may enlighten you in some important ways. Some leaders fear this technique because they are afraid a topic will come up that they aren't able to address. Here you have a couple of options. First, consider whether this could be one of the times to put the work back on the team—perhaps you shouldn't be providing all the answers. Perhaps the team can do a better job of this than you alone. Let them put the item on the agenda and let them solve the issue as well. Remember how in our Seventh Step about employee engagement, the #3 reason for people to be engaged at work was decision-making ability? And the #2 reason was having challenging work? Rather than resulting in an out-of-control free-for-all, when you open the agenda and drive down decision making you are likely to end up with creative ideas being generated by an empowered team. So, we said you had a couple of options if something shows up on the agenda that you aren't able to address—the second option is to talk about it—privately. If an agenda item comes up that can't be discussed for legal reasons, or it's a personnel or other information-embargo issue, simply explain to the team member who suggested it why it can't be addressed in a general session and, if you can, give them some indication of when things might change.

3. Step Up/Step Back

Great leaders help the members of their teams balance their contributions to the meetings. A great tool for this is called *step up/step back*. When you use it, you start by getting your team to agree to a common value around allowing everyone to be heard. The *step up/step back* idea is that each team member works to be aware of themselves and their participation, stepping into the conversation and contributing their ideas and perspective. But they also work on being aware of themselves and their participation so that they *step back out* in order for others to contribute, too.   When groups agree to the principle, and particularly when they define it for themselves, the team leader only need remind the group of their shared value around "step up/step back" at the start of a meeting. It is also helpful to remind the group of that value when one or two members are carrying the conversation and excluding others.

4. Reflect Then Talk

Great leaders know that some members of the team really need to think about a topic before they are comfortable sharing their ideas, thoughts or perspectives with others, particularly publically. So *It-Factor* leaders have team members reflect individually before they start to talk.

You can promote getting ideas on the table by giving team members time to reflect individually for a few minutes prior to diving into a discussion. In particular, this will help those with a preference for introversion come to clearer ideas as they can consider and reflect without interruption. If given time to reflect, extraverts can organize their thoughts so they spend less time in external processing with the group. Provide small notepads, index cards, or sticky notes and pens and instruct members to write down 3-5 ideas prior to you opening the floor for discussion. The introverts on your team will feel more prepared to engage in conversation, and the extraverts will benefit by being able to communicate more efficiently.

5. Engage in Small Groups Before Opening an Entire Group Discussion

Leaders who harvest the most ideas get the work going in small groups first, before opening the floor for discussion in the big group. They know that introverts work best in smaller groups that allow for more equal participation among members. When you divide a larger group into smaller teams with 3-6 members, that structure will allow for a greater variety of ideas to be generated and discussed. Then have the small groups reconvene into the larger one. Start the large group discussion by having each small group share their ideas before the larger group as a whole addresses the issues.

6. Harvest Ideas One at a Time

When you have your team break down into smaller units to generate ideas or concerns, you will eventually need to bring everyone back together to generate the collective thoughts of the whole. Avoid if you can the situation where the first group shares every idea they generated. It is best to let them share one, maybe two, and move on to the next group, going around the room again and again until all the ideas have been offered. Ask the teams to share items that have not yet been mentioned, so that you don't spend time hearing repeats, since most groups will come up with some overlap of ideas. If you let each group share their entire list of ideas, all items will probably be on the table by the time you reach the third group, and you've just inadvertently created dominant groups. Those who don't get to share any of their ideas are likely to feel rather unvalued and unheard. They are less likely to contribute to the discussion next time. So create a culture of conversation by making sure that everyone is heard through harvesting just one idea at a time from subgroups or individuals.

7. Be Comfortable With Pauses

One of Ruben's favorite lessons to teach leaders is how people experience time differently. Routinely we find that talented leaders make the classic error of assuming that everyone experiences time in the same way, the way that they do. When you are leading the group, you need to allow for pauses, at times for 15 or 20 seconds. This can seem a bit strange to an extraverted person, but think about it: a more introverted team member who has been repeatedly cut off by their more verbal peers might be reluctant to venture forth with an idea until they are certain they will be able to speak without interruption. After all, if they have been verbally clobbered time and time again, why would they now try to share what they know or see? It's going to take a pause long enough to make them feel comfortable that they really will be able to share their idea, perspective, information, or material in order to get them to do just that. Leaders need to cultivate comfort with pauses in order to introduce this space into the conversation. Face it, if you aren't comfortable with pauses, then your team won't be either.

8. Invite Participation Into the Discussion

Great *It-Factor* leaders know that sometimes you have to actively draw people into the dialogue. You can invite your quiet team members to contribute. However, this strategy requires a bit more finesse from the team leader, because in essence inviting someone into the discussion who has not participated is calling on them. Done poorly, this can create an uncomfortable situation for the individual and will have a negative effect on the culture of communication. However, by choosing words carefully a leader can promote more equal participation. Particularly after paying close attention to body language, you might say something like, *"Pat, I notice that you haven't had a chance yet to jump in—is there something that you would like to add or that you think needs to be put on the table about this issue?"* This allows the individual the opportunity to contribute or to acknowledge that the vital issues are already being discussed.

9. Round Robin at Strategic Points in the Discussion

It-Factor leaders also know that sometimes you have to use a forced opportunity to get folks to jump in. Therefore, another useful strategy leaders implement is to go around the group at strategic points during the discussion, asking:

> *At this point, I'd like to go around the room and check in with each of you. If there is a point that needs to be on the table that is not, this is the opportunity. I would also remind us all of our value to 'step up/step back', so if you have contributed a lot to the conversation already, please feel free to 'ditto' previous*

comments or 'pass'. If you haven't contributed yet, we'd like to hear from you.

When you give each person a chance to engage in the discussion with no interruptions, you will create a venue where more team members feel they really can participate and contribute ideas or concerns. You can also see here how you can layer these strategies, as in the example of combining the round robin with step up-step back.

10. Pay Attention to Body Language to Draw Participants In

It-Factor leaders know that people say as much without words as they do with them—sometimes even more. Often those who are not participating in the conversation will send non-verbal signals of their interest in the topic. Look for eye contact, facial expressions, or leaning forward. One of your strongest cues that someone wants to say something is that sharp but quiet intake of breath, as if to speak, but then not speaking. You can use these signals to identify those who might wish to be invited into the discussion, as in strategy #8, above.

11. Use Body Language to Your Advantage

Body language can also be an effective tool to help someone conclude their contribution when they are over participating or getting off topic. This works best if the team leader is standing, such as taking flip chart notes, facilitating, or leading the discussion. Moving closer to the participant, particularly while making eye contact, will nearly always cause them to stop talking. The closer you get to their "personal space" the more likely they will conclude their comments.   If absolutely necessary, a light hand placed on the shoulder with a polite "thank you for contributing that" and then redirecting the conversation back to the topic can be helpful to moving the conversation back to within appropriate boundaries. If you have a team member who struggles with "wrapping it up" and tends to over-participate, then structure your meeting so that you will be free to move about the room, such as by volunteering to facilitate and keep track of points on the whiteboard. That way you'll have the flexibility to use this tool, should the need arise.

12. The Talking Stick

When group discussion is derailed by one or a few members who continually fail to allow others into the discussion, leaders can "make the invisible visible" by using an ancient Native American technique called "the talking stick." This has been described as follows:

> *"The talking stick was commonly used in council circles to designate who had the right to speak. When matters of great concern came before the council, the leading elder would hold the talking stick and begin the discussion. When he finished what he had to say he would hold out the talking stick, and whoever wished to speak after him would take it. In this manner the stick was passed from one individual to another until all who wished to speak had done so. The stick was then passed back to the leading elder for safe keeping."[8]*

Usually this technique is utilized when other strategies to create a culture of step up/step back have not been as effective as needed, often because individuals are blind to their own verbal dominance. You can introduce this technique by telling the story of the talking stick followed by a discussion of how the group has struggled with creating the environment to garner equal participation. This technique helps the members visualize the amount of time each member spends contributing. You don't have to use a stick—use a squishable ball, plush mascot, etc. Anything soft and toss-able should do the trick. After a few meetings the technique can be phased out as team members gain skills at allowing others to speak and in respectfully listening to what they have to say.

13. Allow for People to Contact You After the Meeting with Their Ideas

It-Factor leaders make sure there are multiple ways to get ideas on the table. If your introverted team members are frequently cut off or interrupted by others, they may not feel comfortable fighting their way to be heard by the group. We've worked with one leader who said "the hallway meetings after the meetings are just attempts to sabotage the process!" He was irate that the business of the meeting would spill over into the hallway after the session had adjourned. If this happens with your meetings and you feel similar to this leader, then we would like reframe this for you. If people who did not contribute during the meeting are then talking about the topics afterwards, perhaps you (as the leader) haven't created a safe enough venue for them to share their ideas? In our experience (and we'll talk about this more in the Eleventh Step towards becoming a great *It-Factor* leader when we get to "don't shirk the tough talk"), maybe 5% of people (those true bad apples you want off your team bench) are really out to joyously sabotage the process simply for the disruption they cause or the power they believe it brings them. So that leaves 95% of everyone else who are trying to be heard—but the only place they feel they *can* be heard is in the hallway. That's not sabotage: that's the fault of leadership for not creating a culture of conversation where people can actually be a part of it all.

Another thing to watch out for is that when groups have a strong desire to achieve closure they actually can make a rush to judgment, leading to decisions before important matters have been fully investigated or discussed. One way to avoid this outcome is to ask for further insights or ideas outside the confines of the meeting but within a specified time period. Inviting members to submit their ideas via other venues, such as phone, voice mail, email, or in person can help the leader learn more and consider a broader viewpoint than emerges in the convened meeting. That way, if a team member feels shut out of the discussion they still have a way to contribute their ideas and be heard.

14. Use Social Media

Technology today can be a huge boon to the leader who is trying to get great participation from a diverse group of team members. If you have ever been part of a webinar then you are familiar with seeing everyone (virtually) attending the meeting. One person can serve as the speaker, sharing data or slides with everyone in the session. When you adopt this technology, everyone else can vote, give thumbs up or thumbs down, they can applaud (silently, virtually, by using an icon), and they can send a written message to anyone or everyone in the room. Participants can raise their virtual hands, letting the speaker know they want to be called upon. All of this without ever speaking a word. So think about using this technology at your next meeting. Set up a webinar and have everyone bring those ubiquitous laptops and tablets that they are going to bring anyway. Whoever is the speaker can deliver their information and you can create multiple streams of information, contributions, and feedback—multiple ways for people to participate and be heard.

15. Use Open-Ended Listening

All too often when people look like they are listening to one another, in reality what they are doing is formulating how they are going to prove to the other person why they are wrong. They really aren't listening at all. If you want to create a culture of conversation, then you need to *listen with the intensity usually reserved for speaking*[9]. Stop thinking about the conversation like a debate and think about it as communication: hear the message. Practice this yourself. Model it for others. Teach it to the team as a cultural value. More on this when we get to the Eleventh Step towards becoming a great *It-Factor* leader.

16. Don't Shoot Down Ideas

A great way to kill the conversation and stop ideas from getting out on the table is to allow killer statements that shoot down the suggestions or perspectives offered. Once someone feels their idea has been ridiculed or rudely dismissed, don't expect them to offer up another one. And that will also be true for many who witnessed the rough treatment of their colleague's participation. But here's a strategy you can use that is a great help to ending those killer statements. It's called the POINT process, and it was refined by Dr. Gerrard Puccio[10], who studies innovation. This technique was initially introduced in the early 1980s by Diane Foucar-Szocki, Bill Shephard, and Roger Firestien, and called Praise First[11]. We talked about this process in-depth in the Fifth Step to becoming a great *It-Factor* leader (P: Plusses; O: Opportunities; I: Issues; NT: New Thinking), so we won't go over it again here, but we do recommend that you re-read POINT and use it in your groups.

17. Control the Amount of Air Time People Get: Pay to Say

This is an interesting strategy if you have team members in a small group of 20 or fewer—give everyone 5 poker chips, which they have to throw into the center pile every time they want to speak. They have to "pay to say." This can be an astonishing experience for those who speak all the time but are unaware of their behaviors—they will quickly run out of chips and then they will have to just listen to the others. In our experience, this is also a tremendous experience for those who generally won't fight to be heard—now they have guaranteed air time and often find an unaccustomed sense of power and empowerment when they are holding all the remaining chips and know that at last they, too, will be heard.

One thing that is important to understand about creating this culture of conversation is that when you do it right and create a really healthy culture in your organization, you really can't tell the difference between extraverts and introverts in this exercise. When everyone's voice is valued and heard there is no dearth nor hoarding of the chips—they get used pretty evenly by all the participants. In a safe culture, one of trust and respect, everyone is listened to.

18. Shake It Up—Change the Venue

People take a lot of cues from their environments. How often do you have a meeting where people sit in the same seats, as though they have been assigned to them, like in grade school? As human beings we tend to be creatures of habit—so it's natural that you get the same ideas out of a group that thinks the same way, with the same players doing most of the talking...or listening. What can you do to surface new ideas and get everyone involved? One idea is to change the venue—people can't sit in the same old seats in a totally new place. Also, when you change the venue, particularly for an off-site retreat, it helps to change how people participate and what they talk about. It changes the turf and that helps change the conversation.

19. Change the Seating Arrangement: Shake Up the Neighborhood

The 19th strategy is similar to the last, where you change the venue, only this is much easier (and generally less expensive) since it doesn't require you to go out and find retreat space. Shake up the neighborhood! You've probably noticed that people sit in the same seats, next to the same other people, at meetings. This tends to lead you to having the same conversation. But you can use table tents with names on them to mix people up so they sit next to those they either don't know or don't know well. Getting people to sit next to different folks all the time is a basic practice of inclusion—and can help with group interaction, innovation, and idea cross-pollination.

20. Get Away From the Same Old Words
In Fact, Get Away From Words

Another way to get people talking is to focus the dialogue around images, not words. In an "Art Walk," you can have people draw out images, either in teams or as individuals, (usually on flip charts). Or you can use pre-made images. Our favorite tool for this is to use a product by the Center for Creative Leadership, out of Greensboro, NC, called "Visual Explorer"™. This is a collection of a couple hundred pictures of everything you could imagine. What we like to do is to put them all around the edges of a room and then have the participants individually consider (before they look at the photos) whatever the big issues are that face them. We usually pick just two issues to keep it simple. They then go around the room and choose a photo for each issue that resonates with them, symbolizes, or represents the issue in some way. We put them in small groups—three to four people max—and each person has a couple of minutes to share what it was about the picture that caused them to choose that particular image. The job of the others is to listen with Open-Ended listening, described above. No interruptions, no corrections from the peanut gallery. Then, after everyone has gone, one person from each group summarizes the themes of their discussions and shares that with the whole room. This is a pretty quick exercise that surfaces amazing perspectives. Everyone gets a guaranteed chance to talk—so you get more ideas on the table. And when people can't use the same old words they always say, (since they are communicating through pictures) they often talk about the issues in a very different way. The art walk or Visual Explorer can really help to change the conversation and get everyone contributing to it.

21. Create Ground Rules

Often group dynamics become difficult because the group has no group charter of ground rules to guide *how* they will work together. No direction at all can lead to a free-for-all where some members dominate and others abdicate. Team members understanding of how their group will work together is a part of Bruce Tuckman's now-famous "Forming, Storming, Norming, Performing" stages typical for high performing teams.[12] We recommend that when a team forms, or changes significantly, it is good to have a discussion around two questions:

1. What is it that brings us here/what are our goals?
2. How can we create the environment that will allow us to achieve these goals?

Basically, by having the conversation of "How do we need to work together to achieve these goals?" your group will create its own ground rules.   Creating these guidelines and reminding the team of them will greatly help meetings stay on task and help the team achieve their goals.

Some Final Thoughts

Organizations hire smart people for very good reasons, but then all too often they fail to listen to them. Further, they fail to create the venues where all team members can be heard. Anyone who has run a group meeting knows how difficult it can be to get even participation across the group with all members contributing ideas and thoughts to the discussion. The pattern where some attendees are very participative and share a lot of ideas, while others tend to speak up less often, and some not at all, is symptomatic of a poorly nurtured organizational culture of communication. In that culture, many good ideas likely never see the light of day.

When the team environment does not allow for all members to share their ideas, then leaders need to take steps to create a culture of conversation and communication that creates venues for both extraverted and introverted members to share ideas and information. These strategies can help leaders initiate and nurture this type of an organizational culture that promotes ideas, options, creativity, and thought diversity. It's what the great *It-Factor* leaders we've worked with are doing—and you can too.

Your 8th step to becoming a great *It-Factor* leader is to create this culture of conversation.

The Ninth Step:
Speak To Be Heard

Speak to be Heard:
Speaking So Others Will Listen

In our Third Step to becoming a great *It-Factor* leader we talked about how *It-Factor* leaders know how to listen—these leaders also know how to be heard. This is not about speaking loudly—or even about repeating your message. It's about speaking so that different people can key into what you are saying because you "speak their language." In the Eighth Step we explored a lot of ways in which leaders can create a culture of conversation—but applying our understanding of how the human mind works goes much further. The Eighth Step was great for getting people talking to one another. In our Ninth Step, we'll explore how to get people to listen to you.

Leaders must communicate effectively, despite the fact that any audience tends to bring a variety of perspectives with it. Members of your audience probably don't know it, they probably aren't aware of their own preferences, but in reality they are listening for you to make statements that fit their world view (some psychologists talk about that as "fitting their filters"). There are two of these areas that are crucial to understand for those who desire to be a leader with the *It-Factor*: how people gather information and how they use that information to make a decision. If you talk about information—we could call this data—in a way that your audience (your team mate, boss, spouse, work group, etc.) doesn't understand, see, or appreciate then they miss most of what you are saying, and consequently the relevance is lost upon them. If you talk about making decisions along lines that your audience doesn't value, then they will not respect the decisions you make or potentially not even *hear* the decision when you share it with them. Great *It-Factor* leaders don't lose half the people in the room—they make sure they are speaking to everyone and are speaking to be heard.

Let's first examine how to talk about data. An area of significant difference among people is how they appreciate, gather, understand, and use information. The legendary psychologist Carl Jung postulated that individuals prefer either a mental functioning style he termed "sensing" (often denoted by "S") or one termed "intuition" (often denoted by "N"). According to Jung's early theory[1] and a lot of subsequent research[2-4], a person pays greater attention to ideas that fit their innate preference, and correspondingly pay a lot less attention to those that reflect their non-preferred style. It's like if you go to the movies and you like action flicks—you probably don't even register the romantic comedies on the marquee. At a restaurant, if you routinely choose a steak then you probably don't even see what is listed under vegetarian entrees that you could order. In fact, you might not even realize that non-meat options are available. People look for, listen for, see, and hear what they recognize and know first...and then they take in everything else. The challenge for leaders is to speak effectively to audiences where both of these quite opposite preferences are in force—which is going to be almost any medium- to large-sized group you're addressing!

What this means for you is that people with different preferences can listen to the same language, the same statements that you make, and because of their very different filters they can (and often do) hear *different things*. This is mostly because they pick up only part of what you said, and fill in the rest. So what do you do? You "speak the language" of the listeners—the *diverse* language of the listeners. You use what we call "bridging language" to communicate more effectively across this communication divide.

Speak to What Matters

First let's talk about what Carl Jung found out about the human mind and these "Sensing" versus "Intuition" types he researched. What is it that makes one different from another? Jung (and much research conducted after his time) found that Sensing types appreciate facts and are grounded in reality. Common sense and realistic appraisal are key to their view of the world. Sensing types like direct experience, tangible results, and value efficiency and cost-effectiveness. To a Sensing type, the application of ideas is more tantalizing than the ideas themselves. Not surprisingly, many Sensing types will need to see an idea's application in order to fully understand it. Sensing types tend to avoid generalizations and inferences—if that's where you're talking, they stand a good chance of not hearing what you have to say. They also value established methods, traditions, or institutions. They value good technique in that it leads to good outcomes. Sensing types can seem resistant to change, but closer to the truth is that they just need to see the common sense path leading to the change—those definite and measureable steps to take—in order for them to jump on board[1-7]. Does this feel "right" to you? You might be a Sensing type. Recent research by the Center for Application of Psychological Type (CAPT, on the web at www.CAPT.org) finds that 66-74% of the US population feels most at home in this category[8].

But that leaves 26-34% of the population that *isn't* listening to your words for that hard data that derives from what you can see, hear, taste, smell, or feel. They aren't looking as keenly for numbers, isolated events, or "data" in the way you might be talking about it. Those other roughly one-third of the population who prefer the Intuition function can be markedly different in what they appreciate and listen for when they listen to you. Intuitive types enjoy brainstorming and readily make inferences and connections between data and the big picture or the vision. For them, context really matters. If you leave out the context, even if you provide a lot of numbers, they don't see you as a leader. For them, numbers without context are just for bean counters who they worry don't fully grasp the situation. They prefer to focus more on the concept than the application and particularly enjoy new theories or ideas. Innovative, different, or unique ideas are appealing to them. Dealing with hard-to-measure or intangible results does not worry them. They are typically resourceful when dealing with new or unusual circumstances. Intuitive types tend to be naturally future-oriented, and thus they can eagerly support a proposed change just based on the idea, even if the details are not fully worked out. Many engage readily in strategic planning[1-4, 7].

The task you will often face as a leader is to speak with a group that holds both of these perspectives, some of them simultaneously, but most of them preferring just one or the other. You will need to offer a message that appeals to the *particular cognitive filter* of the individuals listening. Here is an example of how to fashion language that will marry both the opposing preferences into a single over-arching statement. In our teaching and coaching work we refer to these as "bridging statements." Combining language in this way draws together the true benefits of *both* preferences and helps gain the attention of those with *either* preference. The words that fall to either preference (S or N) are denoted in all capitals. Here is one of our favorite bridging statements, a tool which many of our leaders have used to preface their announcement of a new project, direction, or plan:

> *While it is important that we be INNOVATIVE, we must also examine the FACTS and seek to make TANGIBLE improvements in EFFICIENT ways. We know that we are well positioned to apply CUTTING EDGE THEORY in PRAGMATIC ways. We can trust in our EXPERIENCE and SKILLS while we work together to CREATE NEW approaches to these COMPLEX problems.*

You'll notice that this particular bridging statement doesn't actually *say* anything, content-wise. A statement such as this can be used to preface the introduction and details of a new plan, strategy, resource allocations, budget cuts, staffing changes, etc. What comes after can differ widely—the purpose of this example is as an introductory statement cueing both sensing and intuitive types that their perspectives are valid and embraced by you, as the leader. This example bridging statement endorses the Sensing perspective, and bridges it to the Intuitive one. One could easily turn the capitalized words around to endorse the Intuitive perspective to a Sensing one, or use other words altogether, as described in the Sensing and Intuition paragraphs above. Of course, bridging statements can also be applied to statements that do relate content about the issue you are discussing or debating.

How well do they work? There are many examples we could share, but one that always make us smile is of Tony, a physician at a large health system. He called for a coaching session, frustrated that he was proposing a great idea, but couldn't get the upper administrators to listen to him. We introduced him to the bridging statement listed above, which he used exactly as written to great effect. When we checked in with him after his big presentation, he reported his success. "They said it was great that I finally made some sense, but I proposed the exact same plan last time, I just opened with that bridging statement this time!" The difference was that now, Tony had his audience's attention.

These bridging statements can be useful in conversation with another individual as well. For example, when someone who sees the world from an Intuitive perspective is trying to advocate for changes in process or policies to someone who sees the world from an opposite Sensing perspective, a statement such as the following might be helpful:

> *We do need a practical solution, one that is efficient and effective, but we also need to be innovative and resourceful as we face these unprecedented challenges. While these ideas on the table might be ones we haven't tried before, how might we implement them, at least on a pilot basis, and measure their effect?*

Someone speaking from a Sensing perspective might advocate to a colleague who sees the world through an Intuitive filter:

> *We are faced with a situation that calls for innovation and creativity. I also want to explore how our newly proposed solutions can be applied to the ground level problems our clients face. What we have tried before has had disappointing effectiveness. How might we work from what we know and use that as a launch pad to develop alternative approaches?*

You can also use bridging statements throughout your conversation or presentation to keep bringing the attention of both groups to the discussion and to help them see the value of the opposing perspective. One of the best things you can do is to create several of these Sensing-iNtuition bridging statements that are relevant to your own organization and situation. You won't gain mastery of this (or any other leadership skill, frankly) without practicing it. An oft-made statement by executive coaches is that leadership is like sports—you don't have to be sick to get better. Of course, without some time in training you will have a hard time competing on the big stage or performing when it really matters. So hone your skills, create your own bridging statements, and master the skill.

Speak to how People Make Decisions

The next area to work on comes from another gem that Jung found out about the human mind: we make decisions based either on our logical, critical thinking skills or on our sense of values, relationships, and harmony. These might not seem totally compatible for you—and indeed, some folks struggle with the fact that others see the world and make important decisions based on very different ways of evaluating information. In our culture shaping work, we often get called in to work with organizations that are in conflict over this very issue—*how do we make decisions?* And *why do we fight over the decisions we make?*

Carl Jung found that some prefer to make decisions using what is called "sequential reasoning," which means that information is looked at following clear rules, premises lead to results, and conclusions are consistent. This is a bit of a "letter of the law" approach, which calls on objectivity and impartiality. This preference falls into what Jung called a

"Thinking" (often denoted by a "T") type, and he postulated that these individuals focus on cause and effect, keeping clear boundaries between issues. Making decisions based on an analysis of the pros and cons is a favored strategy of thinking types, and they tend to be quite confident and clear about both their objectives in situations and their decisions as well. Thinking types like to clarify ideas, and may use many questions to do so, which can at times seem as if they are grilling their colleagues. But they like to be precise and make sure that ideas are vetted thoroughly and any discrepancies are surfaced. Thinking types can get stuck, unable to move forward until their questions are all answered. An important aspect of thinking types is that they tend to separate out emotional considerations from outcomes and instead focus strongly on those outcomes, rather than on the process by which they are achieved.

Jung found that the opposite preference for how people make decisions is strikingly different—he called this the "Feeling function." (often denoted by a "F") Those who make decisions using their Feeling preference tend to have strong skills in empathy—they think about how a decision is going to affect people: will it be in sync with their values? Will it be in sync with *our* values as a group? With our mission? Does it help us "walk the talk"? These "feelers" will weigh those positive and negative feelings in a situation, and that will be crucial for how they make a decision. They like to praise others and hold an expectation of mutual kindness and respect. They see it as a failure of leadership when that much coveted win-win solution does not occur. Rather than using intellectual pressure to get their way, they tend to be warm, be seen as gentle, and see many ways to achieve agreement among the group. The core characteristic of Feeling types is that they "get it" that purely rational decisions don't exist in the real world. The real world is fraught with all the multi-layered, murky, and emotional complexities that real-life humans bring with them. Feeling types want everyone to feel good with the result, or else they worry that the hard fought for result won't stick. To them, "feeling good" about the decision translates into continued commitment of the parties involved.

According to CAPT's research[8], in any room a leader should expect that 40-50% of the group will be listening for logical, objective analysis with their Thinking preference, while the slim majority of the room (at 50-60%) will be listening with their Feeling function for decisions that provide for harmony and are responsive to the overall mood in a group. So what is a leader to do with a room filled with thinking types and feeling types?

Again, as you offer a message or a vision that appeals to the *particular cognitive filters* of the individuals listening, you can marry both the opposing preferences into a single over-arching statement. These "Thinking-Feeling bridging statements" draw together the true benefits of both preferences and help gain the attention of those with either preference. The words that fall to either preference (T or F) are denoted in all capitals. First we will share with you a wonderful, Thinking-Feeling bridging statement that Pamela Shields, one of Claudia's rather gifted graduate students, created while taking Claudia's leadership course she offers at the University of North Carolina at Chapel Hill. Again each of the Thinking or Feeling trigger words are in capital letters.

> *While we have a proven track record of being OBJECTIVE with our clients and ANALYZING each situation in order to make EFFECTIVE decisions, feedback shows that the most satisfied clients FEEL that we CARE about and EMPATHIZE with their INDIVIDUAL needs. Because of this, we will continue to maintain our PRINCIPLES and PRECISELY identify BEST SOLUTIONS with an additional emphasis on expressing APPRECIATION for the INDIVIDUAL client's needs.*

And here is another example:

> *We make SMART products that people CARE about. That HELP people. We bring science and technology to focus on our BOTTOM LINE of MAKING LIFE BETTER. We are GOOD STEWARDS of the resources we use and of the TRUST you place in us.*

And another example:

> *While it may be LOGICAL that we look at the PRECISE policy for wording and description, it is important that we also consider the INTENT of this policy so that we implement it in a way that EFFECTIVELY achieves the DESIRED END POINT, which is to maintain our PRODUCTIVE PARTNERSHIPS and APPRECIATION and LOYALTY of our customers.*

Now, work toward mastery of this technique and create some bridging statements of your own.

Crafting communiqués either for groups or other individuals that appeal to how people think will help you, as a leader, deliver messages that are understood and retained better by your audience. They will improve communication and help support shared, mutual understanding. Bringing these two types together is crucial for leaders, because if you don't create mutual understanding and peace, their disagreements will easily lead to arguing, fighting, name-calling, and otherwise undermine the organizational culture you are working so hard to create.

The Communication Compass

We carefully coach *It-Factor* leaders to make sure they use language appropriately to speak to everyone in the room. But we also want them to go on to the next step. They can combine their understanding of these preferences to be able to communicate with compelling and effective concise messages as well. We call this tool we developed "The Communication Compass," and you will find it a valuable tool in your leadership toolbox—particularly when you want to get your vision across to a group.

You, too, will have this advantage when you create messages that take into consideration how the human mind is thought to function. By using this tool you will appeal to how people think, and thus you will deliver a message with better appreciation, acceptance, and retention[1-4]. The Communication Compass we developed structures effective messages based on an understanding of Jung's work and it goes beyond bridging language by including all four core functions of the human mind: iNtuition (N), Sensing (S), Feeling (F), and Thinking (T). When you take these functions into account as you structure short opening or closing communications, you are more likely to deliver a message that audiences will attend to and remember. To illustrate: since nearly any audience will include those innately wired to hear messages around Sensing, a good communiqué should be structured to include the sensing perspective. However, the same is true for iNtuition, Feeling and Thinking as well. While this may seem complicated, there is a simple formula that leaders can use to structure these messages. The Communication Compass starts with N (like true North on a compass), followed by S, F, T and then returns to N. See the diagram below in figure 9.1.

Open the message with a communication around iNtuition, which addresses the vision or provides context for the situation. Then Sensing, which addresses relevant data or steps to take. The Feeling function acknowledges the noble purpose behind the action (a.k.a. the mission) and the "benefit/harm" perspective. And the Thinking function addresses the logical nature, objective analysis, or the bottom-line end point[1-4, 7]. The final step is to return to the vision statement (iNtuition function). Depending on the communication topic, one can also change the positions of the Feeling and Thinking functions and address the Thinking perspective, followed by the Feeling one, in the cycle.

Figure 9.1 The Communication Compass

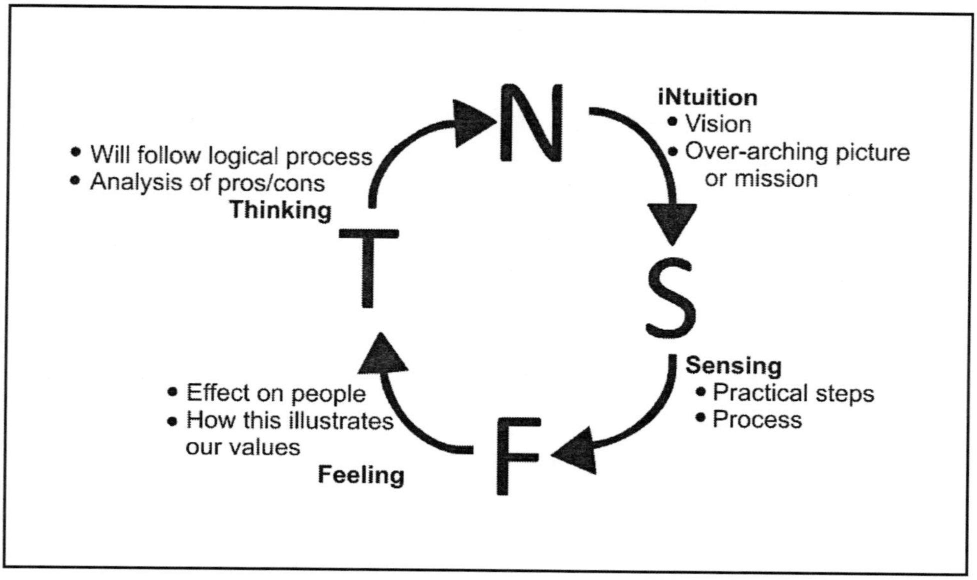

- Will follow logical process
- Analysis of pros/cons
  Thinking

iNtuition
- Vision
- Over-arching picture or mission

Sensing
- Practical steps
- Process

- Effect on people
- How this illustrates our values
  Feeling

Here is an example related to a vision for malaria prevention and treatment. The statements are noted to indicate the particular Jungian functions addressed:

Our vision is to wipe out malaria in the next decade (N). We can do this using the tools we have now, by using our established networks to provide the mosquito nets, the medicines and the newly developed vaccines to those most affected (S). We can save tens of thousands of children, the most vulnerable of the human family, and alleviate much human suffering (F). Given our constraints during this economic crisis, we will implement our best practices, so that our efforts are logical, effective, streamlined— and bottom-line change the world as we know it. We are confident in our ability to make this difference (T). Together with our partners we will see this done within a decade: a world without malaria and the suffering it causes (N).

The next example describes an approach to eliminating food deserts[9], something of great importance to First Lady Michele Obama. This message follows the N-S-F-T-N compass cycle:

We envision an America without food deserts. We see freedom from the tyranny of the bodegas which fail to nourish their customers as they overcharge them for high calorie, low nutrient deli food and snacks. We envision urban environments where fresh, wholesome food is available and poverty is eased. We see this on the horizon within 7 years (N). In these cities we see local supermarkets, urban farming, and farmers markets—a place where everyone can afford and easily obtain healthy produce (S). We value the health of all our citizens. We are one American family. No one should be forced to live in a desert (F). We know there is a direct correlation between the availability of fresh produce and the health of people in the community. Healthy communities—both physically and economically—are in everyone's best interest. By taking these steps and promoting these programs we will encourage economic development in our poorest communities as we wipe out our most pervasive food deserts in the next 7 years (T). Our future is a healthier America— one without food deserts (N).

The next example illustrates a slight manipulation of the Communication Compass formula, presenting the thinking function material prior to that for the feeling function. However, note that the F and T functions—those that relate to analysis and decision making—are still paired here in this illustration. This illustration follows the N-S-*T-F*-N:

Our vision is to create a system that provides pre-natal care for all expectant mothers in our community (N). We know there are many mothers who never see a medical professional until their third trimester or even until their delivery. Through our existing clinics and our partners in local public health, we will open offices in underserved areas. We can create the flexible clinic hours available on public transportation lines and provide care in multiple languages (S). Integrating in this way will make us more efficient and more effective, helping us save resources and support the revenue needed to continue our mission (T). Others may have looked at this as a cumbersome venture, but we are more than a local health system: we are a part of this community and these women and their soon-to-be born children are part of the family of Metropolis (F). Our role and our mission is to provide for all the members of our community family—no expectant mother, nor her baby, need be forgotten. (N).

Apply the Communication Compass to your messages targeted to the public or groups. Members of your audience with strong preferences for the core function pairs of either S/N or T/F will be particularly aware of when you include language regarding their particular preference. Those without strong preferences will be listening for *both* the Sensing and iNtuition or the Thinking and Feeling components to the messages. Using what Jung discovered about how the human brain functions can give leaders a significant advantage when communicating to teams, groups, or the public.

Your 9th step to becoming a great *It-Factor* leader is to speak to be heard.

The Tenth Step: Create Thought Diversity

Create Thought Diversity:
Groupthink Will Lead You to Failure

It-Factor leaders know that they can't do it alone. They can't see everything. They can't think of everything. That's why they create thought diversity on the team. Great *It-Factor* leaders understand that the whole really *is* greater than the sum of its parts. They also get it that when everyone thinks alike, the team comes up with the same old solutions. The same old solution can make you obsolete in no time, and has real potential to lead you to disaster. There's a name for the same old solution when all are of the same mind: *groupthink*. Maximizing the team's pool of options to choose from will often lead to a better solution being chosen.

As a leader it is your job to save your group from derailing because of conformity. Instead you need to create a culture of thought diversity. In this step we'll define groupthink and give you a couple real-life examples of it, then we'll go into 10 strategies you can take to make sure that groupthink can't take root where you lead.

You probably ran across your first example of groupthink without even realizing it—in a fairy tale. In 1837, Hans Christian Andersen's third and final installment of <u>Fairy Tales Told for Children</u> was published, and in it was a story called "The Emperor's New Clothes"[1]. This is a story about an all-too-vain Emperor and two wily weavers who promise the Emperor a new suit of clothes that can only be seen by the wise—they will be invisible to those unfit for their positions, stupid, or incompetent. When they show the Emperor the new suit, which they cleverly stage to be in front of his advisors and councilors, he sees nothing, but doesn't want to admit to that, since he doesn't want anyone to think that he is unfit for his position. Seeing him exclaim how fabulous the new clothes are, his advisors and councilors follow suit, ooohing and aaahhing similarly—no one wanting to admit to looking stupid or incompetent in front of the others. This goes on until *everyone* is talking about the beautiful new clothes, and feeling very wise and smart.

A parade is arranged, at which all the city pours out and admires the Emperors new outfit. Until, at last, a boy, mystified by the behavior of all the grown-ups and completely confused by the concept of pretense, cries out, "but the Emperor's got no clothes on!" With the obvious truth having been said aloud, everyone starts laughing at the nearly naked Emperor, who goes back to his palace much embarrassed and chagrined. Of course, the weavers have skipped town by this time, taking with them the hefty fee they charged for their con. For his part, the Emperor does learn something—he goes home deciding never again to be so vain. Henceforth, he will take his position of leadership more seriously.

This might seem like a cute story but it is a tale of saving face. It offers us some profound lessons. When leaders create a climate where there is pressure to agree, where dissent is seen as disloyalty, and where difference is seen as incompetence, then groupthink is going to take root.

If the culture is one where saving face outranks the truth, then derailment is the next stop.

It-Factor leaders know they must do just the opposite—they must create a climate where truth telling is valued and rewarded or at the very least supported. Objectivity must be a cultural value, as opposed to taking everything personally. In short, leaders must create the climate where any member can (and is expected to) say, "Hey, the Emperor has no clothes!"

In the American story, not all leaders have learned this lesson until it was too late. Let's look at how Groupthink can take hold and then we'll explore how it has manifested in the US.

Hallmark Signs of Groupthink:

Groupthink is a crippling organizational phenomena that occurs when one or two people or personality styles dominate a group's culture so completely that there is no room for those with other styles, perspectives, needs, or beliefs to get their ideas on the table[2]. This can take the form of people hiring only those who think as they do, which shows up as hiring for gut chemistry rather than skill or fit. It also happens when the dominant thinkers badger others into accepting their ideas. Another way this manifests is when members critically downplay the value of others' ideas—you'll hear this in statements like:

> *"Well, she only finished her training two years ago. She doesn't have a lot of real experience."*

or

> *"You know that idea could never work!"*

or

*"Why would you suggest something like that? That's just
not how we do things around here..."*

When all this happens, team members "go along to get along," and new ideas or much needed cautions won't emerge from the group. Of course, when leaders simply fail to listen the ground is ripe for groupthink to take hold as well. If leaders stop listening, the team will stop talking. So all those great strategies we talked about in our Eighth Step to becoming an *It-Factor* leader (get all ideas on the table by creating a culture of conversation) will be useless if you don't listen—and instead fall into the trap of a culture of groupthink taking hold.

Creating an environment ripe for groupthink will make you efficient—in the short run, but it will bankrupt you in the long run. This is because when all the team members think alike, they don't have innovation or creativity—they come up with the same ideas all the time. They usually don't understand it or see it when the world around them changes—they keep doing the same old thing as they become increasingly irrelevant. The problem is that if new ideas are not introduced, if old ideas are not challenged, then organizations make choices from a very narrow field of options and all too often they totally miss the boat.

Groupthink will lead you to develop painful blind spots. A blind spot is when you cannot see a flaw or liability you have, but everyone else can see them quite clearly. Just like we talked about in our First Step to becoming a great *It-Factor* leader: know yourself, *the good, the bad and the fixable*, an individual's blind spot often shows up as an interpersonal issue, such as poor emotional intelligence or poor temper control. Blind spots can even show up as underdeveloped technical skills in an important area. But when it comes to entire organizations, blind spots show up as continuing to produce the same old programs, products, or outcomes while being completely unaware that the world, the client group, the financial structures, the resources, etc., have changed around them. It can be hard and uncomfortable to look directly at the truth, but it is far worse to turn a blind eye to it.

A Painful History Lesson

The history of the United States holds some important lessons for us about groupthink. The term groupthink was actually coined in 1972 by Dr. Irving Janus[3] after an examination of what went so very wrong a decade earlier, when the Bay of Pigs debacle tainted the presidency of John F. Kennedy. Starting in 1960, during the Eisenhower administration, the US government planned and funded an invasion to overthrow the Cuban government of Fidel Castro over our fear of communism. This doomed invasion took place in April 1961, just three months into Kennedy's presidency. Eastern Bloc nations had trained and equipped the Cuban armed forces, which in just three days defeated the US-trained force of Cuban exiles[4]. America was shamed before the entire world. Not surprisingly, this event accelerated a rapid deterioration in Cuban-American relations that has still not completely recovered six decades later.

How could this have happened? How could a huge, powerful country with sophisticated military strategy and tools like the USA be defeated by a tiny country off our coast? President Kennedy wanted to understand that too. A team of psychologists sought the answer. What they found was that no one in the Cabinet or advisors felt they could tell the leadership they were in the wrong or that the plan would not work. It was all too important to maintain harmony. This was *groupthink*. The group created an artificial harmony made up of silence rather than good will, dialogue, constructive conflict, and mutual understanding. Another problem in *groupthink* is that the group believes they are right, often on assumed moral grounds, and they believe that they cannot fail, either because of this moral imperative or because of a history of success. In the 1960s this became evident in our belief in capitalism and democracy as the only "right" way of governing a country, that it was "right" for us to help install a government more acceptable to us, and of believing that our military prowess would see us to victory despite any challenges.   The U.S. was simply too big to fail.

Table 10.1 Hallmark Signs of Groupthink

- A dominant style pervades the group
- Hiring only a like-minded workforce—based on gut chemistry rather than *fit* and *skills*
- Members are badgered into accepting ideas
- Team members "go along to get along"
- Leaders simply fail to listen

And History Repeats Itself

Psychologist Irving Janis devoted many years of work to this concept of groupthink to help us avoid another such blind-sided disaster. His work resulted in several books and many scholarly articles which examine how this phenomena takes hold and destroys communication and diversity of thought. Unfortunately the lessons didn't stick. The next generation had to learn the painful truth of groupthink all over again, as 26 years later national tragedy struck—in what was a preventable disaster.

Thanks to a man named Roger Boisjoly[5], the most famous example of groupthink is the Challenger Space Shuttle disaster. A bit like the renowned Dr. Irving, Mr. Boisjoly is a man who devoted the latter half of his life to helping people like you and me learn a lesson he wished he'd learned much, much earlier. You see, he felt like he just might have been able to prevent one of the worst space disasters we have ever faced.

In case you don't remember all the details, here's what happened. On January 28, 1986, the Challenger Space Shuttle lifted off with seven astronauts on board, including Christa McAuliffe, the first teacher in space. Just 73 seconds after its much delayed late morning takeoff, the Challenger exploded killing the entire crew. The phenomenon is well documented in this case: the leadership heard only what they wanted to hear because the group would not tolerate voices of dissent from within. Just the day before the disaster, engineer Boisjoly and others from the Morton Thiokol engineering group warned that the low launch temperatures might cause the O-ring seals to fail since they had never been tested at temperatures lower than 53 degrees Fahrenheit[5, 6].

On the morning of the launch the tower was encased in ice and the temperature was about 31 degrees Fahrenheit[5, 6]. You can see for yourself how the Challenger looked that morning in Figure 10.1.

But the leaders at NASA wanted a flight and *groupthink* characterized the decision making style of the organization. "Think like a manager!" badgered the leaders until the engineers gave in and consented to a launch.

Two theories predominate about what happened with those oh-so-famous O-rings: either microscopic gaps in the rings allowed superheated fuel to escape or the extreme heat of the launch caused the frozen material of the rings themselves to expand non-uniformly. The

Figure 10.1 Images from the undercarriage of the Challenger Space Shuttle prior to launch, Jan. 28, 1986

Photos Courtesy of NASA

result was, tragically, that they exploded shortly after lift-off. "Thinking like a manager" and valuing an on-time launch was making a narrowly defined choice from a narrow field of options—and it resulted in a national disaster.

Many organizations, particularly in the public sector, like public health, and health care organizations put a very strong emphasis on cultural competence. Groupthink is a key issue here too. When everyone thinks alike and reinforces a narrowly-defined culture then they are unlikely *to even be sensitive to* the differences between themselves and others. When everyone thinks alike, there is no room for alternative approaches, perspectives, needs, or beliefs. When organizations find they have a high turnover of specific population groups, such as women or minorities, they should take stock of cultural incompetence[7] and the impact that *groupthink* might be having on their talent pool and bottom line.

Could disaster happen to your enterprise? To your team? Does your team examine problems from all angles? Or do they take the obvious and easy way out? Does your team rigorously question its actions? Or does it just blindly achieve the next goal, in a rush to complete the task? Remember, inviting narrowly thought out options to rule the day is to put the enterprise at serious risk of groupthink. Use Table 10.2 to consider this more carefully. List the traits, styles, or patterns you see, or the outcomes that have happened in your situation that put your team or organization at risk for *Groupthink.*

Table 10.2 Ways my team is at risk for Groupthink

1.
2.
3.
4.
5.

In Pursuit of Thought Diversity

It-Factor leaders create an organizational culture that prevents groupthink in the first place. The key to avoiding groupthink is a concept called "thought diversity". Thought diversity occurs when you encourage open communication, truthfulness, candor, disagreement, and dialogue—all in an environment of respect and positive personal regard[8]. But *how* to create this can present a quandary. Let's explore how you can make thought diversity manifest in your enterprise.

Just how does an *It-Factor* leader create a thought-diverse organizational culture? How can *you* do this? We offer you 10-strategies that you can use to improve thought diversity with your team. These have worked for the *It-Factor* leaders we have coached. Let them work for you, too. Examine these strategies to see which ones might work for you.

Strategy #1: Encourage open discussions

First, encourage open discussion. In order to do this, leaders must not control the discussion or state their outcome expectations at the outset. Explain that the goals of the process are to *vett* the ideas completely, which requires their thorough examination. You have to get people talking about—not lobbying for—their ideas. They have to be *talking* if you are going to get the maximum ideas generated. If you're not sure how to get open discussion to happen, revisit the Eighth Step about creating that culture of conversation.

The next four strategies work best in the order in which we present them. Groups often want to reach closure—they want a decision made, a course of action specified. But moving to action too quickly can be even more costly than delaying too long. As a leader, you might find that you need to slow the process down enough so that you can examine the ideas that are on the table as well as surface new ones. These four strategies will be incredibly helpful to you.

Strategy #2: Look at what you really do know

Our next strategy builds on encouraging open discussion. You start here by asking questions about the known data, including what facts describe the situation? What can we learn from the past? And what relevant experience do others have that we could learn from? What are the important details to focus on? What are the real costs? Will it work? Can we see how it will work? Does anything really need changing? Here you are looking for the objective, the quantifiable, the *facts.* While all of these are important to know, don't let them drive or dominate the process. They are a part of the process.

Strategy #3: Ask "how is all this connected?"

The next strategy seeks not facts, but a more intangible perspective. This strategy should follow the discussion of "what do we really know?" In looking for this next level of information, the group examines *how* what they know is all *connected*. This means that you look at the implications of this information and you explore any themes that emerge from the data. This may require a bit of intuition or insight as you seek understanding of how the facts and data relate to the big picture. Relating these themes to relevant theories or ideas can help with grasping the critical context in which this information must be understood and also help point out possibilities or options for other strategies. What you are looking for here is an in-depth understanding of how those proverbial dominos are all going to fall. So, as a leader in a group you might ask the following questions:

- What are the implications or themes in the data?
- Are there relevant theories or ideas to help with our understanding?
- What's the big picture?
- What are the possibilities or options for what we can do?
- What else could this mean?
- How is it all interconnected?
- What is a new way to do this?
- What other interesting ideas are there?

Strategy #4: Go for logic

In the next strategy, you logically analyze the situation or the data. This is where you list "pros and cons" of pursuing courses of action. "Going for logic" is the perspective of critical thinking and you are shooting for a vital, objective analysis. Good tools here include listing the criteria for good decision making and charting the pros and cons of each option. Acknowledging the most logical solution will be helpful as well, but a word of caution: be careful not to let logic and critical thinking dominate this process. When *groupthink* does happen, a group has typically engaged *only* in this critical thinking perspective and has completely missed the other crucial steps of the rounding up all the data, looking at how what they know relates to the big picture, and understanding the implications of strategy #5, below. To help elucidate this area, you could ask the following questions:

- What criteria are necessary for a good decision?
- What are the pros and cons of each option?
- What's the most logical solution?
- What are the logical consequences?
- What is wrong with this?
- Why aren't we following through now?

Strategy #5: Make sure you understand who is benefitted and who is burned

Strategies 2 through 5 are linked and for clearest thinking you should pursue them in the order given. After you have surfaced all the relevant data you can bring to light, and after you've understood how it relates to the big picture, and after you've made a critical analysis of it, then you ask the tough question, "if we do this, who is benefitted? Who is burned?" Some unenlightened leaders pooh-pooh this step as only for softies who can't be tough decision makers, but we think that perspective shows a real lack of maturity and an incredibly shallow understanding. Perceiving who is benefitted and who is going to be burned by your actions is crucial to the viability of future partnerships. Yes, it is a perspective that embraces values or a "harmony viewpoint." Emotional Intelligence, which we talked about in our Sixth Step to developing that all important *It-Factor*, has clearly emerged as a key soft skill in successful leaders—and its absence clearly shows up in leaders who derail. Emotional intelligence, or EQ or EI in the popular press, plays an important role in good decision making. Strategy #5 is to brainstorm who else the group must collaborate with, who else they must learn from, and in what ways? Your group should analyze how the proposed solutions will impact the stakeholders—and just where are those stakeholders? Are they within the organization or perhaps the general population?

It is also important to question which solution will promote maximum acceptance and ownership among all stakeholders, both internal and external. Understanding who is benefitted and who is burned by the ideas under consideration will also give you a valuable reality check—and remember that even your own group will be both benefitted and burned by your actions. All opportunities create choices, and choices create opportunity costs. Make sure you well understand the implications of the choices *you* are making. Here are some actual questions you can ask in a team meeting:

- Who else do we need to collaborate with and in what ways?
- How will the proposed solutions impact the various people (stakeholders) in the situation?
- Which solution will promote maximum acceptance and ownership?
- What do we like and dislike?
- How can we make sure everyone gets something of value?

Following these steps and linking strategies 2 through 5 will help your team go far in embracing thought diversity and avoiding groupthink.

Strategy #6: Leave no stone unturned, even if it feels like whining

We've said it already: It is unpleasant to think about what can go wrong, but it can be catastrophic not to. Thus, strategy #6 in encouraging diversity of thought is to assign someone to play the devil's advocate, the person who will ask those critical "reality check" questions. Their job is to help the team leave no stones unturned. Such questions might include:

- What if we fail to achieve this goal?
- What if the current conditions change—and change our resource base?
- Are we measuring success by the right metrics?
- What are the undesirable impacts this endeavor will create?

This devil's advocate function can require a thick skin for the person assigned to it, who might face disapproval, eye-rolling, or ridicule from other group members. They may have something important to point out, but if they feel they are being labeled a whiner or an "Eeyore" will they take the risk of saying what needs to be said?

As a leader, it is critical to understand that this devil's advocate role needs to be played by many in the organization—not just one or two. If only one or two individuals make these comments, the very function of Devil's Advocate will lose its power and effectiveness. Your teammates will probably get labeled as whiners or malcontents. This is a role that must be assigned to ensure that it rotates among the team. All team members will benefit from gaining the skills in respectfully asking the difficult questions that need to be put on the table.

Strategy #7: Reward truth speakers

Strategy number 7 is to reward those truth speakers and make sure that they have the skills to play the whistleblower tactfully and tastefully. It can be enormously uncomfortable to tell the truth in an organization. In many organizations it is too risky to one's job security, with the result that many people know something is wrong, may talk about it at the water cooler, but do not speak up to management. Leaders need to build a climate of trust so that this important organizational function is protected and nurtured. One of the ways to do this is to reward those who have the courage to speak the truth.

Our favorite example situation to get groups discussing is the scenario where a new doctor, medical student, or a nurse asks a senior surgeon if she or he washed their hands. Now what do you think goes on in hospitals all across the country when this actually happens? Do you think the senior surgeon thanks the lower-ranking teammate?

Well, if you're in the Novant Health System that's exactly what happens. Novant is a robust health system in the Southeastern United States and they have hand washing figured out. What might surprise you is that most hospitals *don't* have something as simple as hand washing figured out. How in the world they can open people's bodies and repair or transplant organs and yet still not have something as simple as washing hands conquered beats us, but it's true. As late as 2009 the average compliance rate with hand washing in hospitals, even in intensive care units, was 26-34%[9]. We hope that gives you uncomfortable shivers up your back and that you *never* again are shy about asking a health care professional if they have washed their hands before they touch you. Not only is this totally gross, it's deadly. The famous book <u>To Err is Human</u> put out by the Institute of Medicine in 1999[10] revealed for the first time to Americans that 98,000 of us die every year because of preventable errors, like mistakes and infections caught from the hospital itself. Just where do most of these infections come from? Transferred from patient to patient by the very people who are trying to cure the sick and injured.

But not at Novant. They have figured out that a problem like hand washing takes everyone working together. They have a 100% compliance with hand washing. When a nurse or medical student asks a senior doctor there if she or he washed their hands, well that doctor says "thank you"—and they mean it. That's because they know that they have team members watching their backs—and making sure that *"every patient has a remarkable experience every time in every dimension."* That's the value statement of the organization. Part of having a remarkable experience is *not* catching someone else's nasty infection. At Novant, they aren't about saving face; they are about saving lives.

In your organization, re-define what it means to be a team. Teach your team that you are not about saving face. You are about having each other's backs—and to do that you have to talk truth.

Strategy #8: Embrace the tough talks

Strategy # 8 calls on managers and leaders to equip their whole team with the tools to "have the tough talk." That means you need to teach them the art of the difficult conversation[11]. Everyone needs these skills. As a leader it is part of your job to make sure they get them. It's a huge part of your job to make sure that *you* get them (but more on that in the next Step to becoming a great *It-Factor* leader, where you'll learn twenty strategies of this fine art).

Often people become emotionally invested in their ideas, when they do so it is often difficult for them to hear others criticize their ideas without getting defensive or taking it personally. You need to ensure that you create an environment where it is clear that the discussion is about ideas, not people. These discussions are necessary to ensure that ideas are vetted, thought through, and refined before they are put into practice. There are many books and training programs that can be of huge help. Or have them read the Eleventh Step towards becoming a great *It-Factor* leader in this book.

Strategy #9: Change up the players

We're almost there. In Strategy # 9, if you find that you are having the same discussions over and over, leadership and organizational development expert Meg Wheatley states[12], change the people at the table. Sometimes in order to create a new discussion, you need to inject new ideas from new people into the group. A common practice is to invite an outsider into your group in an advisory capacity. Or you could pose the same problem to an entirely different group, and see if a different solution surfaces. Both Claudia and Ruben have sat on boards, as customers, partners, and as the voices of the competition—talk about non-traditional stakeholders to have at the table!

Strategy #10: Don't rush to judgment

Strategy #10 of this process is to avoid rushing to judgment. Closing the door on a decision will often cost you more time and resources than if you allowed a bit more time for reflection. Hard decisions deserve time to not only contemplate the decision you make, but to think about how you are making the decision. Revisiting the decisions being made and re-examining the processes followed will help ensure that no stones were left unturned. As we always say when we teach: *In the long run it is better to answer the difficult questions about your process of decision making than it is to explain the inadequacies in it.*

For example, when you are dealing with particularly thorny problems, tell the team straightaway that while solving the problem is important, decisiveness will not trump correctness. Therefore, the first or early meetings are to make sure the situation is explored deeply, along with potential strategies that can be taken (in particular, go through the 2nd and 3rd strategies in this Step to *It-Factor* leadership). Invite members to contact you outside of the meeting using a variety of channels—what is crucial is that you hear all that you need to, that all the data that must be examined surfaces so you can deal with it. Give the issue sufficient time to be fully considered.

Think Differently

Thought diversity is about thinking differently. Thinking differently helps you to understand and appreciate the perspective of others.

There are other ways that thought diversity will help your organization. Turnover is one example. Research shows that even though organizations recruit minority team members in order to achieve diversity, they often struggle to retain those employees—and thus to *maintain* their diversity. Recruiting isn't enough—if you have an organizational culture that truly does not welcome others who think differently, have a different perspective, embrace a different view of the world, or hold different values, then you may indeed have an organization ripe for groupthink. There tends to be a high turnover of minority employees in many organizations. If people really aren't welcome in the organization then they will leave. Thought diversity underlies cultural diversity. Without thought diversity as the basis, an organization isn't truly going to have diversity in any meaningful way. But when you do have a thought diverse organization, then you can have true cultural competence and cultural elasticity.

When an organization has a culture of promoting thought diversity, not only does it pave the way for other forms of diversity, it increases the number of options generated to solve any given problem. The more options an organization has, the more flexible and adaptable it can be in adapting to change. But for these options to be generated, the organizational culture must embrace a variety of ideas, encourage exploration and debate of those ideas, and be respectful of disagreement. Further, thought diversity positions the organization to be able to take advantage of opportunities that can keep it on the forefront of its market space, able deliver products and services in more efficient and innovative ways.

As we said at the opening of this book, we have found a strong hallmark of *It-Factor* leaders: they know it isn't about them. They don't create organizations that *think like they do*. They don't create organizations that are just a mere reflection of themselves. Great *It-Factor* leaders understand themselves, they know their strengths and their weaknesses. They take that knowledge and build teams that compensate for weaker areas and create overall balance. *It-Factor* leaders create an organizational culture that prevents groupthink from ever taking hold because they create and nurture thought diversity from within.

Your 10th step to becoming a great *It-Factor* leader is to nurture thought diversity in your enterprise.

The Eleventh Step: Don't Just Talk Tough, Master Difficult Conversations

Don't Shirk the Tough Talk by Just Talking Tough:
Mastering the Art of the Difficult Conversation

In our work coaching and teaching some inspiring leaders, we have found that those we classify as *It-Factor* leaders share a common trait: they don't shirk the tough talk. What do we mean by "tough talk"? We don't mean "talking tough": yelling at someone, or barking at them like you are their drill sergeant. For most people the "talk" that is toughest is the difficult conversation they know they need to have (and yet want to avoid) and those difficult conversations that get sprung upon them, unprepared.

It-Factor leaders know that sometimes difficult conversations are inescapable—and they work to master the art of them. If you would like to master the art of the difficult conversation, there are two things you have to know first: you have to understand what the heck is going on (understanding the dynamics) and you have to have some skills (tools to use). *It-Factor* leaders have both of these down. In this Eleventh Step to better leadership, we will explain how the human mind operates around situations involving difficult conversations and conflict and give you 20 strategies for dealing with the "tough talk" (difficult conversations) that you face.

Let's start with the surprise difficult conversation, where you might feel ambushed by the situation. Perhaps it's happened to you that you've been in a meeting, having a conversation with someone, and suddenly you realize that this is not the calm, constructive dialogue you expected. All of a sudden the tension becomes palpable as you realize this is going to be a difficult conversation. There *are* some clear red flags that a conversation is going to fall into the "difficult" category. One of those is that when people are caught in a contentious issue, they come to the table with their position staked out in the sand: and it's an "I want" position. It could be about budget, space, authority, title, or really just about anything[1].

When you start coming up against strong "I want" positions, think of them as red flags, and be prepared! You are entering what has been dubbed "a crucial conversation"[2]. Difficult conversations are often referred to as crucial conversations because at least one party at the table sees them as high stakes—and they are usually bringing a lot of emotions, wants, or needs to that conversation. It is also thought of as a crucial conversation when people see the issue very differently, often from opposing sides.

It-Factor leaders have the skills to artfully manage difficult conversations and bring about the best outcomes possible, given the circumstances. You simply cannot escape difficult conversations. It is human nature to come to situations with concerns, needs, or desires—and at times those will compete with the concerns, needs, or desires of others.

Without having the right tools, those difficult conversations can feel excruciating, prompting many to employ the ostrich strategy. Many (if not most of us) are tempted to run away from these experiences, but living in denial of the serious problems that exist will only make them fester and become worse in the future. Many an organization, project or team has failed because of the inability of the leaders to face up to reality and address those serious issues. The good news is that with some understanding of the dynamics of difficult conversations, and some tools in your pockets, these conversations don't have to be quite so daunting.

What you want in a difficult conversation is to keep everyone on the same ground of productive conflict. Yes, you are reading this correctly. It is about conflict—and conflict is not a dirty word. However, it can be either productive or destructive. Table 11.1 lists some of the ways this conflict gets destructive, so watch out for signs of those. After briefly visiting the destructive side, we'll spend most of this Step to becoming a great *It-Factor* leader talking about how to make conflict productive.

Difficult conversations go south when they fall into either silence or violence[2]. The silence side is all about *artificial harmony*—where people "go along to get along," but don't truly feel represented in the decision and don't have buy-in for it. The signs of this include masking, avoiding, or withdrawing. The violence side becomes *destructive dialog,* where people end up saying things that they often wish later they had not.

Table 11.1 The signs of destructive conflict

Silence: artificial harmony	Violence: destructive dialogue
Masking: people understate or selectively share (or face) the truth, thus the issues that need to be faced never surface	Controlling behavior: someone interrupts, over-states the facts, speaks in absolutes, or changes topics in order to maintain control of the discussion and prevent productive conflict from happening
Avoiding: people steer the conversation away from sensitive issues, preventing productive conflict from ever happening	Labeling: either the ideas of others or the individuals themselves
Withdrawing: people pull out of the conversation—so you never hear their perspective	Threatening: either verbal or physical threats, belittling others or their ideas.

Adapted from Patterson et al[2]

One of the most important strategies to artfully managing difficult conversations is to keep them safe. If the conversation is not safe, you cannot achieve productive conflict. All of the elements in table 11.1 make a conversation very un-safe.

There is a way to make these difficult conversations safe—John Gottman[3] came up with the idea of an emotional trust account, which operates like a bank account of interpersonal trust. This "emotional trust account" is how your most important relationships operate. In his model, every relationship you have has a level of trust associated with it based on what goes into the deposits-side of the equation. If you have clear expectations of others, show kindness and compassion, keep the promises you make, are loyal to those team members who aren't around, and ask forgiveness when you've dropped the ball, then you will build trust with others.

On the other side of the coin, you'll be withdrawing trust when people have to operate with unclear expectations, or when you show unkindness and discourtesy. Trust is also diminished when you break promises, are disloyal, gossipy, or show duplicity. Instead of accepting responsibility, those who blame others destroy trust, particularly when they blame those who aren't around.

But just like a bank account that holds money, if you make too many withdrawals, or spend your savings frivolously, then you will end up in relationship bankruptcy.   And bankrupt relationships lead to very unsafe conversations.

To make a conversation safe, you need to bring three things to it: patience, calmness, and objectivity (frequently cited by one of our absolute favorite authors, Ronald Heifetz[4]). These experiences require a good dose of patience to create dialogue and mutual understanding. You will need calmness because you need to remember that *it's not about you*. While it is easy to become personally involved, offended, or upset when others are, remember to stay calm. The situation may not be about you at all, even if the anger or hostility is directed at you. It might be much more about "the fairy tale feature" of difficult conversations than it is about the facts of the situation. But more about that in a minute. Another important fact to remember is that when you are a leader, you, in many ways, serve as a lightning rod. You will face a lot of angst and high stakes simply because of the role you play. Remember to separate out your self-concept from the role you fulfill in your organization.

And finally objectivity: perhaps this is the most important part of managing the difficult conversation. You need to, as author Ron Heifetz calls it, "get up on the balcony"[4], or you might have heard this described as "getting a 10,000 foot view" or "the view from the top of the mountain." Gaining objective perspective will help you implement the tools for successfully managing the difficult conversations that you will face. When you can be objective it is easier to see an issue that has many sides to it.

To illustrate our next point, we are going to use a personal story. A true story. Claudia's story.

My grandmother, Daisy, lived to be 103. One of her life goals was to never be put in a nursing home. For a while in my mid-20s, I lived close to family and was able to live with and assist my Grandmother. Working together with my mother and uncle, who each lived about an hour away, but in opposite directions, we were able to keep Grammy in her own home—for a while. But eventually I moved out of state to pursue my dream job at a university several states away—and Grammy had to give up her independence. Talk about guilt! Grammy spent her last five years in a nursing home—a nice one, but still a nursing home. When I came back to visit Grammy for that first time after her move I dreaded it. I felt partly responsible that my decision had caused Grammy to be experiencing something she never wanted—her loss of independence. I remembered that for many years she lectured us to never, ever let her end up "in one of those places." Expecting the worst, I took a deep breath and went for a visit. Grammy greeted me warmly and took me for a sweet, slow, shuffling tour of her new home. She showed me "the cabin that my daddy built for me," the "little church that served lunch every day," and all the little homes in the "village" as we walked around the hallways of the nursing home. The "cabin" was, of course, her own room. The "church" was the dining hall. And the "village" was all the other residents' rooms.

I wondered what was going on here—was she trying to make me feel better after I abandoned her? Was she lying to me? It sounded a little like "la la land," and not connected to reality. My Grandmother taught me a lot and gave me many insights in her life—but none more important than her last gift. My epiphany: what Grammy was doing was making sense of the reality around her. She was taking what she could see and adding a logic to it that helped her understand her world. Her great gift to me was the insight that we all do that. It is hard, if not impossible, to live in darkness and mystery, so we fill in the gaps of the details that we don't know about. We make sense of the story that we see.

Adding these details is so helpful to us, that we do it without knowing that we are. We think it brings light to the situation, but when misdirected it doesn't bring enlightenment. Sometimes we attribute motive to another person or group simply because it makes sense to us. Usually we don't have any idea that we are filling in those gaps—because it makes such perfect sense to us that we never question whether this is reality or not.

This insight gave Claudia and Ruben the idea of a continuum of reality. Certainly we have met people who understood their own feelings and motives, asked for clarification before assuming the motives of others, could describe their feelings and their needs in ways that were assertive and yet neither judgmental nor abusive of others. These individuals could own their mistakes when they made them. And we've had the privilege of knowing quite a few people like these: these are *It-Factor* leaders. We think of these people as very self-enlightened and try hard to learn from them and to be like them.

We also have come across others who hear just a little bit of the story and excitedly "fill in the gaps" from their own imagination (figure 11.1).They quickly explain the nefarious reasons behind why a co-worker or a boss made a decision, and they add dubious information they are sure are facts. On a good day, we think of this behavior as living in the land of unreality, but we've seen behavior that can only be named "soap opera world" at times, too. For these folks, there is just no grounding in fact or reality when they are at that end of the continuum.

FIGURE 11.1 The Continuum of Reality

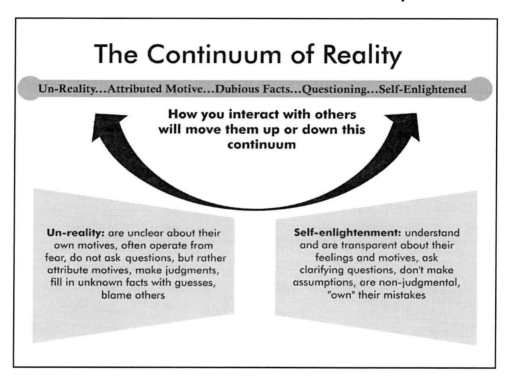

Yet, people who are living in a "soap opera world" are still trying to make sense of the world in which they find themselves. It is human nature to do so, and they likely have no idea they are making up the story. What is important here is that when you are in a difficult conversation, you need to realize that if someone is scared or angry, they might be operating from a bit lower on this continuum—and they might struggle to be *self-enlightened* in that moment. How you treat them, how you handle this conversation, will influence their position on the continuum. If you treat them with dignity and respect, make observations (not accusations) and remain calm you will help them move to the right-hand side of the continuum. If you threaten, justify, and/or defend the actions of yourself or others, then you will likely push them to the left-hand side of the continuum. If *you* do those things, you are probably operating at the un-reality side of the continuum yourself.

You might have to help the other person—and sometimes yourself—see where this "making sense" of the world is founded on shaky ground. We'll talk about strategies that will be very helpful to you when you run into an "I want" position with someone who is not very far along that continuum of self-enlightenment.

This range of reality also gave us insight into two groups we see as being, well, off of any continuum of enlightenment. Far beyond living in a soap opera world of drama are those who live in what we can only call *La La Land*. These are individuals who truly believe the story they tell themselves, but sadly that story is a twisted illusion based on ludicrous facts and disinformation. If you present them with facts that are contrary to their worldview, they disregard them. They simply don't live in reality at all—and they refuse to look at it. For Grandma Daisy, this limited view of the world came about because her nearly 100-year old brain wasn't working as clearly as it had been a mere five years before. But there are those who are not centenarians and have no such biological reason. They live there by choice. They may not realize they are making that choice, but they live in a *la la land* of their own creation.

The other group is more dangerous. Happily we don't believe that there are very many of this group about. However, if you have a long career you may run into at least one or two. For lack of a better name, these are what we call "5-percenters," based on our hope that 95% of the people we all meet and work with will be reasonable folks. But 5-percenters are not reasonable folks. These are individuals who will lie to you, give you false information, or flawed data in the hope that you will screw up and they will advance while you fall behind. These people simply do not share a moral code with most of humanity. They wish to advance themselves or their agenda at all costs. They think nothing of using you or stabbing you in the back—it's all about them.

There is nothing in this book or indeed any of our work that can really help you deal with a 5-percenter. Our leadership work can help you deal with people at the low end of the continuum of reality, even *la la landers*, but not with those who understand reality and *desire* to be knowingly deceptive about it. Our best advice to you: if you have a 5%er on your team, get them off your bench. No organization can function healthfully when they tolerate 5-percenter behavior. And your team, organization, or enterprise will get the behavior it tolerates[5, 6].

Let's relate this idea about the continuum of reality to what happens in difficult conversations. When people come to the table with that *I want* statement, they will present two items in their arguments; *facts* and *fairy tales*[2]. The proportion you get of each depends quite a bit on where they stand on that continuum of reality. The further they are towards true reality and self-enlightenment, the more they will bring facts to the discussion. However, it is very hard when anyone is stuck on the left hand side of the continuum to understand the facts because they are stuck in the fairy tale feature of the story they are sharing.

The fairy tale feature is how one makes sense of the facts, how one strings them together into what they think of as the story. It's a lot like Claudia's Grandmother at the end of her life. She could not understand that the "village" she was describing was, in fact, a fairy tale. Now for Grammy, that fairy tale helped her cope and adjust well in the last years of her life. But for the rest of us, these fairy tales can really get in the way. When we interpret the facts by adding motives or fill in the details that we really don't know, tensions can escalate and we can plunge further into un-reality or "soap opera world." All too often, the *story* may have little to do with *actual facts*.

Consider this example of a fairy tale that can exist in someone's head:

> *"He's a workaholic, but totally self-centered! Sure, he's successful but watch out for him—he will only work with you if it increases his power or if he can get some control over you. What can you do to get a little genuine cooperation around here?"*

It is hard to sift the facts out of this particular story. Perhaps the other person works hard and puts in a lot of hours? One thing we *do know* is that we all carry negative stories around in our heads about others. It is unfortunate but it seems to be a human characteristic.

In this example, "increases his power" and "get some control" aren't behaviors—they are *stories*, value statements, interpretations. But they are not facts. When trying to manage a difficult conversation, the first thing you have to do is separate fact from fiction. But be prepared because even bigger challenges await you.

We talked about the curse of saving face when it came to *groupthink* strangling the truth and creativity out of an organization. In difficult conversations, it shows up again. Back in Step Three, we talked about the phenomenon that once we come to a conclusion or make a decision, we don't like to say that we were wrong. Think of someone you've known who sunk a lot of money into a fancy—but not too reliable—car. Oh how they hate to admit that they made a mistake—and they tell you all the reasons why only true car lovers own this kind of car, that their little baby is just getting a little attention in the shop, that they are "an enthusiast." This dissonance effect[7] happens on a subconscious level—in part because it feels good to make a decision and there is a boost in self-esteem once we have come to a conclusion, and of course, most people feel uncomfortable admitting that they were wrong. How does this translate into the workplace? Well, if you think someone is a jerk you are likely to look for examples of them being a jerk—and unfortunately ignore examples of them being a fair teammate. After you've made your decision that they are a jerk, all your mind looks for is evidence to confirm the decision you've already made. The real problem is that most people have no idea they are making this error of very selectively seeing the world around them. The problem with our filters is that it leads us to collect very selective evidence, and that's a shaky foundation upon which to build our interpretation of the facts. When they do see evidence to the contrary, then for many it can be hard to say, "wow, I made a mistake," particularly if they've been calling that person a jerk to others.

Researchers have studied gamblers and found that once they make a bet their confidence in the bet goes up[8]. They start looking for data that justifies their choice. The same "dissonance effect" happens with everything, especially stories we tell ourselves about each other and conflict. Interestingly, this effect is multiplied the more public the story becomes. If people hear us telling our stories, our need to justify them becomes even stronger. You might have heard this described as people who are "married to a decision" once they've made it. This is about saving face. If you can get over your need to save face, you can become a true *It-Factor* leader.

The fairy tales you tell yourself do more than help you make sense of the world: they shape how you feel about the situation, or the other person, or the world in general. How you feel has a very big impact on how you act. How you act, in turn, impacts how you feel. In the end you are making a substantial contribution to the problem that frustrated you in the first place. In the situations where you are frustrated, angry, annoyed, or upset, always consider how you are a part of your own problem. You create the reality that exists around you. Don't be surprised if you find that you are a *big* part of your own problem.

When you can be objective about a problem, step away from it, witness it from "up on the balcony" (remember that patience, calmness, and objectivity?[4]), you can deal with that problem much more realistically. The balcony is a much more effective vantage point to work from.

We feel this section skims the surface of the dynamics of difficult conversations, but there are some very good books we recommend for that deep dive to learn more. Two are called <u>Crucial Conversations</u>[2] and <u>Crucial Confrontations</u>[9], published by McGraw Hill. Another we recommend is <u>The Practice of Adaptive Leadership</u>, by Ronald Heifetz, Marty Linsky, and Alexander Grasshow[4].

Now that we have some understanding of why those darn conversations become so difficult, let's start to explore some tools to use.

Strategies for Managing the Difficult Conversation: 20 ways to make the tough talk work for you

Strategy 1: Be in touch with your body

The absolute first and incredibly important foundation of harnessing conflict to create productive dialogue is usually overlooked. It is to take stock of how you feel physically. Difficult conversations make most people very tense. If you find they make you tense, then you will probably notice that your muscles tighten up in your hands, face, neck, and chest. Your breathing becomes shallow and rather than doing a deep and relaxed-type of breathing, you are more likely to take quick, sometimes gulping breaths that are just chest deep. This can promote that rather embarrassing tendency to turn bright red when you are upset or tense. Thus, the first thing you need to do is to take a deep breath, breathing all the way down to your abdomen, called "belly breathing." Take a few of these and give your muscles permission to relax. Set your feet evenly on the floor, relaxing the tension in your feet and legs. Feel the chair you are sitting in, feel it supporting you. Take a couple more breaths. It is much easier to think and react calmly when your breathing is relaxed.

Claudia trained as a hypnotherapist earlier on in her career. In her work back then, counseling patients with compulsive eating and eating disorders, she found that the anxiety people experienced around conflict could really be mitigated by learning simple breathing techniques. Deep, relaxed breathing is an essential part of successful hypnosis, meditation, and relaxation. It facilitates acting with intention, rather than *reacting* to a situation. Oh yes, and when her patients were calmer it was much easier for them to choose healthy behaviors too.

Strategy 2: Prepare yourself mentally

The next step is to prepare yourself mentally. Of course, you need to do your research about the situation, but it also means doing your research about yourself—what are your intentions in this conversation? What do you want to result from the dialogue? What is your story? What are the facts and what are the fairy tales you are telling yourself? Just where are *you* on the continuum of reality? If you don't do this essential first homework, it will be hard to use the other tools of managing difficult conversations with authenticity and success.

In Ruben's work as a lawyer, he knows that any attorney worth his or her salt spends a good bit of time doing a self-assessment with the client prior to going into any kind of mediation. Without it, they won't be able to see all the possible acceptable outcomes, and are likely to get stuck on just a singular solution. This, of course, limits the options for success and increases the chances for frustration all around.

Strategy 3: Speak in "I" statements

A powerful tool in mastering difficult conversations is to understand that no one has a patent on "the truth". Even when someone is operating in a world of hurt and fear, and therefore pushed way down on that continuum of being "in touch with reality", the way they see the world is the truth they know. If you can't each share your perspective non-judgmentally, then it is unlikely that the conversation is going to move towards a greater understanding or resolution any time soon. If you hold onto your "truth" like a lifeline, then you severely limit any chance of seeing a bigger or different picture, or of learning more.

When you speak, maintain humility, refrain from telling people what they think, feel, or believe. For example, accusations like "you never believe me", or "you just don't listen when I share ideas", assume that you can read minds and actually know what someone is thinking or feeling. Instead, treat your view as a hypothesis, talk in terms of behavior (see Strategy #5) and ask for clarifications. Table 11.2 translates these accusation-style statements into hypothetical queries.

Table 11.2 Reframing Statements as Hypothesis

Accusatory Statement:	Reframed Statement:
You just don't listen when I share ideas.	I notice that when I tell you an idea for the X project, you seem to engage in other activities such as checking your phone or email. That makes me wonder whether you heard and understood these suggestions, or whether you find them pertinent to the challenges we face.
You don't appreciate the work I do around here.	I have observed a pattern of when you ask me to gather the background research for a proposal, that you don't say thank you, nor do you credit my work with the team. This leads me to think that you don't believe that initial data gathering is useful to you or valuable to the project. Is this the case?
You never believe me.	I notice that even though I presented all of our financial figures at our meeting, you still went to Roz to verify all of my numbers. That makes me wonder whether or not you trust the information that I give you.

Notice how phrasing the statement has a huge impact on how the conversation either unravels or progresses.

Strategy 4: Avoid the hot words and stories

Hot words are the highly emotional terms and the absolutes that trigger strong responses. Hot stories include *the Villain*, that's when you hear someone saying "it's all someone else's fault," *the Victim,* where the individual is saying "it's not MY fault," and *Fate,* which is when people throw in the towel and say "there's nothing I can do"[2, 9]. Find yourself saying *"there is a Villain!"* Really? That's a pretty easy excuse for the trouble you face and awfully one-sided. Sometimes, when the fruit is too low hanging it might be way over-ripe. Watch out for stories you tell yourself that can be rotted at the core. So what could be their real motivation, their perspective of the situation? Villain? Probably not. Having needs you don't know about or understand...now there's a theory to explore.

And you're the *Victim?* Another person or cruel Fate has boxed you in? You're truly powerless? Absolutely owning no responsibility for the situation? Hmmm...probably not. Afraid to act? Maybe. Unsure how to act? Quite plausibly. But incapable of acting....not likely. Completely not culpable for any part of the situation? Here's a clue: If you're living, breathing, and interacting with others then you probably own some of the responsibility for the situation at hand. When it comes to difficult situations, don't buy into your complete innocence. You need to understand your own perspective, motives, needs, biases, and beliefs in order to really be self-enlightened. So if you catch yourself using these hot words or telling yourself these hot stories, challenge yourself to change your perspective—change your position on the continuum of reality.

Strategy 5: Describe the behaviors

All too often, difficult conversations arise from our own attribution of motive to another person. We do that when we ascribe underlying feelings to be the impetus for their actions. One of the most important things you can do in a difficult conversation is to focus on and describe the *behaviors* you see, and not what you *feel* or what you believe the other person thinks. When Ruben went to graduate school for psychology, his teachers pounded this lesson in objectivity into the students' heads. It was such a crucial part working through the conflicts they were learning to dissect and gracefully handle. Here is a typical workplace-based situation:

> "Jo was 5 minutes late today. Jo was 10 minutes late yesterday."

Those are facts. But focusing on a feeling or attributing motive would sound more like:

> "Jo is lazy" or "Jo is so disorganized" or "Jo is not committed" or "Jo is just stealing from us by not coming in on time—it's totally selfish and unfair to everyone else who is here on time!"

Those are fairy tales. These examples attribute motive and add a conclusion, which could be very inaccurate. All too quickly we attribute motive, the human mind seemingly programed to do so—and most of us don't even realize we are doing it. While it makes sense to "make sense" of the world, when you layer on a fairy tale or create a soap opera out of some wisps of truth you are bound for trouble. When you find yourself doing this...*stop*! Challenge yourself to move further along the continuum of reality—stay away from *fairy tales* and move to *facts*. Write down on a piece of paper the story you are telling yourself—and then dissect that story. Identify the facts in the situation and the fantasy. Then concentrate on the facts. As you keep working with this strategy you will find that you can quickly learn to distinguish fact from fantasy in your head, and thus move yourself up further on that continuum of enlightenment. The next trick will be to help others do this too—but you have to start with yourself before you can help others. The skills for managing difficult conversations are a little bit like riding in an airplane—you know when they tell you:

> *...should it be needed, an oxygen mask will automatically appear in front of you. ... If you are travelling with a child or someone who requires assistance, secure your mask on first, and then assist the other person.*

First, you take care of your own needs. Put your oxygen mask on first, before helping others. It is true in many aspects of life: you can't be very effective in taking care of others if you don't take care of yourself first. Once you help yourself realize what the facts are regarding both you and the situation, you will be in a better position to have a more productive conversation.

Strategy 6: Exercise leadership, not authority

One of the mistakes people often make in difficult conversations is to confuse authority with leadership. True *It-Factor* leaders have that difference figured out. Face it, if you could impose your will upon others there would be no difficult conversations, or having them would not present such a challenge. When you can impose your will that is called having *authority*. Authority is very different from leadership. When you use *authority*, others must follow you or suffer the consequences. When we teach workshops on Managing Difficult Conversations, it is common for some participants to bring up the military and the use of authority when conflicts arise. However, our experience in working with military leaders is quite different. They routinely tell us that *influence* always trumps authority, even in their settings. They need the skills to artfully manage the difficult conversation so as to create willing buy-in—relying on authority is often a short and foolish road to derailment. The military leaders we have worked with agree that when you exercise *leadership* others follow you and are engaged in the outcome, and all by their own volition. So do ask, don't tell. Do dialogue, don't order. Do seek to understand, don't dictate.

When you have to manage a truly difficult conversation, you cannot comfortably rely on authority. Even if you *have* the authority, you might actually lose power or effectiveness (or even magnify the problem) by acting on the basis of your authority. When you need others to willingly cooperate, whether they are an external stakeholder or an internal player, you are left with the tool of influence. *It-Factor* leaders work hard to master the skills around influence.

Strategy 7: Be curious

Being curious is also a critical factor in transforming "tough talk" into meaningful dialogue. When you can come to a conversation with curiosity and a sense of open-mindedness rather than being judgmental, it is easier "to listen with the intensity usually reserved for speaking"[10]. Research in communications has found that 50% of whether others will trust you in high stakes situations depends on your listening, caring and empathy[11]. If you find yourself being judgmental, revisit the third and fourth strategies, as you may be living in your own fairy tale. Being able to be curious, and not judgmental, is an essential component of that.

Instead, use curiosity as it is an essential tool for managing the art of the difficult conversation.

Strategy 8: Share internal information

Another clever strategy that actually strengthens trust is sharing internal information. Don't worry, this is not about sharing corporate secrets—it's really about sharing your feelings. Most interestingly, negotiation researchers have found that *sharing feelings* is a powerful technique to use even when the people negotiating are representing big business interests who aren't known for playing nice in these situations. Researcher Neil Rackham of the Huthwaite Research Group found that when coal and steel labor and management negotiators shared information about their feelings during the session, they ended up with better contract outcomes than those who went into the difficult conversations with an iron fist and strictly talking tough[12].

Research has given evidence to support what Ruben has learned in his work as an attorney: when you come to agreement on even very small issues, like when you'll break for lunch or how you will speak to one another, you are more likely to agree on other issues later in the conversation. Agreement begets agreement. Also, giving verbal headlines helps keeps you both organized during these challenging discussions. An example of a verbal headline is when you say, "we have 15 more minutes until we take our first break—let's take a moment to re-assess if we're covering the topics we set as our goals." *It-Factor* leaders use verbal headlines pretty frequently to keep everyone on the same page. When you don't use verbal headlines like these, you are working from information that *you* are aware of, but may not have shared with the other person. You should not assume that the other person shares the information, beliefs or values that you are using as the foundation for your conversation.   By sharing these verbal headlines with the other person, you can come to an agreement on them, and as an agreement often leads to more agreements, that's a good direction to head in a difficult conversation.

Strategy 9: Take personal responsibility

Taking personal responsibility is a good place to start to open the conversation with another person when they are angry at you or at a situation they believe you influence or control. The goal is to open up the dialogue, acknowledging that you are empathetic to the concerns of the other person. By going first, taking the initial risk of being honest, you help build a climate of trust. Here is an example statement for just such a situation, created by Ohio State University law professor, Josh Stulberg[13]:

> *"Thank you for coming in to see me today. I appreciate you taking the time to discuss this issue. I want to start off by apologizing for not noticing earlier that you seem frustrated with this situation. I want you to know that I value you and understand your contribution to the team. I am distressed that you might have been feeling out of sync here while I was distracted by my other responsibilities. However, I hope that now while we are both here, we can talk about the situation and come to some better understanding."*

This type of introduction helps diffuse tensions around the situation and allows the other person to talk about the challenges they have been facing. Josh is a real *It-Factor* leader. His statement takes some responsibility—for "being distracted by my other responsibilities" and not noticing that the person was feeling out of sync. Notice that Josh didn't put "hot" labels on the feeling, like "angry, tense, upset," etc. It is reasonable for a leader to have other responsibilities, so this statement isn't taking *full* responsibility for the situation, but it is a very good invitation to the other party to help them engage in some meaningful dialogue. Try his technique of authentically taking some personal responsibility and see how people open up.

Strategy 10: Open-ended listening

Reflect for a moment on when you last talked with someone and you felt they truly heard what you were saying. How did that feel to you? What happened in that conversation? There is great value in "feeling heard," particularly when one stakeholder is upset or angry. A common name for what we call Open-Ended listening could be active listening, but this technique is more than just active listening. When engaging in Open-Ended listening your mind is quiet, and not creating an answer to their concerns. A fundamental element of Open-Ended listening is that you really embrace that *"It's not about you" perspective* that we've brought up over and over again in this book. You listen without judgment of the person, their interpretation of the facts, or their understanding of the situation. You do not enumerate the flaws in their argument. You listen. The result is that this technique helps people *feel* heard. Feeling heard is a very powerful tool. Don't be surprised if this is the only tool you need to use in handling many of the difficult conversations you face, it's *that* powerful. Some helpful questions to ask start with *"tell me about...,"* *"explain to me...,"* *"describe for me....,"* or *"why"* Those open ended questions will help you listen and learn more. These are called TEDY questions (**T**ell...**E**xplain...**D**escribe...Wh**y**) and are a favorite of our good friend and expert in sales, Dave Roberts, a professor at the UNC Business School[14]. He always teaches TEDY questions as an essential part of handling negotiating—which can be some of the trickiest difficult conversations you'll face.

In case you doubt us, we would point out some very important research by one of Claudia's cherished mentors and colleagues, Dr. Vincent Covello, who is a true guru of the communications world[11]. He runs the Center for Risk Communication in New York. His research indicates that when people are in high stress situations, such as when they are engaged in difficult conversations, they trust you based on your ability to listen, care, and show empathy. You might be surprised to learn that your *competence and expertise* in the issue, even your *honesty and openness* make up only 15-20% each of the trust that others place in you. All other factors—such as *what the situation is*—account for another 15-20% of whether people trust you. When the stakes are high, compassion trumps content. Of crucial importance is that Dr. Covello's communication studies have shown that listeners assess this about you in the first 9 to 30 seconds[11].

So, when the stakes are high, your ability to build trust with others is crucial to you being able to bring the difficult conversation to a successful resolution. Some of the strongest tools in your pocket are listening, caring, and empathy. Open-ended listening will help you, so keep these TEDY questions at hand. Remember these as we dig further into the trove of strategies for artfully managing difficult conversations.

Strategy 11: Rephrasing

Rephrasing is another tool that you will find useful. After you have listened carefully, using Open-Ended Listening, let the person know you heard them by rephrasing what they told you. Put it into *different* words. That will help you gain clarity regarding the situation and the discussion. Remember, this situation is uncomfortable for them and the conversation is a difficult one for the both of you. They are talking with you now because this problem has vital importance to them. People react strongly and feel some sense of crisis around the issues that eventually turn into difficult conversations. When people feel a sense of crisis, they don't always say exactly what they mean and sometimes difficult things are, well, difficult to say. When you rephrase their concerns, you give them the opportunity to say whether what you heard was accurate or not. It also helps you take their concerns out of the realm of the personal and into the objective, as much as possible.

For example, your colleague might say:

> *Did you see Jennifer's proposal for absorbing the latest round of budget cuts? It just further shows how totally out of touch she is with what we do and what the customers and clients expect from us. Doesn't she realize the damage that will occur with that kind of reduction in staff and programs? We might as well just kiss goodbye all the relationships we've developed over the past 5 years.*

As the leader or manager you might respond:

> *I hear you saying you're concerned that the current proposal on the table for cutting the budget might have a devastating effect on programs and services.*

The goal of rephrasing is to help bring clarity to the situation. The "effect on programs and services" may be related to the organization's mission and capacity or existing relationships with external partners. It could have implications for directional or strategic change. It could also signal that the decision-making process for cutting costs may have benefitted from having included other perspectives. By rephrasing you can come to greater clarity about what is the real underlying issue.

However, let's assume that their view, their position, is slightly skewed from reality. Then, the good leader invests in them to help them gain insight into what they are feeling and why they are feeling this way, via listening, reflecting, and reframing, which we'll talk about next. This can help them find the path to a more rational truth of the organization, which hopefully will also be a more satisfying perspective of the organization for them as well.

Strategy 12: Reframing

We just mentioned reframing above —let's define that strategy, or tool, here. This helps the person to see their concerns in another light. Given a different perspective many come to a different opinion on the subject. For example, one *It-Factor* executive we worked with told us how a member of his support staff would spend quite a bit of time with him, mostly chatting. Another executive berated him for "wasting his time" listening to her. Our client wisely explained:

> *"That's how I keep my finger on the pulse of the organization. By listening, I know how people are feeling, what they care about, what they are pleased with, and what concerns them. She might not realize it, but she's one of the best information sources I've got!"*

Reframing from "Why should I listen to their whining?" to "Listening is one of the most important things I do all day" is an important shift in perspective. Being able to reframe a situation or perspective is an important tool for managing the difficult conversation and turning a "tough talk" into meaningful, constructive dialogue.

Strategy 13: Reflecting

Another strategy that will help you create authentic dialogue is reflecting. When restating the person's perspective lands you back to square one, with them repeating the same words over and over again, it might not be their *words* that need to be heard. It might be the *emotional* content that is the energy behind their concerns.

You cannot avoid the emotional side of the conversation. If you're going to excel at the art of the difficult conversation, you have to accept that humans are emotional beings. Some of us are more aware of our emotions than others, but to deny that humans are affected by their emotional state is to deny our humanity.

When using the reflecting strategy, an appropriate statement could be:

> *I hear the frustration in your voice. Please tell me more about what you're feeling here.*

Or

> *This situation seems to be creating a great deal of anxiety. I'd like to understand more clearly how you're feeling and understand why.*

Labeling the emotions attached to the issue can help identify the crisis nature of the concern to the other party. It gives them a chance to acknowledge their feelings or even to correct you (for example, "actually, I'm not frustrated, I'm furious at this situation"). Typically in these situations the emotions will be related to not being heard, not having their perspective given due weight or consideration, or some other outcome that can legitimately be understood as a threat to their basic interests. It is surprising how often difficult conversations become unstuck when you apply this simple strategy.

Strategy #14: Interests vs. positions

The basic concept behind interests and positions is that in any debate, argument, conversation or negotiation, the *I want* statement that people have is their position. When people have a position, there is one—and only one—thing that will satisfy them. However, what you need to understand is that *behind* every position is a much larger field of interest. As a frame of reference, here is a very simple example. Someone might say, "I want ice cream." This is their position and there is only one condition that will satisfy this position: ice cream. But if you get people talking about their larger field of interest you might discover that what they really want is dessert or something sweet after a meal. Ice cream is ice cream—but there are more than a dozen different kinds of desserts that could be just as satisfying.

Let's say you're having a difficult conversation and everyone is talking about what they want—their *positions*. Here's a clue: If you're bargaining over positions, then you *are* having the wrong conversation. Whenever you choose a position, then all you've got is your stake in the sand and you're stuck with very limited possibilities of what could meet your needs or provide solutions to the current challenges you face. The essential problem is that after staking out a position, people feel a need to defend and justify that position—and the more they do defend and justify it, the more committed they become to it. Remember how cognitive dissonance and the need to save face cement people to an idea?[7] Be aware that arguing over positions can endanger the relationship you have with the other person as well.

Consider this: when you're bargaining over positions, the best you can end up with is compromise. In itself, compromise is not a terrible thing, but merely placating everyone at the table doesn't lend itself to creating innovative solutions that really get to the heart of the issue. So when you're in a conversation make sure you're having the *right* conversation.

Probably the most powerful tool in the deck is to explore people's interests rather than their positions. Attorneys are trained in negotiation. Ruben and many other negotiation experts consider positions vs. interests the paramount tool for success. So, how do you find out what someone's field of interest might be? By careful listening, by asking the questions we mentioned earlier of "tell me about….," "explain to me….," "describe for me…," or "why" you can elucidate these fields. It is important to create a conversation covering a range of concerns.

When you create a conversation around interests you are actually defining the problem or challenge. The key point here is that every problem has multiple solutions that can satisfy it. What is a position? In effect, a position is nothing more than getting stuck on just one solution to address a need.

There is a famous landmark example of this in the Mid-East.[15] In the 6-day war between Israel and Egypt, Israel won territory in the Sinai that had been Egyptian for thousands of years. Egypt demanded that this land be returned to them and Israel countered that this land was theirs. It looked like Mid-East tensions would boil over into another war. These were the *positions* of the two countries, their *I want* statement. And peace was going nowhere.

Nowhere, that is, until diplomacy stepped in. President Jimmy Carter, a very gifted statesman, spent two weeks at Camp David negotiating with Israeli Prime Minister Menachem Begin, and Egyptian President Anwar Sadat. He went back and forth between their cabins, personally overseeing the negotiations. He got each party talking about what they really wanted—and it turned out that who owned the sand was not the real issue. Israel's field of interest was much more about security: they didn't want a bunch of tanks poised on their border. Egypt's was much more about honoring their history. After all, the Sinai was a part of the empire of the Pharaohs of ancient Egypt, so while their initial positions could never be satisfied by one solution, their fields of interest actually could be satisfied. The solution was Egyptian sovereignty with a large demilitarized area to provide Israel with security. That was the overlap of their fields of interest—their area of *shared* interest.

When it comes to understanding people's fields of interests, keep in mind that the most powerful interests are basic human needs. Just like in the Sinai, security issues are of fundamental importance to people. Economic well-being—having stable and predictable work—is highly valued by most people. Human beings need a sense of belonging as well. Don't underestimate that as a core part of human motivation. Being recognized for one's work as well as being a valuable person, with personal worth to others, is a key human interest. This adds to having control over one's life. These factor in much larger than other, more tangible elements.

Let's take a moment to look at an example of this with a disgruntled employee: someone who has been with your company for a long time, but you find out that they are now saying vitriolic things about a person, or department, or the company. What do you do? Order him to stop telling people what he thinks? Reprimand him? Fire him? Do nothing? All of these options stem from the position that this kind of behavior is undesirable. Pause for a moment and think about what the *interests* are.

Reprimanding or firing the employee is not likely to make the employee stop his behavior. In fact it may exacerbate the behavior and even make it look justifiable. Think about why the employee has an interest in these behaviors? Are they not coping well with a change? Are they feeling unappreciated, disgruntled, powerless, or voiceless? Maybe he felt he was denied a promotion that he deserved? If so, his *interest* is to become less disgruntled, feel more appreciated, have more power, or to be heard. His goal is not to trash the organization, but to become an engaged employee once again. In fact, as his manager, that's your goal, too! Look at how our leader "Linda" manages this difficult conversation in Table 11.3.

Table 11.3 Example Difficult Conversation

A typical conversation between Wesley, the disgruntled employee, and Linda, the artful leader, might look like this (for the sake of length, this example does not illustrate every tool listed in this section):

Linda: Hi Wesley. I wanted to talk to you today because I am concerned— you seem dissatisfied. Can you share with me what's going on?

Wesley: Dissatisfied? Me? No, everything is fine—why do you ask?

Linda: "Well, Wes, I've heard that you aren't happy and I wanted to know the truth. You've been here a long time and you've accomplished some great things for us. Your team has led the way on many new innovations and your skills are really valuable to me and to the company. I think it would be a shame if you were disturbed about something, really upset, and I didn't know about it. You're a part of my team and I care about you.

Wesley: Oh...well...thanks. You know, I feel I've made a lot of contributions to this company too. I've built a strong team, been innovative—maybe too out of the box at times—but Linda, despite my great track record here I just can't get any traction on the Johnson project. Jo is in charge of that and she won't listen to my advice. She hasn't done one thing that I've told her to do. Given my seniority and experience, I don't understand why this wasn't my assignment!

Linda: Gee, Wes, it sounds like you're feeling unheard and left out of the action.

Wesley: Exactly. I think that project should be given to me.

Linda: I'm sure you would do well with it, but it is important that others have opportunities to manage big projects too. We need a broad, deep bench of experienced and skilled people—we need to invest in them like we have in you. That's one of the aspects of our company that gives us strength in the market. How do you see it?

Wes: Yes, I agree. I see that side of it. Our talent is our people...but....

Linda: I'm glad we share that basic interest at heart—the overall strength of the company. But we still have the situation of you feeling like an outsider in your own company, in a division that you helped build.

Wesley: You have a way of saying it—and, of course, I want a strong company. I have helped build this company and now when the best assignments are being given to less experienced and junior people, where do I fit in? What does it count for that I have done so much?

Linda: You know, our customers need to see us, to know us as a strong and integrated unit. They need to be comfortable with us as a team. When they hear of internal strife it is like bad advertising—and from the quadrant that hurts us the most. I believe we are a good team. I believe there will be other Johnson projects. We are simply too good at what we do to think of this as the only great opportunity. But if customers hear otherwise from us, then we might miss out on those opportunities.

Wesley: Our most important advertisement is our work. It speaks for everything we do. I care deeply about the quality of work we produce. That's why I was surprised when the assignment wasn't given to me.

Linda: Precisely. "Our most important advertisement is our work." precisely! And also *we* are walking billboards for our company. Everything each of us do, everyplace we go, we create the future of this company. *You* create the future of this company. *I* create the future of this company. You help us open doors or shut them. Those are the doors of opportunity to the next big "Johnson project." I'd like to see all our managers have such a fabulous opportunity, but for that to happen rests far more in your hands than mine.

Wesley: So you're saying that Jo's success with this project will be all our success—in potentially very tangible ways.

Linda: Jo is highly talented, but that doesn't mean that the Johnson Project can't still be hurt by other developments, comments, or non-cooperation. While she's highly talented, that doesn't mean her project can't be *helped* by other developments, comments, or cooperation either! That's the nature of being a team. Let me ask you, how do you think Jo is feeling at this point?

Wesley: Hmm, well. Scared! Probably excited. Maybe overwhelmed. I'd guess annoyed—at me that is. (laughs). She does have a lot of great ideas, but some are just too risky!

Linda: Maybe too out of the box at times?

Wesley: Ouch! Well maybe you're right. She does kind of remind me of myself when I was younger.

Linda: The best way to understand how Jo is feeling is to talk with her, and maybe if you have been a little over-enthusiastic in your advice you could offer an apology for that.

Wesley: That might rebuild that bridge I suppose. I probably have really annoyed her.

Linda: I think that's a stellar idea. When it comes to bridges, one of the most important leadership skills we need is the ability to mend them. Now, what do we do about how you're feeling? You are a valued team member and ideally I would like to see you be happy here, and I understand the value of your contribution.

Wesley: I hear what you're saying. This has been helpful. I guess I have been feeling a bit out of sync. I will ask Jo how I can be supportive. Is that the word you always use? Supportive of her success? I guess I have been telling her what to do and I reckon I wouldn't much like it if she did that to me.

Linda: Excellent idea! Putting yourself in her shoes and really thinking about how she feels will probably help you have a constructive dialogue with her.

At this point Linda might discuss with Wesley strategies for feeling more "in sync" with the company, despite the fact that he doesn't now have the "choice" assignment. She might work with him on learning how to mentor —not direct—others. Notice how she did not accuse him of bad-talking the company. After all, she had no first-hand knowledge of that, although she could have shared her concerns more directly if needed. This approach avoided the embarrassment of accusation (which was not needed at this stage of the situation) and allowed for a positive discussion in which Wes could begin to take responsibility for his own happiness and job satisfaction. Linda helped him elucidate his feelings and to understand that his true interests—team work to produce success and a positive view of the company by customers—were vital to his interests of more responsibility and opportunity. Furthermore, her comments helped draw out the boundaries of acceptable organizational culture at the company. Often gentle reminders are very helpful.

Let's look at some of the things that Linda did and did not do with Wesley in Table 11.4.

Table 11.4:
Analysis of Linda's difficult conversation with Wesley

Linda did not:	Linda did:
• Threaten him • Accuse him • Order him to do anything—or to stop doing anything • Give into his demands • Be judgmental • Defend Jo's capabilities to justify the decision • Become defensive	• Inquire about his feelings and help him understand his feelings • Gain agreement on the overall interests of the company and the team • Help him put himself in Jo's shoes • Help him see the larger picture of the situation • Affirm his role in and value to the company • Provide hope for engagement in valued work in the future

Positions vs. Interests is a sophisticated tool and a very powerful one for managing difficult conversations. You will often find that many of the previous strategies we've discussed will fold in quite nicely with Positions vs. Interests.

Strategy #15: Have the Right Conversation

Having the right conversation is an important concept because often we have the same conversation over and over again and yet never come to any kind of a resolution. When that happens take it as a red flag that you are having the *wrong* conversation. The easiest, and we could say most shallow level of discussion to have is about just content. Let's say that your direct report has a temper flare at work. This is when something happens once. For example, you might say to your direct report, "Chris, that event seemed to make you really upset."

That conversation might work to fix the problem. Chris might keep his or her cool after that, since someone noticed and commented on the outburst. But life can be a lot more complicated than it looks on the surface. So if the same *situation* keeps happening again and again, then you'll probably find that you need to have that *conversation* again, only this time you'll need to talk about either process or pattern. In our example, you might then say, "Chris, I noticed that you have spoken very sharply to Pat four times in the past two weeks." Pointing out to someone that a behavior has happened more than once can often make an impact in helping them to put the work into changing it. But if it doesn't, then you need to have a much deeper conversation. In this case, you need to understand much more about why Chris is speaking sharply and managing emotions inappropriately. That conversation could start out something like, "Chris, I notice that there seems to be a lot of tension between you and Pat. You've spoken pretty harshly on more than one occasion and I'm worried for your working relationship. Can you tell me more about what's going on?"

This is a conversation about relationships—and Chris could be feeling professional jealousy, or perhaps Chris feels that Pat has done something untrustworthy. It could also be that Chris is having a rough time lately and that there is no problem with Pat, but that Chris' behavior is inappropriate and misdirected. You won't know until you have this conversation. If there is deep rift here, you won't be able to make headway towards improving teamwork until you have the *right* conversation. The bottom line here is to make sure you are having the right conversation at the right level so that you can address the problem in the right way.

Strategy #16: Shift the Frame of Reference

When agreement is a scarce commodity, part of the problem might be that people are too close to the issue. A great strategy or tool to use is to strategically shift the frames of reference. If people can't agree right now, today, then shift the time frame out. You might shift it by 1 year or by 10 years, depending on the scope of the issue. Usually people can agree to issues that won't be impacting them in their lifetime or career span. Once you get an area of agreement, bring the scope back to a closer time frame. Longer time frames usually apply to environmental or municipal construction issues, shorter time frames to business and industry production issues. For example, strategic plans that introduce large scale changes are often easier to gain agreement on when everyone sees the big changes happening in a 10-year time frame. They argue much more vehemently if that new structure is going to face them in the next 12 months.

You might use a phrase like, "Since we've found agreement on outcomes 15 years out, how would we like the picture to look in 10 years?"   Come to agreement there and scale the time frame back to 3 years out. Once you get as close to the present as possible, you can start focusing on what would need to happen to achieve those goals. That can lead to a discussion of how that path differs from the one the group is on currently. You can use this technique with time, geographic region, number of people served, money, etc. Reversing the direction of the scope can also be helpful. For example:

> *"If we can't agree what we want to do organization-wide, can we agree to how things should work with this team, in this room?"*

Limiting the scope to a very small scale (like a pilot test) can also stimulate the conversation towards dialogue rather than disagreement. The actual words you use can be really helpful too. While a permanent policy or agreement might be too much for people to commit to, you can often get agreement to a pilot program or trial. Rather than try something long term, try it limited in scope. When people can't agree in fact, they can often agree in principle. And if they can't like or appreciate a new structure, they can often live with it[16]. For more on this technique we suggest reading *Getting to Yes,* an excellent guide to negotiation strategy by Fisher and Ury[17].

Strategy # 17: Walking in the other guys' shoes

Our next strategy revolves around helping your team see one another's viewpoints—and advocating for them as well. The strategy of walking in the other guy's shoes is about finding common ground, which is at the heart of the next couple of tools we'll examine. Seeing and advocating for the other person's perspective is particularly effective when your team has reached an impasse in cooperation. You can direct them to put themselves into one another's shoes and then use the rephrasing technique to state a common goal.

Are you thinking this technique is wimpy? We've had people in our leadership sessions say that, or sometimes sigh about the snorting and chuckling responses they get when they ask people to do this. What we advise them is that so much impact is in the delivery. Imagine how the conversation might go if you said something like this:

> *Pat and Chris: I am concerned that you two are not listening to each other at all. So I am going to give you a pop quiz of your listening ability so that you can prove to me that you have actually been paying attention and working towards a solution rather than simply pushing your own points of view. Pat—I want you to argue for Chris' proposal and Chris, you're going to argue for the merits of Pat's proposal. I have heard strengths in both of them—and I expect to hear those strengths reflected in your statements as well.*

Not so wimpy now, is it? Think of how you would respond to that admonition and expectation from your boss. Surely you wouldn't want to have to demonstrate for your boss just how much you weren't listening to your colleague. That is a test you don't want to fail.

Strategy #18: Establish common ground

Establishing common ground is key strategy. When you manage people, you will often find challenges in communicating that lead to

these difficult conversations—and it is your job to help them see where they just might be talking about the same thing. When people see different sides of an issue you can run into exchanges like this:
One team member might complain:

> *He's just advocating for the status quo to avoid change.*
> *How are we going to stay responsive if we don't change*
> *how we do, what we do, based on changes in our*
> *environment?*

And another might retort:

> *Yeah, but you weren't around the last time we embarked*
> *on a similar "little experiment." What a mess that was.*
> *We all had to work twice as hard to regain lost ground –*
> *let alone the lost credibility that we never got back as far*
> *as I'm concerned. It's not that I'm a naysayer, it's just that*
> *I understand the consequences of taking on that kind of*
> *risk.*

How can you use creating common ground to bring them closer together? Well, you might consider saying:

> *I hear the both of you talking about risks we face here—*
> *the risk of not changing and the risk of making a change.*
> *Indeed, both are risks that we have to manage.*

This conversation isn't about one side or the other: it's about managing risk. The key is to get the parties talking about that common issue. In this example, the leader didn't take sides, defend or justify, but instead used some reframing to create common ground that valued the perspectives of both parties to the confrontation. In our example with Linda and Wesley, she used this establishing common ground technique as well.

The key is to keep the parties talking about their mutual interests such as: meeting the clients' needs, developing a deep bench of experienced and skilled team members, working together to solve the inevitable challenges that arise in doing so, sharing best practices, and creating opportunities for each team member to engage in key projects in the future even if they might not be involved in the issue that triggered the current tension.

Strategy #19: Give people a role and a reason

It is always important to make sure that each party has an investment in the long-term picture of the group, organization, or effort that you are working on. If people feel there is a hope for their being involved in a future project that is valued by them and the group, they are much more likely to engage in the adaptive learning process[4] during this "crucial conversation"[2, 9]. There needs to be a good and worthy goal to make it worth it to put the hard work in now, so think about what they value. Give them a stake in the long-term game. Think about how they can play a part that is meaningful to the team (and ideally to them as well) down the road. Help them understand the contribution of the role you are giving them or planning for them. Conflict might stem from misunderstanding and feeling sidelined when actually that perception is more fairy tale than fact.

Strategy #20: Create a common vision

Creating a common vision is key to helping each party grasp the mutual objectives that they share. Show them, or better yet have them describe the larger picture of the situation. Put the work back on them—it shouldn't be just you, as the leader, telling them the common vision of why they need to resolve the current problems. When they help create it they will feel ownership of it and have more buy-in to it. Of course, you will find it helpful to keep those descriptions as broad as possible since you don't want your team to fall into the trap of *positions*. Broadening the discussion helps you stay focused on *interests*, as we discussed above in strategy #14. When people are focused on their own goal or way of getting things done (a position), they can sometimes forget that there are many ways to get up that proverbial mountain. It is helpful to give context to a common vision by reminding the team that there is rarely ever only a single right way to accomplish a task. When it comes to managing conflict and difficult conversations creating the common vision of many paths to success can be a useful instrument in your toolbox.

As the leader, your task here is to gain agreement among the parties on the overall interests and vision of the group.

20 Twenty tools in your pocket

Twenty skills, strategies, and tools is a good number to have in your pocket—you won't use every one of them every time. You'll have to practice and gain mastery over them, and then you'll develop a good sense of when to use which skill and how to layer them appropriately. After having a difficult conversation, write down what worked and how you can improve your skills. Remember the cycle of learning we talked about in our First Step to becoming a great *It-Factor* leader (Figure 1.1). Write down each step of the cycle as it applies to your learning curve. Just like leadership doesn't happen by accident, gaining mastery of these skills comes with practice. *It-Factor* leaders aren't born and they aren't trained either: they are developed. And development comes with attention to practice.

Derailing the difficult conversation

Of course, just like there are steps to success, there *are* steps to *derail* those difficult conversations as well (Table 11.5). Threatening and

Table 11.5: 8 Ways to derail a difficult conversation

Difficult conversation derailment actions to avoid	
Threaten	Accuse
Defend your position or someone else's	Justify either your or someone else's actions
Judge	Be personally defensive
Give in the demands of others	Give orders

accusing parties at the table will quickly end cooperation, as will becoming judgmental, defensive, or defending and justifying the actions of others or yourself. Since you cannot simply resort to giving people orders to start or stop a behavior when you are having a difficult conversation, you will need a great deal of discipline. Giving orders is relying on positional power, which you may not have, and even if you did, it probably wouldn't be effective when it comes to people's perspectives, beliefs, needs, or behaviors. You need to actively engage them in the *dialogue*. You will need to convince them through influence and persuasion. You will have to lead them through the process of adaptive change[4], to help them work constructively with the larger group. It is hard work: part of the hard work of leadership. While it may seem tempting at times to just give in to the demands, that is merely sowing the seeds for greater trouble later on and is not exhibiting leadership.

Managing a difficult conversation is difficult. It is part of the hard work of leadership, but it is a skill that sets *It-Factor* leaders apart from others. As you work on these skills, you will gain greater comfort and ease with them. Always remember that these conversations are not about you, even if you do feel defensive, offended, hurt, frustrated, or annoyed. You need to practice each of these skills on yourself as well. It's not about you. Take a deep breath and embrace the discipline of setting yourself aside during these conversations. After all, that's exactly what you are asking the other parties to do as well.

Like great *It-Factor* leaders, you too can use these tools to make difficult conversations much easier for everyone while you craft win-win or at least workable solutions that the parties can get behind so that you can keep your efforts as an organization, a team, or a group moving forward.

Your 11th step to becoming a great *It-Factor* leader is to master the art of the difficult conversation.

The Twelfth Step: Take Charge of Change

Take Charge of Change:
How to Manage Organizational Change

It-Factor leaders don't let change happen to their organizations: they take charge of change. They lead change. They make it a thoughtful, intentional process. Weak leaders are unprepared for change and are battered by its currents when it happens.

Research shows that there are 10 elements that positively affect change, and 10 that negatively affect it[1]. As a leader, you need to be aware of these positive change promoters as well as these change busters so that the change you lead does not get derailed.

Leading change is one of the toughest challenges that you will face. Your enterprise must be responsive to changes in the environment, the evolving needs of those you serve, or who make up your customer base. You have to respond to competition and changes to your revenue streams, market share, or budget strength. The inability to successfully lead change is a major derailment factor for leaders today.

For more than a decade we've known what the strong strategies for leading change are. The Grenell Group studied what factors support the sweet victory of success as well as those that contribute to the agony of defeat for organizational change[1]. What they found holds true today. We'll go through these factors, but first take a stab at making your own top 10 list of change promoters and change derailers. List them in Table 12.1.

Table 12.1: Promoters and derailers of organizational change

Change Promoters/Supporting Factors	Change Derailing Factors
1.	1.
2.	2.
3.	3.
4.	4.
5.	5.
6.	6.
7.	7.
8.	8.
9.	9.
10.	10.

10 Supporting Factors in leading change

It-Factor leaders get it that leading change is one of the most difficult challenges they can face. They rely on these 10 factors to help them with the process.

Vision

Change is hard. People have to know the destination in order for them to be on board with the change process.   Creating and communicating a clear vision is a critical element for success. Making this a shared vision is also a crucial step. You will have to communicate this vision often and in a variety of methods—verbally, written, and if you can, even in a graphic or symbolic format. You might find that creating a physical tangible object to symbolize this vision will help you make your idea of change more concrete in the eyes of stakeholders. In Figure 12.1, we share with you an example of how *It-Factor* leader Dr. Bobby Moser used a physical, tangible object to help him communicate his vision for change. He was Dean at The Ohio State University's old School of Agriculture and used this symbol to great effect. This tangible object embodied his vision for a new, improved College and he used it, rather than a lot of words, to persuade a very reluctant group of stakeholders to embrace this bold new version of the enterprise.

Figure 12.1

As you can see in the picture, Bobby and his team created a four-sided pyramid, a very strong structure, which, of course, symbolically indicates the strength of the school. The four sides are labeled with four core values: environmental sustainability, production efficiency, social responsibility, and economic viability. The base bears the new name of the school, and suspended in the center, rests a globe. The clear acrylic of the pyramid represents transparency. Everything about this object symbolized the new paradigm for the College. This new paradigm was complicated to talk about. Difficult to describe. But actually very easy to hand to you or put on your desk.

This visual symbol is an excellent example of how a clear vision supports successful change. Of course, Dean Moser did more than visually symbolize this change: he traveled across the state promoting it and left one of these pyramids everyplace he went. Symbols help. Tangible objects will give you an advantage. *Vision* is at the top of the list for a reason. You need a clear vision and you need to say it over and over again. For an example of just how much reinforcing of the vision a successful change process takes, see our highlight right after this Twelfth Step to becoming an *It-Factor* leader, which details how Dr. Moser led the College of Food, Agriculture and Environmental Sciences at The Ohio State University through this complex and high-stakes process. When you are leading change you cannot over-communicate the vision. If you aren't just about sick of talking about the vision, then you aren't talking about it enough[2]. Consider how you can say your vision for change, how you can write about it, how you can depict it graphically, and how you can symbolize it as well.

Trust

Your followers must have trust. We addressed many elements to building trust in our Eleventh Step, all of which will be helpful to you in leading high-stakes, emotion-fraught change processes. But this picture of trust is bigger than just trusting you as an individual. It isn't just about you. As a leader, you represent the organization. You are the face of the organization. Followers need to trust that there is transparency in the system. They need to know that information is being shared. And fundamentally important is their trust that leadership is ethical, informed, and capable of taking the group through this change process. Research has shown that trust is paramount. Claudia did her dissertation on the experiences of leadership success and failure of chief medical officers in large health care systems—and the ability to create trust emerged as the most important leadership strategy for these boundary-spanning leaders. Even if you are not in a healthcare setting, trust is paramount when it comes to change.

Motivation

Do you assume that the people in your organization are motivated just because they smile at you and say "good morning"? Don't second guess it—motivation is crucial to the success of the change you are leading. People aren't going to be motivated from the authoritarian standpoint of "because I said so" (and by-the-way, that's actually a threat, not a motivational speech).   People need to understand a sense of urgency around change ("why is this important?") and have positive motivation to put in the work required to reach the goal ("I *want* to do this"). Think about what motivates people—if you don't know by now, you might re-read the Fourth and Seventh Steps to becoming an *It-Factor* leader about understanding motivation and engaging those on your team.   Above all, don't misinterpret "create urgency" to mean "threaten."   Rather than motivate them, you'll get the opposite: it will ruin motivation and engagement, and drive your best talent right out your doors.   If there are aspects of your enterprise that do threaten people, such as internal competition, or abrasive management, then you will need to address these in order to truly motivate your team. Remember what we said earlier, the work of the brilliant W. Edwards Demming clearly teaches us that 85% of the problems in organizations belong to the system, not to the bad apples[3]. As a leader, system problems are *your problems.* It is up to leadership to fix the systems issues—and problems like groupthink, abrasive management, internal competition, lack of meaningful feedback, poor communication structures—those are leadership problems. Motivation won't be present in the absence of leadership.

Commitment

When you are taking charge of change, you need to create the commitment to the goal (that being the vision we talked about above). Part of creating the commitment is to reinforce and reward the positive behaviors that will enable the team to reach that goal. Study the most critical behaviors that are necessary for the goal to be met—these are often called *vital behaviors*[4]. It is these vital behaviors that will be most crucial to your success. Also look at the system and see how it reinforces and rewards the actions that people take. And remember that systems reward those bad behaviors you really want to extinguish as well as the good ones you want to promote. Make sure you understand if the system is creating rewards for the behaviors you don't want. For example, when you have internal competition for bonuses, raises, or other opportunities, then people are far less likely to share information with one another, and that could derail any goals of shared learning, creating a learning organization, and promoting innovation.

Here's a very real example alive and well in our top universities across the country. Universities don't have deep benches: they have broad ones. Typically in a department they have one specialist in an area, unlike businesses which have a cluster of expertise. This means that in a University department you have a collection of individuals who might not share interests or speak one another's language very well. It's like having a collection of experts who "Captain their own ships," a group of CEOs of their own research projects. Yet, when we work with academic organizations their leaders always tell us they want their faculty to work in teams, across departments, and to collaborate. They want think tanks with a cross-pollination of ideas. Academic leaders want their faculty to be inspiring teachers and to push the cutting edge of knowledge down to the student level, involving the next generation of leaders in the research. Many want them to push innovations to the population, stimulating the economic development in their states and benefitting the health and well-being of millions of citizens. Indeed our universities, particularly our public universities, are one of the engines of our success as a nation.   However, what they reward is not teaching. It's not collaboration. And it has nothing to do with being inspiring or sharing knowledge with others outside of one's field.

If you are a faculty member at a major U.S. university you can't get promoted (they call it "getting tenured") unless you generate research dollars and publish the results of that research in journals that are read by people who do the same work you do (remember, you probably don't have many people at your university doing the same work that you do). None of these journals are read widely by the population. Only a few are even looked at by journalists, who share news with the wider population. This is because most of the population would not care about these scientific studies. It's not that these studies aren't important; it's just that they are highly specialized. For the faculty member, this is a lot of effort to connect and share knowledge with a tiny sliver of the population who all live far away. Not that research isn't important—but what happens is that these faculty are turned into researchers; not teachers, not collaborators, not idea-generators, and not economic development stimulators. They are rewarded when they embrace a very narrow slice of that vision of why that major University exists.

Let's say you are a faculty member at one of these top-of-the-line institutions who loves teaching—you excel at teaching. But you don't publish the pre-requisite five articles a year in scientific journals? And you don't bring in big grants on a routine basis? Then your fate will be to get turned down for tenure. Do you know that means? It means you are invited to leave your job. No matter that you could be the best, most inspiring teacher in the department. No matter if you share your ideas in important ways outside of your field or collaborate across the silos of the school. You are fired unless you publish, and publish a *lot*. That means that there is a huge level of anxiety for young faculty, and they quite literally "publish or perish." In order to stay at their jobs they need to be completely focused on their research, their publications, and their notoriety—or they lose everything. University faculty are driven by Promotion and Tenure (called P&T) and because the rewards are so great (and the punishments so devastating) many find that they cannot focus on teaching. They may love teaching. The school may say teaching is valued. But you get what you measure in organizational life, and if what you actually measure is publishing papers, you get a lot of people with very narrowly focused interests who publish. What gets measured (and rewarded) gets done.

Many faculty in our most heralded institutions tell us that teaching can be a punishment because teaching classes distracts from their ability to get tenure. Some schools are struggling to change this system. Smaller colleges are ahead of the curve partly because teaching is more aligned with their mission than research. However, many more of our big name colleges and universities are only waking up to what the system of "P & T" costs them. The take away here is to create commitment to the change you are leading, make sure your organizational systems also support this goal.

Behavior change

If organizational change is going to take hold, you simply can't have a "this is the way we've always done it" attitude. Behaviors have to change, thus people need to know what the new behaviors are *and* they have to have the skills to implement those new behaviors. Changing behaviors is hard. It is easier to change the rules and procedures than it is to change personal behavior. Your team will need to be taught, see, and practice these new behaviors. They will need to get feedback on how they implement them, and they will need to practice again in order to gain mastery of the new skills. Development of new skills is a crucial part of leading a successful organizational change. If you think back to our Seventh Step to becoming a great *It-Factor* leader (about employee engagement), it was development of skills that ranked as the fourth most important factor for retaining your valuable employees, right after career advancement opportunities, the fact that other high-caliber people work there, and the overall work environment.

When it comes to this area of leading change, one of the behaviors *you* might need to change is your own visibility. All too often leaders stand atop the mountain and wave the flag but they don't routinely visit the trenches. As the leader you need to be out and in front of the process and be visible, leading it. That will be an important ingredient to the ultimate success of that change-goal. You need to talk to people. You need to be out, to be seen as leading the change. However, don't misinterpret this advice. As the leader you don't necessarily need to control the process, and in fact, over controlling it could be extremely damaging. But being visible, present, even if you don't say much, especially if you are listening, will be very powerful. And if you aren't there, the weight of your absence will be mighty indeed. It will speak volumes about your lack of commitment to the process, your lack of interest in the people affected by it, your lack of attention to the mechanics of change, and your lack of concern about the outcome. How can you expect others to buy into your change process if you don't? When it comes to behavior change think of those behaviors you are looking for organization-wide, but don't forget to look at your own behaviors as well.

Values

Did values show up on your list? Consider how important values are in leading change successfully. *It-Factor* leaders know that people's values need to be in congruence with the change, as well as with the mission and vision of the organization. And vice versa—the change you are leading needs to be in alignment with the mission and vision *and* with people's values. It works both ways. Values have taken an interesting turn—recent history can teach us a lot. Close to the turn of the 21st century, engagement at work was led by leadership, learning, and empowerment. But now in the post-Enron, post-Arthur Anderson, post-Leman Brothers, post-Goldman-Sachs, post Bernie Madoff, post-mortgage-backed-securities-global-financial-meltdown, post double dip recession-era, the engagement research shows that people don't want to work for scum anymore. They are tired of corporate (and personal) greed. For the first time, *Corporate Social Responsibility* has shown up in the top list of factors engaging employees[5, 6]. At last, the good guys win. And engaged employees want to know that they are working for the good guys. It is both the values you hold *and* how the organization's values support and are aligned with the change, that become vital factors in the success of that change.

Tenacity

How about Tenacity? Did it show up on your list? Like we said, "change is hard" and it takes time. It is not for the meek-hearted leader—but then again, leadership itself requires a degree of resilience. In our experience, *It-Factor* leaders have tenacity. Dr. Bobby Moser, of The Ohio State University, describes his leadership job as *"I'm a lightning rod,"* a lot of energy gets directed toward him when he is in his leadership role. He has to be personally resilient to hear the message, but not let the energy of its delivery burn him. Both the leader and the team need to have the tenacity to see things through when the going gets rough. It's also important to realize that organizational barriers will regenerate without ongoing attention—you will need to have the tenacity to return again and again to the systems that are supporting—or derailing—your change. You need to think of it like a garden—it will need constant watering and frequent weeding. You can't just scatter the seeds of change and then abandon them. So be tenacious in tending to and supporting the change you are leading.

Attitude Change

Attitude is everything! Sometimes successfully leading change means that attitudes need to change. These might be the attitudes toward "this is the way we've always done it," or to a new client base, new partners, new products, or new processes. We have seen teams that balk at change saying, *"we don't make that"* or *"we don't serve X market"* or *"we can't work with them…they're the competition!"* At times these beliefs can be so ingrained that people aren't even aware of how they are limited by them.

Think about the attitudes that need to change at your organization, and those attitudes you would like to preserve. Write these down in Table 12.2.

Table 12.2 Attitudes to Preserve and Change in my Organization

Attitudes to Preserve: constructive and supportive keepers	Attitudes to Change: destructive and non-supportive ones to drop
1.	1.
2.	2.
3.	3.

What are the elements that support those destructive and non-supportive attitudes that you targeted to eliminate? After all, they don't exist for no reason. If you want to take charge of change, understand what contributes to negativity at the workplace. Remember, people don't usually leave a job—they leave people *at* the job (usually a boss or manager[7-9]). Take a good look at the skills on your team and assess how they contribute to the attitudes you see. Remember, you can't change people, but you can change the system, and 85% of the time, the problem is with the system. People's behaviors will follow the system.

Do the same with the attitudes you want to preserve. What factors support those positive contributors to effective aspects of your organizational culture? How can you ensure that those factors will be in operation during and after the change you are leading? If one or some of these factors that support the good attitudes will be impacted by the change, then you need give some careful thought to what else you can do to keep supporting the positive and constructive attitudes that are so essential to teamwork and productivity.

Character

Every *It-Factor* leader understands that the character of the leaders themselves has a tremendous impact on the character of the organization. Leaders set organizational culture. As they do, so others will follow. When leaders show exemplary character, honesty, integrity, and loyalty, change processes become much easier. If you want to lead change successfully, then do what great *It-Factor* leaders do: show personal character. Don't confuse these descriptions of character with showing your religious devotion—we've run into leaders who make a big deal out of their personal beliefs but then turn around and show disloyalty, self-centered behavior, intolerance for others, or dishonesty. While having a moral guidepost is a great thing, showing your true character will carry across in your deeds, more than your words, the jewelry you wear, the signs in the office, or other indicators of your faith. When you are honest, loyal, reasonably tolerant, and truly focus on the greater good of the team, enterprise, and customer, then others are more likely to follow and support your change. As we noted in our First Step to becoming a great *It-Factor* leader: the person who is going to give you the most trouble each day is the one who looks back at you out of the mirror each morning[10]. It is worth noting that the person who can make a huge difference to the team, organization, or enterprise by setting a clear example is also reflected in that same image. Character counts. Character matters. Character is contagious in organizations. Make it contagious in yours.

Self-Discipline

Lastly, Self-Discipline joins the list. It is critical because change is so difficult. Doing things differently, learning new skills, or implementing new behaviors takes an appreciable amount of self-discipline. Gaining personal insight and growing in one's understanding requires this important skill as well.

After you have made the path to change clear and addressed other key factors such as learning new behaviors and motivation, then you need to focus on this area of self-discipline. *It-Factor* leaders create structures to help individuals in the enterprise hold themselves and others accountable for the changes. Organizations that have the self-discipline to use constructive metrics will be able to assess where they are in the change process relative to their goals. That makes celebrating success or getting back on track much easier. In this book we've already talked about a few tools that will foster accountability and self-discipline. In our Third Step to becoming a great *It-Factor* leader, we talked about the process of using a team-coaching model to help peers share goals with one another and support one another's learning and development. In our Fifth Step to becoming a great *It-Factor* leader you were introduced to how to create your individual development plan. In the Sixth Step on emotional intelligence there were quite a few tools to monitoring yourself and your behaviors which can help promote accountability, self-insight, and self-discipline.

Table 12.3 presents the combined list of the 10 factors that Grenell's research has found to undergird successful organizational change. Take stock of where your team or enterprise stands on each of these variables.

Table 12.3: Assessment of where my organization or group stands with the 10 assets for change

Assets for change:	Poor	Fair	Good
Vision	❏	❏	❏
Trust	❏	❏	❏
Motivation	❏	❏	❏
Commitment	❏	❏	❏
Behavior Change	❏	❏	❏
Values	❏	❏	❏
Tenacity	❏	❏	❏
Attitude Change	❏	❏	❏
Character	❏	❏	❏
Self-Discipline	❏	❏	❏

Obstacles that block organizational change

We've talked about the assets for change that leaders need to have—now let's talk about the liabilities leaders need to cope with. There are also many obstacles that block organizational change. If you haven't yet, take a moment and go back to Table 12.1, listing what you think these are.

What topped your list of change-busters? Research shows that 10 issues loom large when it comes to the most potent factors for blocking successful organizational change. We will share some points about each of these.

Resistance to Change

Perhaps being resistant to change is just a part of the human condition. Certainly most leaders will face this resistance when they work to bring about change in their teams, groups, or organizations. If you've been through a reorganization at work then you've seen the resistance and foot dragging that can occur. When you have to lead a change, be it with how your team works together, your customer base, what you produce or how you produce it, then selling the change message will be a key strategy you must employ to reduce the resistance and get everyone on board. Author Ronald Heifetz offers tremendous insight[11, 12] into why people are so resistant: when facing a significant change, even at work, people feel the impact of it on their very identity. Work is a huge part of the lives of professional staff and many support staff, too. Changing how and what they do, with whom, and for whom upsets how they know themselves and their relationships at work. Changing their team or the clients they serve might make them feel disloyal to the people they've known for a long time or even the company they are proud to be part of. They might feel incompetent because they just don't know what to do in that brave new world you're leading them to. No one likes to feel uncomfortable or incompetent—as Heifetz so wisely points out: no wonder they resist the change. You will need to make the change safe for them, or at least help them understand and have some buy into that change in order to lower the resistance.

Conflict Aversion

Being conflict averse is toxic to organizations. Living in denial of the truth or being afraid to have difficult discussions has run many organizations aground—whether they are going through a change process or not. Leaders need to address conflict constructively—and they need to make sure that others in the organization have the tools to artfully manage the difficult conversation as well. All too often, when people don't have good tools and skills to address conflict, they substitute "talking tough" (abrasive, overly-directive, or accusatory language) for engaging in the *tough talk* of difficult conversations. Revisit the Eleventh Step to remind yourself of these skills. Don't lapse into talking tough and don't shirk your duty to address conflict—rather embrace that tough talk and make difficult conversations work for you instead. Make sure your team has the skills to harness conflict and turn it into constructive dialogue. Realize, too, that if you won't address significant issues at work because you avoid conflict like the plague, then you are sending a message to your team that they aren't worth the effort for you get out of your comfort zone for them. You need to role model good conflict management techniques for them.

Impatience

Another factor that derails change is impatience. We live in a fast-paced society. It seems that many people are used to immediate gratification and quick results. Well, change can take time, a lot of time, and it certainly takes patience. Reminding the team of the vision, that hard work, behavior change, and that patience will be required will all be helpful. We agree with the *It-Factor* leaders we have worked with and also advise you to create and celebrate early wins to keep folks motivated[2, 13]. Making sure these wins are team-based will be particularly helpful.

It is also helpful to have an assessment of your change process by a respected outside stakeholder who can help everyone see how far you've come as an enterprise. While you could hire an expensive company to come in and assess where you stand, that is usually not helpful unless you feel that the change has been stymied or perhaps you need a significant mid-course correction. What we're talking about here is more of a "blessing" of the change process. A shot in the arm of confidence for the organization—and that should not cost you a fortune. When you can bring in a stakeholder, like a customer or a partner, and show them the real status of change, have them assess your progress, and listen to their remarks about what they see, then you can help address the impatience issue because people begin to see and hear about metrics being met—in other words, "progress"[13]. Celebrate those early wins! That will help mitigate the impatience. It will also be helpful to set realistic expectations—setting goals too high will increase both impatience and frustration. Of course, metrics that demonstrate measured progress against your goals will also be your ally in change.

The Rumor Mill

Rumors can derail your organizational change attempts, particularly when they are coupled with cynicism, which we'll address next. Using transparent and frequent communication will help dispel any rumors. Also addressing rumors as they come up can help shorten their lifespan. When you are lucky enough to find the person who instigates a rumor, it is crucial to talk with them about it. They may not realize the impact of their actions and may not have intended a rumor to start. If starting a rumor does turn out to have malicious intent, then it is all the more important to have what is known as a difficult or courageous conversation with that individual. There is an example of such a difficult conversation in our Eleventh Step to becoming a great *It-Factor* leader. A big lesson here is communication: any communication vacuum will be filled—and quickly! If you don't control the story it will be controlled by someone else. So proactively communicate and don't give the rumors a chance to get off the ground.

Cynicism

Cynicism is toxic. When people attribute self-interest as the primary motive for all the leader's behaviors, and particularly when they express this sentiment in sneers and sarcasm, it is an organizational culture killer. Many for-profit corporations really struggle with cynicism, since those who work in the lower levels of the enterprise can feel that their considerable efforts and productivity results in financial rewards for their bosses, rather than for the team. Leaders who are perceived as being goal directed for their personal benefit, willing to cast aside others who either get in their way or don't have enough to offer tend to be seen as "users" of others, which contributes to a broad band of cynicism on the team. On the contrary, organizations that focus on the greater good and non-profits struggle less with the culture killer of cynicism. In many cases, their very structure and the nature of the mission being central to operations contributes to a more positive working atmosphere. The financial rewards in non-profits tend to pale by comparison with their corporate counterparts, undermining the ability for cynicism to take as strongly to root. In either kind of enterprise, it will help you greatly to create a culture of *assuming positive intent* with one another on the team. According to Marty Linskey and Ronald Heifetz[11, 12] people who become cynical once had a quality of heart we would call innocence. But the battering innocence takes over the years transforms it into cynicism. Of course, people say they are "realistic," since no one really wants the label of being cynical.   Being cynical of the leader's motivations is bankrupted trust. As you demonstrate that you deserve their trust, you will help address the problems with cynicism.

Apprehension

Interestingly, apprehension is also on this list of change-busters: Fear of change is often far worse than the change itself. Help people reduce their apprehension by making the vision clear, as well as the steps they need to take to reach the destination. Metrics can serve as virtual milestones so people know where they are and how they are doing in the change process. Make sure there is a way for them to learn and master the new behaviors they will need in order to be successful in this new, changed landscape. That will greatly help to lessen the apprehension surrounding the change. As the leader you need to take action to reduce fears. Apprehension is real and ignoring it won't make it go away.

Mistrust

This list is quite an amazing one. It's not surprising that mistrust undermines successful organizational change. One of the reasons character is so important in leaders is because ethical and competent conduct can help to build trust with all stakeholders. Of course, so does listening to others, considering their views, and remaining objective, as we talked about in our previous Steps to becoming an *It-Factor* leader. Key ways to engender mistrust include threatening or accusing parties at the table, becoming judgmental, defensive, or defending and justifying the actions of others or yourself. *It-Factor* leaders don't let themselves fall into that trap, and neither should you.

Inertia

Many are surprised to find inertia on this list of change busters. All organizations (and you might even say people) are used to functioning at a typical velocity or speed (organizationally you can think of this as "productivity level"). When change needs to happen usually the pace of work needs to pick up considerably. This can run smack into the face of organizational inertia. The "this is how we've always done it" mentality can lock an organization into a set pace—and that pace may no longer be competitive or realistic given changes in the larger world. For example, when times are economically good, organizations tend to become less efficient. Revenues or profits are easier to manage. Without even realizing it, organizations often relax their desire to constantly learn and improve their processes during these easy times. They tend to become less innovative— feeling "why should we stress over changing it up? Things are good." However, when the economic pendulum swings, these organizations are caught in this inertia trap. Suddenly they have to become far more efficient and lean just to survive. Changing when you have to, when it becomes survival of the fittest, can be very painful indeed.

You will lessen the hold that this inertia has on your organization if you foster an organizational habit of continually examining your processes and implementing best practices. You should also have your group discuss the following, admittedly, difficult questions:

- How do we compare against the benchmarks in our industry?
- Are we doing the right thing?
- Are we doing it the right way?
- In what ways are we relevant to the market?
- In what ways are we losing relevance to the market?

Egocentricity

One of the biggest mistakes a leader can make is to fall into what we call the "it's all about me" trap. When leaders run an organization like "it's all about them" they kill organizational culture, they stifle creativity, and promote groupthink, which we addressed in our Tenth Step to becoming an *It-Factor* leader about creating thought diversity. To be successful as a leader, it is critical to remind yourself of the mantra, "it's not about me." Make sure you ground yourself in your life outside of your role at work as well. If you only know who you are as your work title, you are very likely to derail through errors brought about through egocentricity. Having a full life outside of your work role will give you much better judgment when you are in that work role. While we recognize that work-life balance is the butt of many a joke in the corporate sector, it is important to realize that that balance does serve as a check against out-of control egocentricity, and against the kind of obsessive over-work that can lead to burnout and even dying on the job. It also helps to protect against those egocentricity-based-behaviors that lead to derailment through lapses of moral judgment and corruption.

Over Control

This one can be a tough one for leaders. Many want control. Many tell us they feel they can't steer the ship without it. While it might feel uncomfortable or even downright scary to you, it is important to accept that you simply cannot control everything. You must delegate. And those to whom you delegate cannot control everything either. Too much control kills innovation and the ability of an organization to deal with unanticipated issues as they emerge. It's not what you know that is going to give you the most difficult challenges: it's what you don't know. If the team has no experience, no ability to lead themselves and learn from their mistakes, then they will have no skills in thinking on their feet and managing the unexpected crisis. Leaders who over-control also don't live forever. When they leave an organization, either for a new position, or totally burned out, or because their Type A personalities and work-a-holic ethic led to serious health problems, the teams they leave are often crippled from inexperience and lack of direction. A leader's need for over-control can ultimately run the entire enterprise aground. You need a broad base of talent. Growing that talent only comes from loosening the grip on the reins. *It-Factor* leaders know how to let go. They share the spotlight, the responsibility, rewards, and the work.

Derailing change through over-control can be a tough one for a lot of leaders. Good intentions are usually based in a desire to make sure the change process rolls out exactly as planned with as little risk as possible— but over-control lends itself to rigidity rather than flexibility. Leaders can get bogged down in many small details, which calls into question exactly what they are focused on in their jobs.

By way of example, a newly appointed government director in the Northeast attempted to bring unity to the 20,000 employees in the department by issuing a new email signature policy. Employees could only electronically sign their names in 11 point, black, Arial font, with no logo, no background, no personalized quote or division slogan, no bold or italics font. While trying to comply, workers struggled with computer systems that were 10 years out of date, complaining that the underfunded department's old Word 2003 programs could not comply with the edict. There was particular worry in that the staff was told that employees who failed to adhere to or implement this policy may be subject to personnel actions and procedures at the director's discretion. Information Technology staff worked to assist nervous department employees, who could not get their systems to comply—or even to open the .docx file in which the new policy was sent, all while they fretted over how they were ignoring their primary work functions while they worked to adhere to this new rule.

This multi-page email policy followed a strict dress code rule released the previous month, requiring male managers and executives to wear suits with dress shirts, and female directors to wear slacks or skirts. This statement also specified the dress codes for non-managerial staff, along with requirements for daily bathing and grooming. Certainly, the idea was to lead changes intended to bring a sense of unity in a department that had vast numbers—but the outcome was a sense of micro-managing on the part of higher leadership, and instead led to employee apathy, disengagement, and derision of the leader. Unfortunately, the good intentions went awry, and so did the change process. The widespread ridicule led to a quick rescinding of the dress code policy and a blame game from the leadership office trying to deflect responsibility.

You can really sum up many of the problems of dealing with change as an *inability to cope with the non-linear, experimental and ambiguous nature of the change process*. We've said already that change is hard, right? Well, on top of that it is not always predictable. Sometimes you have to lead the group, team, or organization into uncharted waters. Sometimes you have to lead them through events you've never faced before. People need to be prepared to cope with the non-linear, somewhat experimental and ambiguous process ahead of them. The inability of people to cope, to be flexible, and "figure it all out together" is a potent obstacle to organizational change. If they are conflict averse, impatient, cynical in their mistrust of leadership's egocentricity and over-control, then the apprehension and resistance to change that will be engendered will win out—and the change process will fail.

How might all of these issues affect your organization? Reflect on the risk your team faces by using table 12.4 on the next page

There is something quite key to deduce about all of these factors. Did you figure out what they all have in common? Whether they are success factors or derailment ones, what we call "change busters," note that they are mostly psychological factors. Success in leading change is not based on having the newest computers, the latest technology, or an expansive budget. And it's not about having authority or even superior knowledge or skills. It is based on the very human factors that leadership impacts.

Leaders set organizational culture—for better or for worse. It is one of the most important contributions they make to an enterprise. Remember that it's not just the leaders at the top who do this—it is leaders throughout the system—leadership at every level—which is key to a positive culture.

Table 12.4 Assessment of where my organization or group stands with the 10 factors of change derailment

Risk of my organization for:	Low Risk	Moderate Risk	High Risk
Resistance to Change	❏	❏	❏
Conflict Averse	❏	❏	❏
Impatience	❏	❏	❏
The Rumor Mill	❏	❏	❏
Cynicism	❏	❏	❏
Apprehension	❏	❏	❏
Mistrust	❏	❏	❏
Inertia	❏	❏	❏
Egocentricity	❏	❏	❏
Over Control	❏	❏	❏
Coping with the non-linear, experimental and ambiguous nature of the change process	❏	❏	❏

Your 12th step to becoming a great *It-Factor* leader is to take charge of change. Now let's meet an *It-Factor* leader from academia who really knows how to lead change successfully.

Meet An *It-Factor* Leader: Bobby Moser

When it comes to taking charge of change, Dr. Bobby Moser faced a monster of a task. As a Dean at The Ohio State University, it fell to him to lead his college, the beloved School of Agriculture, through a restructuring process and a name change. Now if you don't work at a public university then this might not seem like such a challenge. Businesses do it all the time, right? Just put up a new sign, create some new graphics, print some new letterhead. What could be so complicated? Well, it's a little more involved than that in any enterprise, but in university life, it's a whole lot more complicated.

Leading change at a public university, particularly a *land grant* institution, is not like leading change any place else. Not only are universities incredibly large and complex places, you see the Land Grant ones were set up in President Abraham Lincoln's time, and since that time they belong very much to the people. At least that's the way everyone involved in any aspect of Ohio's agriculture saw it when Dean Moser wanted to rename and restructure their school.

It became pretty clear to Bobby when he became Dean that much needed to change if the school were to serve its mission, the students, and the citizens of the state—but the changes he saw as necessary went smack up against the traditions and history of the school. The faculty were not enthusiastic about the proposition of their school being 15% leaner. And as for the agricultural producers in the state, well they were determined to stop the process dead in its tracks. A cold Tuesday on the *Ides* of March saw a letter arrive on the Dean's desk. Fourteen of the state's most powerful commodity groups had signed it, stating their discomfort with the transformation taking place, disappointed with the College's failure to serve the needs of industry. They didn't see this new "School of Food, Agriculture, and Environmental Sciences" as being their school at all—their school was the School of Agriculture. Period. This new entity was too research-oriented for them to back and the letter suggested that industry might not be able to support the proposed budget requests in the state legislature—money that was critical to the continuing operations of the College. Many leaders would have relented to a tide that was too big to turn, but not Bobby. Bobby is an *It-Factor* leader.

In his mid 60s, Bobby has far more experience than gray to attest to his age. His easygoing friendliness, farm-boy accent, and tanned-in-the-sun skin make him comfortably approachable by farmer, student, faculty, and legislator alike. When you talk to Bobby, you can tell he is listening. He is a man of spare words—an introvert you might call him, but when he talks you can tell that all that wealth of experience is stored away in a razor sharp and perceptive mind. Bobby Moser could (and probably should) write the book on "it's all about relationships." Even before he assumed the role of Dean he went to every county fair, he met every farmer he could, as well as met every agricultural educator in every school in the state of Ohio. He crisscrossed the state, listening, talking, meeting people. Building relationships—as it turns out he needed those relationships!

He was determined to bring his school up-to-date and called this organizational change process "Project Reinvent." He saw that OSU's College of Ag needed to be nimble, flexible, and responsive to the quickly changing world of agri-business—and much leaner. Universities are like very large ships with itty-bitty-tiny-rudders: they tend to turn in a geologic time frame. Yet he didn't have eons to make this change happen. He faced all the traditional obstacles to change we listed in our Twelfth Step—there was ample resistance to change: rumors, cynicism, and impatience that threatened to derail the process. Key stakeholders, being conflict averse, walked out on an important discussion. Bobby got them to return to the table. He faced mistrust and apprehension, all on top of the incredible inertia of a large organization.

So what did this *It-Factor* leader do when he faced all these change busters? He created trust through tenacious listening—625 people gave nearly 14,000 hours of "people time," as he gathered input from a myriad of stakeholders. He created motivation and commitment by bringing together the opposing sides and putting them side-by-side on committees. He created a welcoming space for all ideas to be put on the table. What happened? Both the faculty and the industry groups collaborated.

"Their role in Project Reinvent ultimately helped them shape what we look like," Dr. Moser told us. Eventually, the groups came up with a new paradigm for the school and a symbol that spoke its values and that you can see today. A very large version sits on Bobby's desk. Small versions decorate desks all over the state of Ohio. One sits on ours as well. Bobby brought vision to the process—and communicated it often. The new symbol of the reinvented school became known as the "Moser Pyramid." This clear acrylic pyramid has one side representing production efficiency, a second economic viability, a third social responsibility, and the fourth environmental compatibility. We shared a picture of it in our

Twelfth Step. Bobby remarks, "These sides together form a structure with a programmatic strength greater than if they stood alone"[1]. At the base of the pyramid the plaque reads: The School of Food, Agriculture, and Environmental Sciences. Bobby reminds the long standing stakeholders, "Agriculture is the center of our college." In the midst of the pyramid hangs a globe, suspended in the balance of these values, supported by the school. It is poetic. It is simple. It is the product of many people who could have drawn a line in the sand but instead, working together, built one of the strongest schools in the country.

Bobby addressed people's attitudes, values, and behaviors. As an *It-Factor* leader, he had the character and integrity that invited people to follow him. He worked well with his stakeholders. Even the faculty themselves gave him the thumbs up with an 82% approval rating. He unveiled a new vision: a school of Food, Agriculture, and Environmental Sciences in place of where the old College of Agriculture used to be. Bobby Moser understood what it takes to lead change, even when it runs against the tide. He gives us a great example of how to address change busters while capitalizing on the factors that promote change.

Great *It-Factor* leaders like Dr. Bobby Moser know how to be effective and keep stakeholders engaged and on board.

The Thirteenth Step: Know How to Make a Powerful Apology

The Powerful Apology:
The Dialogue of Mending Damaged Relationships

There are many skills a successful *It-Factor* leader needs[1-3]. According to research by the Center for Creative Leadership, an internationally recognized organization specializing in studying leadership, there are 10 factors in which successful leaders shine. We talked about these in our First Step to becoming a great *It-Factor* leader: know yourself—the good, the bad, and the fixable. As a reminder (so you don't have to go flipping back through the book) great *It-Factor* leaders have the ability to maintain their straightforwardness and composure as they create participative management, which captures the best of everyone's ideas while creating buy-in and a shared sense of ownership. They also balance their personal life and work while they manage change. They are decisive while being self-aware: their blind spots do not catch them by surprise. They confront problem employees, and excel at putting people at ease. They shine at doing whatever it takes and they are decisive, with an ability to keep projects on track by making the critical decisions in good time.

Likely the most important, they understand that it isn't just about building relationships—at which they excel. They also realize that they must be able to *mend* those relationships. Let's face it—it is likely that you'll come up against some competing needs with at least some of your stakeholders. Competing over scarce resources can cause bruises to professional relationships—a key leadership skill is to mend relationships when they do get bruised. Thus, an *It-Factor* leader also knows how to make a powerful apology.

It is unfortunate but true that in life and work things don't always go as planned. Sometimes mistakes get made. When that happens, good relationships can become damaged. *It-Factor* leaders realize how important it is to mend those valuable relationships: with co-workers, partners, customers, or the public, and to do so in a way that is meaningful and restores trust. One of the actions to take in mending relationships is the powerful apology. It is important to note that this is not a one-time statement. The Powerful Apology is a conversation—it's the opening to a dialogue of healing. When the need to apologize arises, great *It-Factor* leaders do so powerfully. They open with a statement that follows these guidelines, but they don't drop it there. When you need to apologize, be like an *It-Factor* leader and make your powerful apology, opening with a strong statement that invites and cultivates this ongoing dialogue—it can help you successfully mend a damaged relationship, not to mention save your organization's reputation.

Table 13.1 lists the seven parts of an apology that make it powerful—and if any of these are missing it makes your apology weaker. While the situation you need to apologize for, legal issues, and the audience will all influence the different components, you need to think of each of these seven components when you create this all-important statement. Thinking through these aspects will help you to make a considered, thoughtful, and authentic apology. When done well, this can markedly help to improve those wounded relationships and restore trust.

Table 13.1: The Seven Components of the Powerful Apology

1: Timing
2: Responsibility
3: Explanations
4: The fix
5: Ask for forgiveness
6: Connect personally
7: Acknowledge compassion

Before we get started, it would be good for you to think about a situation in which you could or should make an apology—either personally or on behalf of your group. After all, this lesson in *It-Factor* leadership will be much more meaningful if you apply it to a situation that is relevant to you. You can use Table 13.2 to note the situation that you can work on.

Table 13.2 My Powerful Apology Example to work on:

Now that you have a situation in mind, let's go through each of these in turn.

Part 1: Timing

You've probably heard the saying, "timing is everything." Timing is the first element of the powerful apology. If you give a great apology—but it's long after the event, then no matter *what* you say it will not be a powerful one. Delays are costly. Getting the timing right is one of the hardest parts of the apology—you need to make your statement as soon as you can, as soon as you have enough information to have clarity on the situation. When liability is involved, more time may be required to gain this clarity before you can make a full and powerful apology. If that is the case, then you can use a qualified apology that expresses your concern for those involved, for the outcome, and pledges what you are doing about the situation, including how you are learning about the situation. But if all the 7 elements aren't included, know that your apology will be weaker.

Part 2: Responsibility

When you owe others an apology, it is crucial that you take responsibility for those events or outcomes that belong to you. If you have made a mistake—own it. When you don't take this crucial action your powerful apology can come across as merely "duck, dodge, bob, and weave" avoidance strategies. As Ruben learned in law school, research in negotiation outcomes shows that when people take at least some responsibility for the events at hand, it increases trust and the willingness of others to engage in the conversation. For example, while you might not be totally responsible for the distress an employee is feeling at work, you can make a statement such as the one attorney Josh Stulberg of The Ohio State University uses when he teaches[4]:

> *I want to apologize for not noticing the distress you were feeling here while I was distracted by my other responsibilities.*

This is a great example of taking some responsibility but not owning the entire situation. Recent research[5] has shown that Westerners, particularly Americans, don't want to apologize because they are afraid that making an apology means expressing culpability. They are more afraid of being sued than they are motivated to preserve the relationship, which is ironic because preserving the relationship reduces your chances of being sued! It is important to understand that not everyone sees apologizing in that same light. In Japan an apology is seen as expressing sorrow that an event happened and showing compassion for those involved. Not surprisingly, the Japanese apologize a lot more than Americans do, who tend to equate an apology with culpability. If you work globally, you need to understand these cultural differences, or risk being seen as completely insensitive. And if you're so willing be seen as totally insensitive, defending your (or your company's) actions by refusing to offer an apology, then don't be surprised at the trail of bruised and broken relationships and partnerships that follow you. Don't be surprised when business doesn't follow you.

You can make an apology acknowledging the situation and any part you have in it, even if your part is small. When you really have dropped the ball and you do own the entire situation, when the mistake or error truly has been your fault, then you *need* to take responsibility for it. When you engage in avoidance—the "duck, dodge, bob and weave" game of shifting the blame—you will come off as untrustworthy. Trust lost is very difficult to regain. Just look at the mess at Penn State University[6] in the wake of the totally mishandled Sandusky child abuse scandal of 2012. Before that, a famous historical example is, of course, Watergate[7].

Part 3: The explanation

The next component of the powerful apology is the explanation. Explain how this situation happened. Provide whatever details you can, those that don't cross a line legally, or compromise an ongoing investigation. That helps people understand the situation and how it came about. If you keep people in the dark and withhold information, then people will begin to attribute motive to you—saying that you are being cagey, untrustworthy, secretive, or manipulative. Potentially worse, they will "fill in" those gaps in knowledge with the details they either imagine or guess to be in there. Often, they will have no conscious awareness that they are doing this, they will simply 'fill the void' and then believe *that* story to be the true one (remember how we covered that interesting aspect of human psychology in our Eleventh Step to *It-Factor* leadership?) So if you don't explain, don't for a minute believe that you actually leave people in informational limbo—they won't wait around for you to finally share what you know. You will simply lose control of the story. Then you'll be facing the situation, and on top of that you'll be facing misinformation as well.   When it comes to information there is no such thing as limbo. There never was, even before the information age. People always just made up the parts they didn't know and put that on the grapevine as truth. The only difference today is that the grapevine is faster and more globally connected. The gossip mill has gone global through social media at the speed of a tweet.

Part 4: The fix

After you've taken the appropriate responsibility in a timely fashion and explained how an event happened, then you address what you or your enterprise are going to do to make it right with those who have been affected. Another important component of *the fix* in a powerful apology is to illustrate how you've learned from the experience. Share what you are doing to prevent the problem from ever happening again. Make sure that while the past may have been flawed, you are helping your audience to understand how the future will be different.

Part 5: Ask for forgiveness

All too often when someone makes an apology they say, "I'm so sorry." Or worse yet, they say, "I'm so sorry that you feel that way." That statement suggests that what the other party is feeling is wrong, at least in your eyes. The blame, the fault, is on them. That generally doesn't work too well when you're the one who owes the apology. The statement, "I'm sorry" is much more an indication of "I'm sorry that happened," like when you accidentally step on someone's toes when standing in a crowded line. They usually say, "oh, that's all right" and the exchange that's really happening here is that you both agreed this unfortunate event just occurred. It doesn't have anything to do with taking responsibility, explaining, making it right, or preventing the error from happening again. And, probably most important of all, when you say a simple "I'm sorry," you hold the power.

Our colleague, business psychologist Roger Hall[8] insists that what you need to do is to give the offended party the power. We could not agree with him more. He counsels the executives he coaches to ask for forgiveness after committing a major offense. We also think this is an important part of *the powerful apology.* This is very different than saying you're sorry. This takes some real humility and gives you the opportunity to show authentic contrition. An essential difference here is *power.* After all, when you ask the other party to forgive you, they can say no. They might not be ready. Whenever you give the other party power, you increase trust.

Part 6: Connect personally

Another aspect of the powerful apology is to connect personally. That will help you both feel and show empathy for the wronged group or person. There are many ways to do this, either by aligning yourself based on human experience, like saying, "As a parent of a child myself," or as a member of a community, by saying: "As someone who lives here and is affected by this decision...," or as someone who has experienced and can understand the emotions in the room, for example, "I can well imagine how frustrated you must feel with this outcome..."

And there will be times when you might not be able to make this connection, because you simply have not shared their experience. In that case you can connect with an empathetic statement such as: "I cannot begin to imagine the sorrow and grief you are going through at this moment..."

An apology becomes more powerful if you can make this personal connection, and particularly if you have a relationship you can build on with the person or group.

Part 7: Acknowledge their compassion

It is crucial that you follow through with this final component— which is to acknowledge the compassion that the other party shows you. Remember, that if they forgive you, or show you this compassion, that is a gift *to you.* A gift they have given you *after* you or your organization has wronged them in some way, and that is significant. There are many ways you can make this acknowledgement in your apology conversation. You can simply say, "...thank you for your kind understanding." Or, when you are mending the relationship, you could express something like "I appreciate your ability to allow us to move on from here."

To help illustrate this for you, we'll share a real life screw up—not from one of our hundreds of case studies, but from one of us. So here is a real life example of a screw up that Claudia did. The situation is that a highly sought after year-long senior leadership development program awards a $10,000 training scholarship plus travel to selected Fellows each year. Understandably, there are many applications for this program. An organization that partners on the Fellowship selects a number of candidates and presents them with the scholarship in their name. There are also a number of candidates who are selected and given the scholarships in the name of the program itself, but everyone applies through a central system. The error that happened was that the Partner's applicants were accidentally kept in the data base—and when it was time to send out the regrets letters to the non-selected applicants, well, the Partner's candidates also got these letters, even though the Partner was in the middle of interviewing their candidates. So, here were people who were *still* being interviewed via Skype or phone for the award, and sometimes *during* the interview they received an email letter of regret that they could not be included. Ooops! While thankfully neither of us work in life-or-death situations, this error did have national implications and could have damaged relationships that bring nearly $2 million to the organization where this program is housed. It was a serious human error of the type that could cause a lot of bad press and result in fewer partners at the table in the future if not handled according to the powerful apology guidelines. Certainly, this was a situation that required a powerful apology.

Claudia wrote the following note individually to every applicant who she had unintentionally wronged (we'll refer to the partner organization as XYZ):

> *I am writing with a most heartfelt apology for a terrible mistake I made—that I only in the last 10 minutes realized. Much to my horror, I realized tonight that I accidentally forgot to take all the of the XYZ applicants out of the data base prior to sending my note to all the non-XYZ applicants whom we could not accommodate this year in the program. Since XYZ makes the selection of your group's members of the Fellowship I actually have no idea of the status of ANY of the XYZ members—I'll find out tomorrow myself. I am so very sorry for the error I made and I can only hope that you can forgive me. I know there is such a great deal of hope and excitement about being given a seat in the program. I apologize for the angst I caused you with my error. I anxiously await the news of your status in the program as well!*
>
> *Most sincerely and most apologetically,*

Of course, she signed it.

And the result? Nearly everyone wrote back very quickly, none of them hostile, all of them understanding and many of them saying things like, "Wow, that was the best apology I've ever been given!" At that point, Claudia then wrote them a thank you for their kind understanding (that's the "acknowledge the compassion" part of the seven components), as she reiterated her contrition over her mistake. Although this letter was sent about seven hours after the mistake was made, which functionally put it into the next business day for most recipients, note how the letter says "in the last ten minutes". By changing the frame of reference from when the mistake was made, to when it was noticed, it gives the impression of being much more timely. This was important because a) people were angry, and b) a quick response indicates that the issue is important. While "real time" could not be changed, the perception of time related to the importance of the issue could be addressed.

Some public examples

There have been many memorable and very public apologies that have won praise and goodwill—and those that didn't go so well and have been very costly to their organizations. Let's take a quick look at some of the winners and some of the losers.

The Winners

On the winners side: David Letterman. While no one could condone what he did, having an affair with his staffer both while he was married (and newly a father) and while he was in a position of authority over the staffer in question, his on-air apology to his wife for that highly inappropriate relationship won him admiration from his viewers. He would rather have lost face before all of America, and potentially have lost his job, than to be blackmailed[9]. There were many who thought this would be the end of his highly successful career—but he was able to mend some of the bruises to those relationships and begin to heal some of the trampled trust through his apology.

That was an apology for a personal behavior. But what about when the issue is a corporate one and on a much larger scale? A far more compelling example of an admirable powerful apology happened back in 1982. James E. Burke was Chairman of the Board and CEO of Johnson & Johnson during the tragic cyanide poisoning in Tylenol capsules that killed seven innocent and unsuspecting people. Mr. Burke set the standard for corporate apologies as he handled the unprecedented crises. He took responsibility in ads and the company voluntarily recalled the product, destroying 31 million capsules, at a $100 million-dollar cost—in 1982 dollars! Again, many thought a company could not survive such an event, but today Johnson & Johnson remains a large and powerful conglomerate, and one of the most trusted names in the marketplace[10].

And to round out the winners, let's look at a popular food company and how their leadership used the powerful apology to try to save the relationship with their customers because of a persistent quality issue with their product. In 2010, after much criticism about their cardboard crust and ketchup-like sauce, Domino's pizza took a surprising advertising approach—a very successful on air apology, citing the complaints and providing explanations of the improvement remedy as they asked their customers to give them another chance[11]. Company CEO, Patrick Doyle explained this apology approach in the following way:

We're proving to our customers that we are listening to them by brutally accepting the criticism that's out there. We think that going out there and being this honest really breaks through to people in a way that most advertising does not.

This unconventional approach worked very well for Domino's as critics gave them high marks for their honesty and forthrightness.

The Losers

Unfortunately, there aren't many great examples of well-done and public powerful apologies. This is probably due to the fact that a) they aren't easy, b) leaders aren't trained to do them, and c) when the powerful apology is implemented quite well it tends to reduce fear and anxiety, build trust, and thus helps keep the story under wraps and out of the press. So while there are some great untold stories out there, the fact that they are hard to find is a testament to how successful they were. Another significant factor in their rare public appearance is the potent fear of litigation in the United States—a fear that drives some organizations to make very bad decisions around not apologizing. We only need to go back about a decade to look at a total disaster in public relations[12]. Back in late 2004, the Duke University Health System discovered that an elevator maintenance company had found some empty detergent barrels while doing repairs at Duke University Hospital. The purpose of the detergent was to clean surgical instruments. The empty barrels had not yet been picked up. Thinking these were convenient empty containers to store their used hydraulic fluid, the elevator repair crew filled them—and then for unclear reasons left them on site. The drums were later picked up by employees from other hospitals in the system and used as if they contained real detergent. After all, the barrels were left with all the new and unopened barrels of detergent. The elevator maintenance company neither marked the barrels clearly as to their change in contents nor told anyone about them. The containers were opaque and thus from just looking at them one could never tell that the fluid inside was anything other than what the label said. So the poor hospital workers had no idea the stuff was really the dirty hydraulic fluid. Rather horrifically, they delivered the barrels to the other hospitals and for two months those hospitals washed surgical instruments with that dirty hydraulic fluid rather than surgical instrument detergent.

When the detergent barrel is hooked up tubes are stuck in the small holes in the top—the huge barrels are not poured out like milk containers, so no one ever saw the actual fluid—they just saw the clear-ish liquid (the assumed "detergent") going through the tubes and into the washing machines. No one washing the instruments had any way of knowing that a group so wholly removed from them had dumped their waste in those detergent barrels. But the surgical teams noticed the results. Surgical teams complained about greasy instruments that left a yellow stain on the tray liners—and to their credit, many of them re-washed them in the operating rooms. In all, between the two hospitals and over the 2 months this was going on, 3,800 patients had been exposed to these not-so-clean-as-intended surgical instruments when they were undergoing procedures. Now, it's important to note that no one died from this medical error. Of course, after learning about the error quite a few people complained of illnesses, but there were no more people with post-operative issues who were exposed to the surgical instruments under question than routinely have side effects or lingering complaints after undergoing such a major health event with perfectly sterile tools. Happily, the data support that no one was physically harmed by this horrible and disgusting mistake.

So what would you do if you were the Duke University Health System? Well hopefully you would get out in front of this public relations nightmare. Duke did not. They made no apology. They simply remained silent. Duke is a great hospital. Their communications team, however,— not so great in this instance.

With no apology at all—well, that pretty much breaks every guideline of The Powerful Apology. So what happened in the aftermath of this serious error? When the Duke University Health System said nothing, other people jumped right into that communications vacuum—as anyone would have predicted would have happened. Most of these came from patients and the media. That painted Duke into a very bad light of looking guilty and using the "duck, dodge, bob and weave" strategy we talked about earlier. A once-trusted health system now looked like it was trying to conceal the facts or evade responsibility, when really this was unfortunate, this shouldn't have happened, but it wasn't something that they could reasonably predict or prepare for. They were liable, but not exactly at fault. A bit like Johnson & Johnson with the Tylenol poisoning— they were liable but they hadn't actually caused the problem. But J&J got ahead of this PR nightmare. Duke didn't learn the lesson. J&J was strengthened by their experience—Duke was damaged.

Here's an example that many would argue tops the "loser" list of botched apologies. Tragically, on April 20th, 2010 an oil rig operated by BP exploded, killing 11 workers and creating the largest oil spill in the history of the petroleum industry, and as everyone now knows, it went on unabated for 3 months! Pristine waters and beaches were severely contaminated, there were massive wildlife die offs, entire industries were disrupted, and economically this was devastating to the area. The White House Oil Spill Commission report blamed BP and its partners for making a series of cost-cutting decisions and the lack of a system to ensure oil well safety.

The apology approach by CEO Tony Hayward was…unusual, to say the least. His May 30th, 2010, statement of *"I'm sorry. We're sorry for the massive disruption it's caused their lives. There's no one who wants this over more than I do. I'd like my life back"* didn't follow the Powerful Apology guidelines, nor was it very effective. In particular, the "I'd like my life back" didn't ring well with the families of the deceased, who were sure their loved ones would like their lives back too, quite literally. His absences to go yachting during the crisis suggested that he did not feel empathy or contrition. BPs repeated insistence that only a very low rate of oil was leaking, about 5,000 barrels a day, when in reality it was ten times that much at about 53,000 barrels a day (as scientists increasingly pointed out), caused an expensive public relations nightmare for the company. Of course, their nightmare was nothing compared to all those who reside along the coast and had to live with the aftermath of the oil spill every day for years afterwards, not to mention those who had to live the rest of their lives without their loved ones. Their nightmare doesn't end. Tony Hayward's never started. He made it obvious that it was never his crisis from the beginning.

Much later, after its own internal probe, BP admitted that it made mistakes which led to the Gulf of Mexico oil spill. In June 2010 BP set up a $20 billion fund to compensate victims of the oil spill. In the short time between then and July 2011, the fund paid $4.7 billion to 198,475 claimants. In all, the fund had nearly 1 million claims and continued to receive thousands of claims each week.

Tony Hayward was reassigned within BP, demoted from CEO, sent to Siberia, and later left the company. Last seen, he was back in the oil business in Iraq. BP's logo is now seen almost as often in its oil spill satire format as in its original clean sunburst (see Figure 13.2). Much like Exxon after the Valdez accident, BPs name will be associated with the worst environmental disaster for decades to come.

Occasionally we get asked questions like, "is it better to make an insincere apology or not to make an apology at all?" The issue here is how to make a powerful apology. No apology at all is not powerful. For Duke it was a disaster. An apology that you don't mean—that is, to lie about your apology—well, that will not be a powerful one either. It wasn't for BP. It was just another disaster.

Figure 13.2 The satirical form and the original of the BP logo

We've looked at a healthcare crisis and an environmental disaster, for a full picture, let's examine a legal debacle as well. In a legal case that also made national headlines an exotic dancer accused three male college students of rape, alleging the attack occurred when she was working at a sports team party that took place in 2006. There was an incredible rush to judgment on the part of college faculty, school administrators, and most crucially the city district attorney, who was facing re-election. Everyone assumed the guilt of the three young men. This was not helped by the fact that team members and the dancer were of different races and socio-economic backgrounds. In the South, which struggles with its history of racism, and the difference between the haves and have not's (now often referred to as the 1% vs. the 99%) this controversy had tensions at the boiling point. The University forced the sports team coach to resign and cancelled the rest of the team's 2006 season. When speaking about the case, the City District Attorney, Mike Nifong, was quoted as saying, "There's no doubt in my mind that she was raped and assaulted at this location." However, he had failed to interview the accuser or review the defendants' case, and was later found to have hid the DNA evidence that actually exonerated the three young men. A major, major mistake, error of judgment, and violation of integrity that deserved, well, an incredible apology.

With all of this in mind consider his apology. Many found it to be woefully inadequate:

> *To the extent that I made judgments that ultimately*
> *proved to be incorrect, I apologize to the three students*
> *that were wrongly accused. I also understand that*
> *whenever someone has been wrongly accused, the harm*
> *caused by the accusations might not be immediately*
> *undone merely by dismissing them. It is my sincere desire*

that the actions of Attorney General Cooper will serve to remedy any remaining injury that has resulted from these cases.

An attorney for one of the accused student athletes commented:

You can accept an apology from someone who knows all the facts and simply makes an error. If a person refuses to know all the facts and then makes a judgment, that's far worse... particularly when that judgment destroys lives.

Soon thereafter the State's Attorney General, Roy Cooper, declared the students completely "innocent" of all charges—a decision that carries a very powerful message about how completely wrong everyone was since there actually was *no evidence* at all to support the accusations everyone assumed were true. If there was ever a reason to extend a series of apologies this is it.

But Nifong didn't get it right. He was disparaged in the press and disbarred in June of 2007[13] and the University made an undisclosed settlement with the three men who were wrongly accused.

We hope that these three cases illustrate to you that a failure to apologize is very expensive—indeed, in just about every way expense can be measured.

There is one more event that made national news in 2012 that is worth examining. In early 2012, Georgetown University law student Sandra Fluke testified before Congress about the lack of coverage for oral contraceptives by health plans. She was testifying about a fellow student who had been prescribed these medications for control of a painful and debilitating condition known as ovarian cysts. We've checked with OB-GYN doctors, asking just what these painful cysts are. We've been told that for some women the normal process of ovulation goes very wrong—and internal abdominal bleeding occurs, called a "chocolate cyst" because of the dark blood that collects. One doctor described it to us as "writhe-around-on-the-floor kind of bad pain." You can't attend classes with bleeding ovarian cysts. You can't work. Heck, you can hardly stand up. Birth control pills prevent ovulation. They prevent the internal abdominal bleeding. They prevent the disability. Even though the young woman's physician said she needed these medicines her school's health plans objected on the basis that they *also* served as a method of birth control. Because the side effect meant that she couldn't get pregnant, the treatment for her disease was denied her.

A week later, radio commentator Rush Limbaugh called Ms. Fluke a slut and prostitute, making a series of shocking statements about her character, relating her personal use of birth control pills as recreational. He had never met Ms. Fluke or heard of her prior to her testimony before Congress. Obviously, he has never had a ruptured, bleeding, "chocolate" ovarian cyst, or he might have expressed more empathy for this situation.

Despite a rather immediate reaction of shock and dismay from both sides of the political aisle, Mr. Limbaugh did not offer any apology initially—in fact he continued his statements for another two days. On March 3rd, 2012, after much public criticism, including from the President of the United States and the Speaker of the House (who were from different political parties), he made the following statement:

> *For over 20 years, I have illustrated the absurd with absurdity, three hours a day, five days a week. In this instance, I chose the wrong words in my analogy of the situation. I did not mean a personal attack on Ms. Fluke.*

He then went on with 118 more words defending his point, and then concluded with the statement,

> *My choice of words was not the best, and in the attempt to be humorous, I created a national stir. I sincerely apologize to Ms. Fluke for the insulting word choices.*

So, what do you think was the outcome of this apology approach? How many of the seven components did Rush Limbaugh use? Two days later Mr. Limbaugh offered yet another apology, as advertisers started to pull their support from his program. His apology was to his audience, and he stated:

> *...I don't expect...morality or intellectual honesty from the left. They've demonstrated over and over a willingness to say or do anything to advance their agenda. It's what they do..... But this is the mistake I made. In fighting them on this issue last week, I became like them. .... I became like them, and I feel very badly about that. I've always tried to maintain a very high degree of integrity and independence on this program. Nevertheless, those two words were inappropriate. They were uncalled for. They distracted from the point that I was actually trying to make, and I again sincerely apologize to Ms. Fluke for using those two words to describe her.*

This apology has been shortened by removing some sentences that continue to place blame and point the finger at others[14], but you can see how this format does not follow the guidelines for the powerful apology. In particular it does not show contrition or any indication that it won't happen again. In the end, it wasn't very effective. His sponsors continued to leave the program and he was dropped by some of the stations that carried it.

One thing about this particular event that was so powerful is that social media played a huge role in the reaction to his statements and these successive apologies. They played a huge role in businesses and radio stations hearing from customers and listeners dismayed with their support of the program. Additionally, in reaction to the events there was significant fundraising for the political party Limbaugh did not support.

When you or your organization has made a serious error—you owe those who have been wronged a serious apology. Put into that apology conversation the thought it deserves. Make sure you consider how you'll make the apology in the appropriate time frame, how you'll take responsibility, explain what happened and show how you've learned from this error so it won't happen again. Don't *just* say you're sorry, also show contrition and ask for forgiveness for the error you've made. Whenever possible, connect personally with the other party. And if they do forgive you and continue to work on the relationship or partnership they have with you, make sure you thank them. That is showing compassion for your error, and that is a gift to you. So be appropriately grateful.

Remember, a *powerful* apology is not a one-shot statement. It is a conversation. A conversation that helps heal bruised and damaged relationships. It's not possible to go through a career without making any mistakes. *It-Factor* leaders don't escape mistakes and you won't either. Hopefully you and your organization can avoid the big ones, but if not, then you can go far to mend those valuable relationships by making a powerful apology.

Your 13th step to becoming a great *It-Factor* leader is to master the art of the powerful apology.

Conclusion

Great Leaders are not born, they are developed

We have now traveled 13 crucial steps along that path to becoming an *It-Factor* leader, an enlightened place to be. These steps are how individuals become great leaders. Once people thought great leaders were born with that *special something*, an elusive *"It-Factor"* that pre-destined them to become leaders. Now we know you don't have to be born with "it." Those who have that special *"It-Factor"* don't magically wake up one day with the skills and talents for the job. Great leaders are developed, not born. They learned it and you can learn it too. You can hone the skills of leadership and become an *"It-Factor"* leader yourself. The path we've laid out for you contains 13 Steps to build your own sophisticated set of leadership skills and take you further down that road to leadership enlightenment.

Through reading this book you've now been introduced to more than 100 strategies and learned the tools and skills that allow you to make a difference in your particular situation, whether it be with your team, your organization, or your community. Of course, *reading* and *doing* are two different things. The *It-Factor* takes practice and, as you develop your skills, your own rhythm emerges. Use the charts in this book to help you create Your Individual Development Plan (an example is in our Fifth Step: "Build a Great Team"). Share your skills and your progress, perhaps with a mentor, an executive coach, or a colleague. Get feedback. Be open. You are traveling the path to better leadership! You can *FastTrack* your development by following the steps in this book and always keeping yourself open to ways you can continually improve.

Support is helpful as you move along the path of leadership enlightenment. Enrolling in a leadership development program (like those we offer at *FastTrack*) or applying for a spot in a Leadership Institute can escalate your skill development—no matter whether you are an emerging leader or at the senior level. Some people find having an executive coach helps them master these skills quickly, but that can become expensive. So if your organization doesn't offer these services through a human resource department, consider adopting the peer coaching method we shared with you in the Third Step. You can work through the steps together, give each other feedback, and support each other's development. It's like forming a leadership book club—only skip the wine and stay on track with the topics. Reading the steps and working on the strategies and tools will give you an immediate leadership boost. Don't forget to come back to the steps of special interest to you again and again. You probably won't master 100+ strategies, tools, and skills with just one read—when we coach professionals we work to refine skills, often hitting them three or four times. We have many leaders who had early access to these materials tell us, "I keep the notebook on my desk and refer to it every day." What's really important is that you find the supports you need to keep you moving down the path to becoming an *It Factor* Leader.

The "It-Factor" is not about you

We opened this book discussing the concept that, "it's not about you." It's a good way to close out our thoughts as well. Just like this book makes a progression into deeper and more sophisticated skills as you move into later chapters, there is a progress of self-understanding and self-enlightenment that follows suit. For example, reflection is a key process so that you can come to know yourself—your talents and assets as well as your rougher spots. You need to gain objective perspective on yourself so that you are not "had" by your own personality or skill limits. It is insufficient to merely understand yourself, or how you prefer your world to be. You need to see how others perceive you, to understand how your words and actions are received by them. When we teach we often advise, "you need to know yourself, you need to get over your-own-bad-self, to help everyone ease on down the road together." Know yourself—but also understand how others think and feel (the Ninth Step is helpful for that). Master the language that might not be innate to you, but will help you connect with others. When you can bridge to how others see the world, to use those skills to communicate effectively with them, then you are really on your way. When you can understand yourself and use that to leverage an even greater understanding of others, then you are on the path to what we call enlightened leadership.

A Basis in Research

Of course, you might be thinking, "Well, these all sound like good ideas but how do I know they work?" Good question! This book would not exist without the incredible input from the hundreds and hundreds of the amazing leaders we've worked with. Claudia is a university professor—and her field is leadership development. She's been teaching these skills and collecting data on leader improvement for several years. Her research shows that not only do leaders *like* learning the material, they find they *use* what they've learned, because it's *relevant* to the challenges they face every single day. According to testing on 20 key leadership domains, leaders noted significant development in their skill levels in every single category.

In studies investigating the return on investment for leader development, Claudia found that participants used their newly developed skills to impact thousands of people in a variety of ways:

- altering state laws to better benefit public interest,
- gaining more revenue and funding for programs,
- making the crucial "right hires" to build a more effective team,
- markedly improving the development and competence of the teams,
- making connections with new markets and partners, and
- individually moving up into positions of higher authority with better paying jobs.

This path to becoming a better leader was not developed lightly; it comes from a solid foundation in research. The material is tested and refined as we continue to work with executives, leaders, and managers, individually and in teams. Our leadership institutes build these skills. We hear back from leaders who use these skills and we know how they play out in organizations. We are confident that they will be useful to you.

Follow the Path

The path to becoming an *It-Factor* Leader has a definite beginning, middle, and at the end of the journey a culmination of nuanced and sophisticated skills. Leaders who use this path find their skills markedly improved as they develop. These 13 Steps are carefully and intentionally laid out. They build upon one another in important ways: self-reflection (our First Step) leads to self-awareness and this knowledge brings 1) an understanding of one's assets and 2) the realization of areas that need further development. When you understand and appreciate how you are the same as—and different from—other people, you gain insight into how to create the kind of organizational culture that gets the best ideas and efforts from everyone on the team. This accurate self-understanding and assessment brings the ability to make both the right career moves to get on the right team, and to select candidates wisely as you build your own team. All too often poor leaders make bad selection choices because a basic lack of self-awareness prevents them from hiring diverse strengths onto their team. Selecting teammates for personal chemistry rather than for fit and skill results in the need for painful hiring corrections down the road. Follow that Second Step on the path to make sure you get the right team fit.

Once you have self-knowledge and understanding and you find your team fit, the other skills start coming into play. Learning to "do ask, don't tell" (our Third Step) is an important set of behaviors to employ with your team. Use the skills of intentional and persuasive listening to foster both problem solvers and to build good business relationships. This ability to listen acutely will help you understand the next step in the process, which is what motivates people (our Fourth Step). We talked about that as focusing on the mortar (or positive personal regard) that holds the bricks (the technical skills) together. Capitalize on motivation at work to get the best out of everyone and to meet their needs, too.

The first four basic steps are to know yourself, get (or get on) the right team, listen persuasively, and understand what motivates people. From these, the path becomes an intricate web of steps that relate to one another in complex ways. While all the subsequent steps build on the first four, they are independently related to one another as well.

The Fifth Step addresses ways of building a great team—how to promote development of skills and learning to improve performance. In our Sixth Step, we explored emotional intelligence and how to practice and refine these skills. Emotional intelligence connects in a web-like fashion throughout this path of skills, which is why it is at the center of the book and the most involved chapter. When you develop the skills within your team and create an emotionally intelligent environment, it becomes much easier to understand and engage your employees, as we addressed in Step Seven.

Once you have progressed in developing your own set of *"It-Factor"* skills, the next tier of steps come into play. Creating a culture of conversation, discussed in Step Eight, gets all the ideas on the table, while Step Nine teaches you how to get your message across with eloquence, grace, and brevity – it's important that you *be heard* by your audience. Creating thought diversity, explored in the Tenth Step, helps prevent the disasters that come from "going along to get along" or those uber-dominant types in your group ruling the day, every day. When leaders create thought diversity they embark down the road to innovation and ingenuity.

Creating the environment where ideas are surfaced, explored, and investigated can also bring tensions and anxieties in the group. Thus, managing the art of the difficult conversation, as discussed in the Eleventh Step, is a staple skill for any *"It-Factor"* leader. Yet this step comes towards the end of the book rather than at the beginning. It should not be the first skill one tries to develop. Successfully managing difficult conversations requires many layers of sophisticated skills. Self-reflection and understanding are crucial to success, as are listening, emotional intelligence, and creating an environment where everyone can be heard and new ideas are welcomed—and not simply tolerated while being accompanied by deep sighs and eye-rolling.

Taking charge of change and knowing how to save a relationship through making a powerful apology when necessary are the final, most nuanced and challenging steps along this path to becoming an *"It-Factor"* leader, and are discussed in our Twelfth and Thirteenth Steps, respectively. The higher the leadership position the more these critical leadership skills will come in handy. They are skills that are heavily reliant on those steps that come before them in the path.

We hope that you find these tools, strategies, and skills helpful to you in your leadership life. We have learned of their key importance from *It-Factor* leaders who have shared their lessons of experience with us. Use this book as your own personal workbook, a "coach on the shelf", that you can consult whenever you run into the kind of thorny problems that leaders so often face. May they help you, as well, on your path to becoming a great leader, an enlightened leader—an *It-Factor* leader.

Notes

References and further notes: Steps to becoming an *It-Factor* Leader

Step 1: Know Yourself: The Good, The Bad, and the Fixable
1.   Van Vleet DD, Yukl GA. (1989). A century of leadership research. In: Rosenbach WE, Taylor RL, eds. Contemporary Issues in Leadership. Boulder, CO: Westview Press; 65–90.
2.   McCauley C, Van Velsor E (eds) (2004). The Center for Creative Leadership Hand-book of Leadership Development. Jossey-Bass; San Francisco, CA.
3.   Hogan, R., & Hogan, J. (2001). Assessing leadership: A view from the dark side. International Journal of Selection and Assessment, 9, 40-51.
4.   Leslie, J. & Van Velsor, E. (1996). A look at derailment today: North America and Europe. Greensboro: Center for Creative Leadership.
5.   Lombardo, M. M., Ruderman, M. N., & McCauley, C. D. (1988). Explanations of success and derailment in upper-level management positions. Journal of Business and Psychology, 2, 199-216.
6.   McCall, M. & Lombardo, M. (1983). Off the track: Why and how successful executives get derailed (Tech. Rep. No. 21). Greensboro, NC: Center for Creative Leadership.
7.   Edmondson, Amy C. (2008) The Competitive Imperative of Learning. Harvard Business Review, July-August, 60-67
8.   Berrey C., Avergun A., Russ D.,Highly Responsive Teams and Your Competitive Advantage. Journal for Quality and Participation September 1993 Vol. 16 No. 5 pp. 72-76
9.   Moss-Kanter, R. (1995). Concepts, competence and connections: the keys to success: address to the Congress of Cities, Opening General Session, National League of Cities. Gale, Cengage Learning. Available at: http://www.thefreelibrary.com/Concepts,+competence+and+connections%3A+the+keys+to+success.-a017927856, accessed December 26, 2012.

10.   Dr. Leah Devlin, comments given at the Leadership Panel for MCH 790 Fundamentals of Leadership, The University of North Carolina at Chapel Hill, January 7th, 2013.

11.   Aanstad J, Corbett P, Jourdian C, Pearman R. (2012). People Skills Handbook: Action Tips for Improving Your Emotional Intelligence. Acorn Abby Books, Winston-Salem, North Carolina.

12.   Leadership Skills and Emotional Intelligence," Center for Creative Leadership, Research Synopsis Number 1, 2001.

13.   _____. (2003). Breakthrough ideas for Tomorrow's Business Agenda. Harvard Business Review: Apr;81(4):92-8, 124.

14.   U.S. Senate. House Committee on Energy and Commerce, Subcommittee on Oversight and Investigations. Senate Panel Investigating the Financial Collapse of Enron Corporation. Testimony of Jeffrey K. Skilling. February 7, 2002. Available from Findlaw.com; Accessed 1/1/2013.

15.   Twenge, J M, Campbell, W K, Freeman, E C. (2012). Generational Differences in Young Adults' Life Goals, Concern for Others,and Civic Orientation, 1966–2009. Journal of Personality and Social Psychology, Vol. 102, No. 5, 1045–1062

16.   Simpson C. (2012). Beyond the Obvious—Unlocking the Hidden Psychological Drivers of Leadership Performance. Presented at the HR Leadership Forum October 05, 2012, NRECA Conference Center, 4301 Wilson Blvd., Arlington VA.

Step 2: Get (Or Get On) The Right Team

1.   Spencer LM Jr, Spencer SM. (1993). Competence at Work: models for superior performance. John Wiley and Sons, New York.

2.   Fernandez CSP. (2010). The behavioral event interview: avoiding interviewing pitfalls when hiring. In: Baker EL, Menkens AJ, Porter JE, authors. Managing the public health enterprise. Sudbury, MA: Jones and Bartlett Publishers. p. 23-29.

3.   Lombardo MM, McCauley CD. (1988). The Dynamics of Management Derailment. Greensboro, NC: Center for Creative Leadership; Technical Report No. 34.

4.   Wacyk C. Diagnosing and addressing leaders derailment—the role of the executive coach. Available at: www.nelson consulting.co.uk/Articles/exec-coach. Accessed August 30, 2006.

5.   McCall MW Jr, Lombardo MM. (1983). Off the Track: Why and How Successful Executives Get Derailed. Greensboro, NC: Center for Creative Leadership. Technical Report No. 21.

6.   LaFasto F, Larson C. (2001). When Teams Work Best. Thousand Oaks, Calif: Sage.

Step 3: Shut Up and Listen

1. Dr. David Steffen, the University of North Carolina at Chapel Hill, UNC Gillings School of Global Public Health, personal communication

2. Branden, Nathaniel. (1998). Self Esteem at Work: How Confident People Make Power Companies. San Francisco, CA: Jossey-Bass.

3.   John Barkai, The Barkai Chorus, The University of Hawaii, available at: www2.hawaii.edu/~barkai/aals/CHORUS.doc · DOC file, accessed September 25, 2012.

4.   Cooper JM. (2007) Cognitive Dissonance: 50 Years of a Classic Theory, Sage Publications, Ltd. London, England.

5.   Jung, C. (1971). Psychological Type. Princeton, NJ: Princeton University Press.

6. Barker, J. (1992) Paradigms: The Business of Discovering the Future. Harper Collins, NY.

7. Stevick RA, Martin K, Showalter L. (1991). Importance of decision and post-decision dissonance: a return to the racetrack. Psychological Reports: vol 69(2). Pp 420-422.

8. Rackham, N, (1998), SPIN Selling: The best-validated sales method available today. Developed from research studies of 35,000 sales calls. Used by the top forces across the world. McGraw Hill, NY.

9. Walton M, Demming WE. (1986). The Deming Management Method. Perigee Books, New York.   Also see: Demming, EW. (1994). The New Economics for Industry, Government, Education - 2nd Edition. Massachusetts Institute of Technology, Cambridge, MA.

10. Senge, P. (2006). The Fifth Discipline: The Art & Practice of The

Learning Organization. Doubleday, NY.

Step 4: Focus on Mortar, Not Bricks

1. Fernandez CSP. The power of positive personal regard. J Public Health Manag Pract 2007;13(3):321-3.
2. Weiner, B. (1972). Attribution Theory, Achievement Motivation, and the Educational Process. Review of Educational Research, Vol. 42, No. 2 (Spring, 1972), pp. 203-215.
3. Koch R. (2008). The 80/20 Principle: The Secret to Achieving More with Less. Doubleday, NY.
4. Musselwhite, WC. (2006). Discovery Leadership Profile Facilitator Guide. Discovery Learning Press, Greensboro, NC.
5. Shutz, WC. (1958). FIRO: a three-dimensional theory of interpersonal behavior. New York: Holt, Rinehart and Winston.
6. Hammer, AL, Schnell ER. (2000). The FIRO-B Technical Guide. Consulting Psychologists Press, Inc, Palo Alto, CA.
7. Waterman JA, Rogers J. (2004). Introduction to the FIRO-B instrument. Consulting Psychologists Press, Inc. Palo Alto, CA.
8. Shell, ER. (2000). Participating in Teams: using your FIRO-B results to improve interpersonal effectiveness. Consulting Psychologists Press, Inc. Palo Alto, CA.
9. Thompson HL, Shutz W. (2012). Element B Behavior: A FIRO-based instrument. Certification Course Manual. High Performing Systems, Watkinsville, GA. *Also of potential interest:* Thompson HL (2000). FIRO Element B and Type (Part I): Why FIRO Element? Bulletin of psychological type, 23,2,18-22.
10. Loop, Floyd D. (2009) Leadership and Medicine. Firestarter Publishing, Gulf Breeze, FL.
11. Aanstad J, Corbett P, Jourdian C, Pearman R. (2012). People Skills Handbook: Action Tips for Improving Your Emotional Intelligence. Acorn Abby Books, Winston-Salem, North Carolina.
12. Leadership Skills and Emotional Intelligence," Center for Creative Leadership, Research Synopsis Number 1, 2001.

13. _____. (2003). Breakthrough ideas for Tomorrow's Business Agenda. Harvard Business Review: Apr;81(4):92-8, 124.

14. 2003 and 2011 Towers Perrin Talent Reports. 2003 Report accessible at: http://www.towersperrin.com/tp/jsp/masterbrand_webcache_html.jsp?webc=HR_Services/United_States/Press_Releases/2003/20030528/2003_05_28.htm&selected=press *or search for* "Towers Perrin Talent Report 2003"; accessed October 23, 2006.

Step 5: Build a Great Team

1. Edmondson, Amy C. (2008). The Competitive Imperative of Learning. Harvard Business Review, July-August, 60-67

2. Byham, W., Smith AB, Paese MJ. (2002). Grow Your Own Leaders: How to Identify, Develop, and Retain Leadership Talent. Development Dimensions International. Bridgeville, PA.

3. Pedler, M., Burgogyne, J. and Boydell, T. (1997). The Learning Company: A strategy for sustainable development. 2nd Ed. London; McGraw-Hill.

4. O'Keeffe, T. (2002). Organizational Learning: a new perspective. Journal of European Industrial Training, 26 (2), pp. 130-141.

5. Logan D, King J, Fischer-Wright H. (2008). Tribal Leadership: Leveraging Natural Groups to Build a Thriving Organization by Dave Logan, John King and Halee Fischer-Wright. Harper Business, NY.

6. For a list of great quotes by Coach K, see http://coachk.com/coach-k-media/quotes/

7. Collins J. (2001) Good to Great. Harper Collins Publishers Inc. New York, NY

8. Working today: understanding what drives employee engagement.; http://www.towersperrin.com/tp/getwebcache; doc?webc=HRS/USA/2003/200309/Talent 2003.pdf

9. Mayer, D. (2013) Encouraging employees to report unethical conduct internally: It takes a village. Organizational Behavior and Human Decision Processes 121, 89–103

10. Walton M, Demming WE. (1986). The Deming Management Method. Perigee Books, New York.   Also see: Demming, EW. (1994). The New Economics for Industry, Government, Education - 2nd Edition. Massachusetts Institute of Technology, Cambridge, MA.

11. POINt is an outgrowth of work by Dianne Foucar-Szocki, Bill Shephard and Roger Firestien, who called it PPC (Pluses, Potentials, and Concerns). Then it became PPCO, where the O stood for Overcome (the concerns). It is reported that Bob Moore at Pfizer, came up with POINt, which is what most people who teach creativity use currently.

12. Dr. Gerrard Puccio and THinc Communications, Evanston Illinois. The FourSight tool is available at www.FourSightOnline.com

Step 6: Build Your EQ

1.   Daniel Goleman has many great works published on emotional intelligence. See Goleman D. (1996) Emotional intelligence: why it can matter more than IQ. New York: Bantam Dell. *Also see:* Goleman D, Boyatzis R. (2008). Social intelligence and the biology of leadership. Harvard Bus Rev. September pp 74-81. *And finally you might like:* Goleman D. (2000). Leadership that gets results. Harvard Business Rev. 2000:78–90.

2.   Goleman D, Boyatzis R, McKee A. (2001). Primal leadership: the hidden driver of great performance. Harvard Bus Rev. December. pp 42-51.

3.   For relevant works by Roger Pearman see: Aanstad J, Corbett P, Jourdian C, Pearman R. (2012). People Skills Handbook: Action Tips for Improving Your Emotional Intelligence. Acorn Abby Books, Winston-Salem, North Carolina. *And:* Pearman R. (2002). And Introduction to type and emotional intelligence: pathways to performance. Palo Alto (CA): Consulting Psychologists Press. *And:* Pearman R. (2003). Emotional Intelligence For Self-Management and Enhanced Performance v 5.2 (Bar-On Emotional Quotient Training Manual). Qualifying.Org. Winston-Salem (NC).

4.   Stein SJ, Book HE. (2006). The EQ edge: emotional intelligence and your success, (2nd edition). Toronto, Canada: Multi-Health Systems.

5.   Stein, SJ. (2011). The Complete EQ-I $^{2.0}$ Model (technical manual). Toronto, Canada: Multi-Health Systems. Accessed at http://ei.mhs.com/eq20_manual/part1/Intro.html September 21, 2011.

6.   Bar-On R. (2002). EQ-I technical manual. Toronto, Canada: Multi Health Systems. *Also see:* Bar-On R. (2006).The Bar-On model of emotional-social intelligence (ESI). Psicothema. Vol 18 Suppl, pp 13-25. Available at:www.eiconsortium.org.

7.   Fernandez CSP. Emotional intelligence in the workplace. J Public Health Manag Pract 2007;13(1):80-2.

8.   Fernandez CSP, Peterson HB, Holmstrőm SW, Connolly AM. (2012). Developing emotional intelligence for health care leaders. In: Di Fabio A, editor. Emotional intelligence – new perspectives and applications. InTech. p. 239-60. ISBN: 978-953-307-838-0. Available from: http://www.intechopen.com/articles/show/title/developing-emotional-intelligence-for-healthcare-leaders.

9.   Mayer, J.D., Roberts, R.D., & Barsade, S.G. (2008). Human abilities: Emotional Intelligence. Annual Review of Psychology, 59, 507-536.

10.   Mayer, J.D., Salovey, O., & Caruso, D. (2000). Models of emotional intelligence. In J.D. Parker & D. Goleman (Eds), The Handbook of Emotional Intelligence. San Francisco: Josey-Bass.

11.   Phineas Gage Information Page, Maintained by Malcolm Macmillan, School of Psychology, Deakin University. Victoria. Australia; http://www.deakin.edu.au/health/psychology/gagepage/; accessed September 24, 2012.

12.   Dement WC, Vaughn C. (2000). The Promise of Sleep: A Pioneer in Sleep Medicine Explores the Vital Connection Between Health, Happiness, and a Good Night's Sleep. Dell Publishing, New York.

13.   Roger Hall, PhD. Business psychologist. Compass Consultation Ltd. CompassConsultation.com; personal communication, February 2013.

14.   Hayden T. Renaissance Resources, Brunswick County, NC. The Star-News. Available at: www.wilmingtonstar.com. Accessed July 23, 2006.

15.   Kouzes J, Posner B. (1988). The Leadership Challenge: How to Get Extraordinary Things Done in Organizations. San Francisco, Calif: Jossey-Bass.
16.   Leadership Skills and Emotional Intelligence, Center for Creative Leadership, Research Synopsis Number 1, 2001.
17.   _____. (2003). Breakthrough ideas for Tomorrow's Business Agenda. Harvard Business Review: Apr;81(4):92-8, 124.

Step 7: Engage Your Employees

1.   Working today: understanding what drives employee engagement.; http://www.towersperrin.com/tp/getwebcache; doc?webc=HRS/USA/2003/200309/Talent 2003.pdf;; http://www.keepem.com/doc files/Towers Perrin Talent; 2003(TheFinal).pdf. Accessed September 25, 2012.
2.   Walker Loyalty Report, November 2005. http://www.walkerinfo.com/walker-loyalty-reports.asp; http://loyaltyreports.walkerinfo.com/studies/employee05/factsheet. cfm Accessed September 25, 2012.
3.   Fernandez CPF. (2007). Employee Engagement. J Public Health Management Practice, 13(5), 524–526.
4.   Harter JK, Schmidt FL, Killham EA. Agrawal S. (2009). Q12 Meta-Analysis: The Relationship Between Engagement at Work and Organizational Outcomes. Gallup, Inc. Available at: http://www.gallup.com/strategicconsulting/126806/Q12-Meta-Analysis.aspx; accessed September 25, 2012.
5.   Tarr-Whelan L. (2009). Women Lead the Way. Women Lead the Way: Your Guide to Stepping Up to Leadership and Changing the World. Berrett-Koehler Publishers, San Francisco, CA.
6.   Walton M, Demming WE. (1986). The Deming Management Method. Perigee Books, New York.   Also see: Demming, EW. (1994). The New Economics for Industry, Government, Education - 2nd Edition. Massachusetts Institute of Technology, Cambridge, MA.

7.   Byham WC, Smith AB, Paese MJ. (2002) Grow Your Own Leaders: How to Identify, Develop, and Retain Leadership Talent. Financial Times Prentice Hall, Upper Saddle, NJ.

8.   Aanstad J, Corbett P, Jourdian C, Pearman R. (2012). People Skills Handbook: Action Tips for Improving Your Emotional Intelligence. Acorn Abby Books, Winston-Salem, North Carolina.

9.   Leadership Skills and Emotional Intelligence," Center for Creative Leadership, Research Synopsis Number 1, 2001.

10.   _____. (2003). Breakthrough ideas for Tomorrow's Business Agenda. Harvard Business Review: Apr;81(4):92-8, 124.

11.   The 2011 Towers Perrin study can be found at: http://www.towerswatson.com/assets/pdf/3848/Towers-Watson-EmployeeSurvey_power-of-three[1].pdf

12.   Blessing White (2010). Employee Engagement Report 2011. Beyond the numbers: A practical approach for individuals, managers and executives available at: http://www.blessingwhite.com/eee__report.asp; Accessed September 11, 2012.

13.   2007 Walker Loyalty study (Source: www.walkerinfo.com/pics/wlr/Employee_ExecSumm_07.pdf

Step 8: Build a Culture of Conversation

1. Fernandez CSP. (2010). Creating thought diversity: the antidote to groupthink. In: Baker EL, Menkens AJ, Porter JE, authors. Managing the public health enterprise. Sudbury, MA: Jones and Bartlett Publishers. p. 71-74.

2. Jung, Carl. Psychological Types. Princeton, NJ : Princeton University Press, 1971.

3. Briggs Myers, Isabelle. (2003). MBTI Manual: A Guide to the Development and Use of the Meyers-Briggs Type Indicator. 3rd Ed. Mountain View : CPP Inc.

4. Hartzler, MT and McAlpine, RW. (2005). Introduction to Type and the Eight Jungian Functions. Introduction to Type and the Eight Jungian Functions. Mountain View : CPP Press. pp. 1-42.

5. Quenk, Naomi L., Hammer, Allen L. and Majors, Mark S. (2001). MBTI Step II Manual: Exploring the Next Level of Type with the Meyers-Briggs Type Indicator Form Q. Mountain View : Consulting Psychologists Press.
6. Center for Application of Psychological Type. Estimated Frequencies of Types. CAPT.org. [Online] 2011. http://www.capt.org/mbti-assessment/estimated-frequencies.htm. Accessed July 2013.
7. Schein, EH. (2010) Organizational Culture and Leadership. Josey-Bass. San Francisco.Locust, Carol. The Talking Stick. Acacia Artisans. [Online] 1997. http://www.acaciart.com/stories/archive6.html , accessed October 5, 2012.
8. Locust, Carol. The Talking Stick. Acacia Artisans. [Online] 1997. http://www.acaciart.com/stories/archive6.html.
9. Dr. David P. Steffen, a close colleague, adjunct at FastTrack and valued friend—this is one of his favorite sayings and we love to quote him.
10. Puccio, G. Mance M. Murdock MC. (2011) Creative Leadership: Skills that Drive Change. Sage Publications Inc. Thousand Oaks, CA. also: Gerrard Puccio and THinc Communications, Evanston Illinois. You can also check out Dr. Puccio's tool on innovation and creative thinking: The FourSight tool is available at www.FourSightOnline.com
11. POINt is an outgrowth of work by Dianne Foucar-Szocki, Bill Shephard and Roger Firestien, who called it PPC (Pluses, Potentials, and Concerns). Then it became PPCO, where the O stood for Overcome (the concerns). It is reported that Bob Moore at Pfizer, came up with POINt, which is what most people who teach creativity use currently.
12. Smith, M. K. (2005). 'Bruce W. Tuckman – forming, storming, norming and performing in groups, the encyclopaedia of informal education. http://infed.org/mobi/bruce-w-tuckman-forming-storming-norming-and-performing-in-groups/. Retrieved: July 2013.

Step 9: Speak to be Heard

1. Jung, Carl. (1971). Psychological Types. Princeton, NJ : Princeton University Press.

2. Kummerow, JM and Quenk, NL. (2003). Understanding Your Step II Results. Understanding Your Step II Results. Mountain View : CPP Press. pp. 1-27.
3. Hartzler, MT and McAlpine, RW. (2005). Introduction to Type and the Eight Jungian Functions. Introduction to Type and the Eight Jungian Functions. Mountain View : CPP Press. pp. 1-42.
4. Briggs Myers, Isabelle. (2003). MBTI Manual: A Guide to the Development and Use of the Meyers-Briggs Type Indicator. 3rd Ed. Mountain View : CPP Inc.
5. Lawrence, G and Martin, C. (2001). Bulding People, Building Programs: A Practitioner's Guide for Introducing the MBTI to Individuals and Organizations. Gainesville : Center for Application of Psychological Type.
6. Martin, CR. (1997). Looking at Type: The Fundimentals. Using Psychological Type to Understand and Appreciate Others and Ourselves. Gainesville : Center for Application of Psychological Type.
7. Quenk, Naomi L., Hammer, Allen L. and Majors, Mark S. (2001). MBTI Step II Manual: Exploring the Next Level of Type with the Meyers-Briggs Type Indicator Form Q. Mountain View : Consulting Psychologists Press.
8. Source 10/2010: www.capt.org/mbti-assessment/estimated-frequencies.htm. Accessed July 2013.
9. Horwich-Scholefield, S. (2010, September). Ending Food Deserts in Brooklyn and Beyond. Retrieved October 25, 2011, from Brooklyn the Borough: http://www.brooklyntheborough.com/2010/09/ending-food-deserts-in-brooklyn-and-beyond.

Additional References of Interest:
- Pearman, Roger R. Albritton Sarah C. (2010) I'm Not Crazy, I'm Just Not You: The Real Meaning of the Sixteen Personality Types. 2nd ed. Nicholas Brealey Publishing, Boston MA.
- Martin, C. (1997). Looking at Type: The Fundamentals. Using Psychological Type to Understand and Appreciate Others and

Ourselves. Gainesville, FL: Center for Application of Psychological Type.

- Timmins, F. (2001). Managers' Duty to Maintain Good Workplace Communication Skills. Nursing Mangemen. Vol. 18, p. 30.
- Hemmer, PR, et al. Leadership and Management Training for Residents and Fellows: A Cirriculum for Furure Medical Directors. Arch Pathol Lab Med, 2007, 131 pp. 610-614.

Step 10: Create Thought Diversity

1. In 1837, Hans Christian Andersen's third and final installment of Fairy Tales Told for Children was published, and in it was a story called "The Emperor's New Clothes". Since original editions are hard to come by, here is a good reference for this story: Haviland V, Andersen HC, Haugaard EC. (1983). [and Haugaard EC (1974), First Anchor Books Edition] Hans Christian Andersen: The Complete Fairy Tales and Stories (Anchor Folktale Library), Random House, NY.
2. Fernandez, C. (2007). Creating thought diversity: the antidote to group think. J Public Health Management Practice, vol 13, issue 6, pp 679–680.
3. Janis, IL (1972). Victims Of Groupthink. Houghton Mifflin Company Boston, 1972, and Janis, IL. (1982). Victims Of Groupthink. Houghton Mifflin Company Boston, 1982
4. Kornbluh P. (1998) Bay of Pigs Declassified: The Secret CIA Report on the Invasion of Cuba (National Security Archive Documents) The New Press, New York, NY.
5. Boisjoly, Roger M. 1987. Ethical Decisions -- Morton Thiokol and the Space Shuttle Challenger Disaster. American Society of Mechanical Engineers Annual Meetings. Webpages created by Jagruti S. Patel and Phil Sarin, "Engineers and Scientists Behaving Well" Online Ethics Center for Engineering 6/9/2010 National Academy of Engineering URL:http://www.onlineethics.org/Topics/ProfPractice/Exemplars/Beh avingWell/RB-intro.aspx, accessed July 15, 2011.
6. Report of the Presidential Commission on the Space Shuttle Challenger Accident, Chapter VII: The Silent Safety Program, URL:

http://history.nasa.gov/rogersrep/genindex.htm
URL:http://history.nasa.gov/rogersrep/51lcover.htm, accessed July
15th 2011. Part [70] Findings. 10.c.

7. Tarr-Whelan L. Women Lead the Way (2009). Women Lead the Way:
Your Guide to Stepping Up to Leadership and Changing the World.
Berrett-Koehler Publishers, San Francisco, CA.

8. Fernandez CSP. (2010). The Power of Positive Personal Regard. In:
Baker EL, Menkens AJ, Porter JE, authors. Managing the public health
enterprise. Sudbury, MA: Jones and Bartlett Publishers. p. 45-49.

9. McGuckin M, Waterman R, Govednik J. (2009). Hand hygiene
compliance rates in the United States--a one-year multicenter
collaboration using product/volume usage measurement and
feedback. Am J Med Qual. May-Jun;24(3):205-13. Epub 2009 Mar 30.

10. Institute of Medicine (1999) To Err Is Human: Building a Safer
Healthcare System. National Academies of Science, Washington, DC.

11. Fernandez, CSP (2010). Managing the Difficult Conversation. In Baker,
E.L., Menkens A.J., Porter J.E. (eds), Managing the Public Health
Enterprise. Jones and Bartlett Publishers, Boston (MA). Pp 145-150.

12. Wheately M. (1992). Leadership and the New Science. San Francisco,
Calif: Berrett-Koehler Publishers.

Step 11: Don't Just Talk Tough, Master Difficult Conversations

1. Fernandez, CSP (2010). Managing the Difficult Conversation. In
Baker, E.L., Menkens A.J., Porter J.E. (eds), Managing the Public
Health Enterprise. Jones and Bartlett Publishers, Boston (MA). Pp 145-
150.

2. Patterson K, Grenny J, McMillan R, Switzler A. (2009; 2012 2nd ed)
Crucial Conversations Tools for Talking When Stakes Are High, Second
Edition. McGraw Hill.

3. Gottman, JM. (2011). The Science of Trust: Emotional Attunement
for Couples. WW Norton & Co. New York

4. Heifetz R, Linsky M, Grashow A. (2009). The practice of adaptive
leadership: tools and tactics for changing your organization and the
world. Boston (MA): Harvard Business Press. See Also: Heifetz R.

Leadership without easy answers. (1994). Cambridge (MA): Harvard University Press.

5.   Loop, Floyd D. (2009) Leadership and Medicine. Firestarter Publishing, Gulf Breeze, FL.

6.   Porath CL, Pearson CM. (2009). The Cost of Bad Behavior. Organizational Dynamics. Vol 39. Issue 1.pp 64-71.

7.   Festinger, L. (1957). A Theory of Cognitive Dissonance. Stanford, CA: Stanford University Press. See Also: Tavris, Carol; Aronson, Elliot.(2007). Mistakes Were Made (But Not by Me): Why We Justify Foolish Beliefs, Bad Decisions, and Hurtful Acts. Harcourt, Inc. Orlando, FL. See Also: Cooper, Joel M. (2007) Cognitive Dissonance: 50 Years of a Classic Theory. Sage Publications.

8.   Knox and Inkster (1968). Post decision Dissonance at Posttime. Journal of Personality and Social Psychology 18 : 319-323. Thousand Oaks, CA.   See Also: Younger, Walker, and Arrowood. (1977) Postdecision Dissonace at the Fair. Personality and Social Psychology Bulletin 3: 284-287.

9.   Patterson K, Grenny J, McMillan R, Switzler A. (2005). Crucial Confrontations. McGraw Hill, NY.

10.   Dr. David Steffen, the University of North Carolina at Chapel Hill, UNC Gillings School of Global Public Health, personal communication

11.   Dr. Vincent Covello has conducted essential research on communications and trust. He has published numerous articles and training guides. Learn more at: http://centerforriskcommunication.org/

12.   Neil Rackham, John Carlisle, (1978) "The Effective Negotiator — Part I: The Behaviour of Successful Negotiators", Journal of European Industrial Training, Vol. 2 Iss: 6, pp.6 - 11

13.   Josh Stulburg, J.D. Personal communication and address on "Handling Difficult Conversations" given to the Fellows of The Food Systems Leadership Institute, session held at The Ohio State University 2006 and 2007.

14.   Professor Dave Roberts, The Kenan Flagler School of Business, The University of North Carolina at Chapel Hill. Personal communication, May 2013.

15.   Carter, Jimmy. (2007). The Blood of Abraham: Insights into the Middle East. University of Arkansas Press, Fayetteville, AR. See Also: Stein, Kenneth W. (1999). Heroic Diplomacy: Sadat, Kissinger, Carter, Begin and the Quest for Arab-Israeli Peace. Routledge, London.

16.   Dr. Mitch Owen, President, Mitchen Leadership and Organization Development. Raleigh, NC.

17.   Fisher R, Ury WL, and Patton B (ed) (2011). Getting to Yes. Penguin Books. New York.

Step 12: Take Charge of Change

1.   Original research by Grenell Consulting Group, Liverpool NY. 2003; online at: www.grenell.com

2.   Kotter J. (1996) Leading Change. Harvard Business School Press. Cambridge, MA.

3.   Walton M, Demming WE. (1986). The Deming Management Method. Perigee Books, New York. Also see: Demming, EW. (1994). The New Economics for Industry, Government, Education - 2nd Edition. Massachusetts Institute of Technology, Cambridge, MA.

4.   Patterson K, Grenny J, Maxfield D, McMillan R., Switzler A. (2008). Influencer: The Power to Change Anything. McGraw-Hill, NY.

5.   2003 and 2011 Towers Perrin Talent Reports. 2003 Report accessible at: http://www.towersperrin.com/tp/jsp/masterbrand_webcache_html.jsp?webc=HR_Services/United_States/Press_Releases/2003/20030528/2003_05_28.htm&selected=press or Google "Towers Perrin Talent Report 2003"; accessed September 23, 2012.

6.   Blessing White (2010). Employee Engagement Report 2011. Beyond the numbers: A practical approach for individuals, managers and executives available at: http://www.blessingwhite.com/eee__report.asp; Accessed September 11, 2012.

7. Aanstad J, Corbett P, Jourdian C, Pearman R. (2012). People Skills Handbook: Action Tips for Improving Your Emotional Intelligence. Acorn Abby Books, Winston-Salem, North Carolina.

8. Leadership Skills and Emotional Intelligence," Center for Creative Leadership, Research Synopsis Number 1, 2001.

9. _____. (2003). Breakthrough ideas for Tomorrow's Business Agenda. Harvard Business Review: Apr;81(4):92-8, 124.

10.   Dr. Leah Devlin, comments given at the Leadership Panel for MCH 790 Fundamentals of Leadership, The University of North Carolina at Chapel Hill, January 7th, 2013.

11. Linsky M, Heifetz R. (2002). Leadership on the Line: Staying Alive Through the Danger of Leading. Boston (MA): Harvard Business Press.; See also: Heifetz R. Leadership Without Easy Answers. (1994). Cambridge (MA): Harvard University Press.

12. Heifetz R, Linsky M, Grashow A. (2009). The Practice of Adaptive Leadership: Tools and Tactics for Changing your Organization and the World. Boston (MA): Harvard Business Press.

13. Dr. Samuel H. Smith, former President of Washington State University, former President of the NCAA. In his address, Advice from an Insider in Higher Education, at The Ohio State University session for the Fellows of the Food Systems Leadership Institute (www.FSLI.org), February 2013. Dr. Smith advises leaders to celebrate early wins when leading change processes.

Meet Bobby Moser

1.   An Agricultural Call to Arms: Addressing Society's Concerns, by Bobby D. Moser, Vice President for Agricultural Administration and Dean, College of Food, Agricultural, and Environmental Sciences; http://ohioline.osu.edu/paradigm/a0.pdf; accessed October 5, 2012.

Step 13: Know how to Make a Powerful Apology

1. Van Vleet DD, Yukl GA. (1989). A century of leadership research. In: Rosenbach WE, Taylor RL, eds. Contemporary Issues in Leadership.

Boulder, CO: Westview Press. 65–90.

2. McCauley C, Van Velsor E (eds) (2004). The Center for Creative Leadership Hand-book of Leadership Development. Jossey-Bass; San Francisco, CA. 2004.

3. Lombardo, M. M., Ruderman, M. N., & McCauley, C. D. (1988). Explanations of success and derailment in upper-level management positions. Journal of Business and Psychology, 2, 199-216.

4. Josh Stulburg, personal communication. The Food Systems Leadership Institute, 2006.

5. Maddux WW, Kim PH, Okumura T, Brett JM. (2013). Why "I'm Sorry" Doesn't Always Translate. Harvard Business Review, June. Pg 26.

6. Sisak MR. Year in Revew: #1 Penn State Scandal, published December 30, 2012. http://citizensvoice.com/news/year-in-review-1-penn-state-scandal-1.1422706; accessed January 11, 2013.

7. Sussman B. (2010). The Great Coverup: Nixon and the Scandal of Watergate. Catapulter books. You can also learn more about the Watergate scandal at http://www.corporatenarc.com/watergate.php (accessed January 11, 2013), or at http://en.wikipedia.org/wiki/Watergate_scandal (accessed January 11, 2013).

8. Roger Hall, PhD. Business psychologist. Compass Consultation Ltd. CompassConsultation.com; personal communication, November 2012.

9. Video and transcript of David Letterman's apology to wife, Regina Lasko, and current staff, October 5, 2009. Accessible at: http://starcasm.net/archives/18382; accessed January 11, 2013.

10. Kaplan, T. Tylenol case study; The Tylenol Crisis: How Effective Public Relations Saved Johnson & Johnson, accessed August 27, 2012 http://www.aerobiologicalengineering.com/wxk116/TylenolMurders/crisis.html

11. Dominos Pizza Apology, available at: http://www.perfectapology.com/dominos-pizza-apology.html; accessed January 11, 2013.

12. Duke reaches settlement in hydraulic fluid cases, reported April 29, 2008 available at: http://abclocal.go.com/wtvd/story?section=news/local&id=6111423; accessed January 11, 2013. See also: Posted: June 19, 2008 See also: Duke Health settles claims from elevator-fluid lawsuit. Posted June 19, 2008. Available at: http://www.wral.com/news/state/story/3068813/; accessed January 11, 2013.

13. Setrakian L. and Francescani C. Former Duke Prosecutor Nifong Disbarred. ABC News Law & Justice Unit, Raleigh, , June 16, 2007; available at: http://abcnews.go.com/TheLaw/Story?id=3285862&page=1 ; accessed January 11, 2013.

14. A Statement from Rush, available at: http://www.rushlimbaugh.com/daily/2012/03/03/a_statement_from _rush; accessed April 15, 2012. See also: http://www.rushlimbaugh.com/daily/2012/03/05/why_i_apologized_ to_sandra_fluke; accessed April 15, 2012

Fast Track Leadership

FastTrack Leadership, Inc. is a partnership of professionals dedicated to promoting leadership in organizations that contribute to the greater good. It is headed by Ruben Fernandez, who serves as its President. *FastTrack* offers customized programs for teams or entire organizations. Programs range from one-half day learning events to several day retreats.

Our *FastTrack* Leadership Development Programs are designed to significantly expand self-awareness and quickly build practical skills for effectively leading, managing people, and building partnerships. We Train Leaders to improve leadership capacity and we'll teach you how to create the kind of organizational culture that engages and motivates others.

We support ongoing development through our online learning, private and confidential executive coaching, and interactive distance-based learning events. We offer creative solutions to put your leadership on the *FastTrack*.

Our faculty are all doctorally-prepared, assessment-certified executive coaches with extensive experience working with mid-to-senior level leaders and managers. We have more than 15 valid and reliable leadership assessment tools to offer, as well as a variety of simulations that can help your team gain skills and insight into more effective functioning.

We are online at WeTrainLeaders.com. Please visit us.